DO NOT TRAVEL THERE!

My dear friend
Ethel

Ed Reynolds

DO NOT TRAVEL THERE!

Tourist Travel in Department of State
"Do Not Travel" Countries.

By ED REYNOLDS

ISBN: 9781736396100

Editing by Laurie Hensley
Cover and interior design by Vanessa Perez

CONTENTS

PROLOGUE

When I talk to people about traveling to all the countries in the world, they often ask about my experiences in the countries that have been listed on the U.S. State Department "Level 4 -Do Not Travel" list.

Level 4 is defined as: *"This is the highest advisory level due to greater likelihood of life-threatening risks. During an emergency, the U.S. .government may have very limited ability to assist. The Department of State advises that U.S. citizens not travel to the country or to leave as soon as it is safe to do so."*

I have had the urge to see the world, meet the people and visit every country in the world since I can remember. The wanderlust was inherited from my mother and was influenced by my stepfather. He was a US Civil Servant and, in the early 1970s, took an assignment at the Aviano Air Force Base in Northern Italy and extended to an assignment in Tehran, Iran. They drove their car from Aviano to Tehran via Bagdad, Iraq, and sent me pictures and stories of their adventure. While in Iran, they were able to take "space available" flights on the US Air Force "Embassy Flights" and visited most of the countries in Africa, Europe, and the Middle East. I was jealous and wanted to visit the same places they described in their letters.

In 2006, on a cruise down the west coast of Africa, I met Bob and Cathy Parda, who had a small travel company called *Advantage Travel & Tours*. I met the people traveling with them, many of whom Cathy called her "AT&T Family" of travelers. I would travel with the AT&T Family on many adventures during the next nine years to complete my quest to visit every country in the world.

Bob and Cathy introduced me to the *Travelers' Century Club (TCC)*, a club limited to those who have visited one hundred or more countries of the world. It was first organized in Los Angeles in 1954, by a group of the world's most widely traveled people. The idea attracted the interest of world travelers everywhere and the club now has members throughout the United States, as well as many foreign countries.

The motto of the club is "World Travel...the passport to Peace through Understanding.

If there is left in the world any hope whatsoever that man can live in peace, despite the terrible weapons they have created to destroy each other, that hope lies in a better understanding among peoples. Understanding is not possible without extensive personal contacts. Personal contact can only be made by traveling."

Bob and Cathy gave me a copy of the TCC list of countries, and I discovered that I had already visited 100 of them. I was motivated to visit the rest and found a group of like-minded travelers in the AT&T Family. I enthusiastically joined the group.

As I discussed my desire to visit all the TCC countries, I soon learned that it wasn't as easy as it appears: it is difficult to obtain visas to many countries, and the Department of State does not encourage travel to some of the countries.

Yet I was determined. This book tells my stories and experiences in Department of State "Level 4 -Do Not Travel" countries, including Afghanistan, Iran, Iraq, Libya, Mali, North Korea, Pakistan, Somalia, South Sudan, Syria, and Yemen.

Countries are continually added and removed from the "Do Not Travel" list. Some on the current list were not on the list at the time of my travel and therefore are not included in this book.

Many people have traveled to these countries, but my unique experience is that I took this travel as a tourist, not as a journalist, government employee, contractor, NGO employee, or backpacker.

My trips were prearranged tours through US travel agencies and, for the most part, included prearranged local tour guides.

Why did I choose an agency to book my travel as a tourist? For four reasons: 1) I am an independent IT consultant and need to coordinate my work and travel. 2) They provide airport pickups, make hotel reservations, and arrange local tour guides, all valuable efficiencies. 3) They provide a degree of security traveling in Level 4 countries. Knowing my schedule, they could alert authorities if something happened to me. 4) Someone back in the US could adjust my schedule if flights were canceled or connections missed.

With that said, most of the 300+ TCC countries I have visited that are not profiled in this book were not arranged through tour agencies.

I have visited all the 193 countries in the United Nations plus those "want-to-be" countries. Most of those visits and my travel as a member of the military for 22 years and post-military work as an International IT Consultant for 35 years are not included in this book, nor are my trips to islands. Those are documented in a separate book.

Even though Bob and Cathy arranged and took many of the tours themselves to Level 4 countries, the Arab Spring uprisings that began in 2010 made them reluctant to arrange travel in countries with active armed conflicts. I found another agency, *Universal Travel Systems*, that would arrange tours to those places.

During this period, the CEO of the Travel Century Club (TCC) was Klaus Billep, who also owned *Universal Travel System (UTS)*. As president and owner of *UTS*, Billep called himself a specialist in creating "international trips to obscure countries," and arranged single and group travel to off-the-beaten-path destinations around the world.

As with *Advantage Travel & Tours*, *Universal Travel System* preferred to limit group sizes to a dozen or less to ensure an intimate experience. In this way, Billep was able to arrange tours to "obscure" nations for me, including Libya, Yemen, Somali, and Afghanistan.

PERSONAL BACKGROUND

I did not have a normal upbringing. In 1939 my father built a house in Weston, CT. In January 1942, due to gas rationing, my parents separated to move closer to their work, my father to NYC, and my mother to Stratford, CT, but decided to have my younger brother and me continue attending the Weston school. There was a Boys Camp adjacent to our family home, so my brother and I spent the war years living at the Boys Camp, which included British and Dutch refugee boys our age.

From the age of 6 to 11, I lived without daily parental contact. I had a heavy dose of world affairs as my campmates heard from their parents in Europe, and I loved the illustrations and pictures in the London Times they received, and followed the war in Europe in more detail than my school mates. From that experience, I developed a sense of adventure and independence without fear. As an example, at the age of 10, I spent the summer in a solo pup tent at the Camp's satellite location on Lake Winnipesaukee, NH, to enjoy an independent adventure.

I had a great curiosity for the unknown, a desire to explore and learn about other people and cultures: What caused WWII? Why was there anti-Semitism? Why did the Southern states require "colored" to use separate restrooms and drink from separate fountains (having been raised in the north this was something I didn't understand)? Etc.

As I grew up and served in the US Air Force, I expanded the questions with a desire to understand: Why were people drawn to Communism? Why can't the various Muslim sects get along with each other and with other religions? Why has religion caused so much divide and conflict in the world?

I could get many answers to my questions by reading or lectures. But to complete the picture, I felt I needed to visit every country in the world and meet the people in those countries, see their living conditions, their villages, how they lived, what they ate, and who they were.

CHAPTER 1

IRAN

My mother and stepfather had been posted to Iran in the early 1970s. I had worked in Saudi Arabia in the 1980s and 1990s and developed a desire to explore the countries of that region more fully. I received *Advantage Travel & Tours'* newsletter in early 2007, offering a tour of the 5 *'Stans and Iran* in the spring and the fall of 2007. Once their spring trip was completed successfully, I reserved a spot on the fall tour.

Crossing the Iranian Border

Wednesday, October 31, 2007, I had just completed a tour of the five 'Stans with a small group of 10. We had visited Kazakhstan, Kyrgyzstan, Tajikistan, Uzbekistan, and Turkmenistan, and now I was scheduled to spend a week in Iran. The group had largely followed the Silk Road, visiting all the major cities except Mary, Turkmenistan. Three members of our group returned to the US, and seven of us were to travel on to Iran.

Our group included my roommate Jerry Ray, a chiropractor, from Wytheville, Virginia; Ed and Gloria, a couple from Tulsa, Oklahoma; "IQ" and Maggie, an Arab couple now living in Los Altos Hills, CA; and Louise, from Bethesda, MD.

Ed and Gloria had taken early retirement at age 50 and had been traveling for 15 years. They spent years without a fixed home touring the US, Canada, Mexico, Europe, Australia, and South America in motor homes. Gloria writes travel articles for RV and Travel Magazines, and they have co-authored books on the Rocky Mountain passes.

"IQ" was a Jordanian who attended the University of California-Berkeley in the 1960s and stayed in the US working as an electrical engineer. Maggie was from a south Lebanese Catholic family that immigrated to Egypt, where she was born. She followed family members to the US and graduated from USC. She taught French in Palos Verdes and then Arabic in the Military Language School in Monterey, California.

Louise was 80 years old and had traveled all over the world on Earth Watch projects.

Our ride to the Iran border turned out to be one of the worst rides I have ever taken. We were crammed into a van that reeked of gas fumes, driven by a burly Russian. The road through the mountains had a lot of hairpin curves, and our driver sped as fast as he could, mostly on the wrong side of the road. I was in the front seat, asking him to slow down, and he would turn to me and grin, and I swear he would drive faster. To compound the situation, the ladies in the back kept asking me to tell the driver to slow down.

We eventually arrived at the border and had the traditional hassle, going through first the exit of Turkmenistan and then the entry into Iran. Walking between the Turkmenistan building and the Iranian building, we were met by our Iranian guide, Ali, a muscular man in his 30s, wearing blue jeans and a tight t-shirt.

The exit from Turkmenistan had gone quickly. The officials did show surprise that we were Americans, and some asked what we thought of their country.

The entry into Iran, however, was a problem. Because the US was fingerprinting arrivals entering the US, the Iranian government decided they should fingerprint US visitors entering their country. We were the first Americans to cross the border at this crossing point since the fingerprint requirement was made, and they did not have the forms or the fingerprinting equipment. We were told we would have to wait several hours while they had the forms faxed to them and enough copies made for the seven in our group.

As we waited, the immigration officials invited us upstairs to their offices for a tour of their facility and to have lunch in their lunchroom. It was one of the best meals I had experienced since leaving the States two weeks earlier.

Eventually, the forms had arrived from their headquarters in Tehran, and we were sent downstairs to start the immigration processing again.

The fingerprinting was a joke—they used a black stamp pad and pressed our fingers on the pad so hard that the imprint on the paper was just a big blob of black ink. But they did not complain since they had no procedure to use our prints in any way, and the requirement was simply retaliation for the US policy. Ali told us he had spent 4 hours at JFK the previous month entering the US. He had spent extensive time in the US, living in Santa Monica, Seattle, and New York, working for relatives who owned or managed Persian restaurants along the west coast of the US. He returned to Iran to be a tour guide, primarily escorting Iranians on tours of the United States, but also guiding Americans and Europeans on tours of Iran.

Mashhad, Iran

The ride from the border crossing to Mashhad took 4 hours, half the distance over winding mountain roads at a slower, safer speed than the drive up the mountain. Ali also had the driver stop for photos in the Kurd villages, which had adobe houses. The second half was on a four-lane divided highway, and the houses became more westernized.

We finally arrived in Mashhad, a major religious site for Shiite Muslims, and the most important pilgrimage site in Iran. Considered Iran's holiest city, it provides a real glimpse into the religious life of the people and boasts some of Iran's best shrines. We checked into the Homa Hotel in Mashhad. The hotel had large rooms with wireless internet!!

The Iranian officials and people had been very friendly. At one checkpoint, the police stopped us just to welcome us to the country.

Holy Shrine of Imam Reza

Thursday, November 1, 2007, was our first full day in Iran, in the city of Mashhad in the northeast area of the country. Mashhad is the site of the Holy Shrine of Imam Reza, the eighth Imam of Twelver Shiites. It is the largest shrine in the world for one individual and is in a 185-acre complex of buildings and plaza known as Astan-e Qods-e Razavi in the center of Mashhad. A large portion of the complex is off-limits to non-Muslims. Mashhad has a population of about 3 million, and over 12 million pilgrims visit the Shrine every year. It is the holiest place in Iran and for Shiite Muslims.

Ali obtained head coverings for the women in the group, which a helpful passer-by fitted on the women's heads correctly. It took Ali a long time to get the approval for the group to enter the complex. While we waited, Iranians would approach us and ask us where we were from. When we told them we were from the US, they welcomed us to Iran and told us how glad they were we were visiting their country. They shook our hands, had the women hold their babies, and took pictures of us shaking their hands. We had just spent two weeks in the five 'Stans and didn't once receive this type of notice and reception. Gloria was wearing a blue and white striped top, which stood out in the crowd, and when she had difficulty keeping her scarf on, she received a few negative comments and was asked to cover-up.

Eventually, we entered the complex with the men and women passing through separate entries where we were patted down and our bags were searched. Several years earlier, a Sunni terrorist had smuggled in a bomb that killed many people. On this day, the crowds were heavy, but Ali told us it was nowhere near as heavy as when school is out. A sign outside listed the things you are not supposed to take into the complex. The pictures included standard items, like guns, knives, cell phones, and cameras, **plus donuts, hamburgers, and French fries**.

Inside we walked through the plazas as they were laying down large rugs for the upcoming noon prayer. After seeing the beautiful mosques and buildings, we entered the museums. The first museum we visited was called the "Museum of Carpets," but it also contained gifts presented to the Shrine from all over the world, such as paintings, vases, models of Mecca, etc. The last museum we visited was the *Muze-ye Markazi* (Main Museum), which displayed historical items, costumes, weapons, dioramas of historical periods, and more.

Lunch at the Moein Darbary Restaurant

After the tour, it was lunchtime, and Ali took us to the Moein Darbary restaurant, the best restaurant in town (according to the guidebooks and the Iranian Americans we met there) for "kabob." The friendly staff sat us at a long table with Iranian and American flags at the end. They served a delicious salad, soup, and excellent meat on platters on the table, so we passed them around to serve ourselves. We arrived before the normal lunch crowd, and when we left, people were lined up down the block to get in. To facilitate fast turn over, the tables have a dozen heavy, clear plastic table covers: after a meal, they dump the leftovers on the cover, remove the dishes, and bundle up the trash, and there is a new table cover in seconds.

Fly to Shiraz

After lunch, we returned to the hotel for a short siesta and a 14:00 checkout. We had six and one-half hours before our flight, so, we stopped at the Bazar-e Reza next to the Shrine. The bazaar has two long corridors, four blocks long, containing the same types of shops we had seen in the five 'Stans. Small stalls were staffed by two or three people with one standing in front to invite you to see their goods, such as clothes, food, cooking items, etc. Nothing caught my eye to purchase.

We arrived at the airport two- and one-half hours before our flight. There were only four check-in counters. Flights aren't processed until 90 minutes before the flight time, so we sat in chairs, waiting for our flight to be listed. When it finally was, there was a mad dash to line-up. Ali was at the head (he had our tickets), and we waited 30 minutes before someone started processing us.

All this caused Gloria to suffer an anxiety attack which continued throughout the flight and the next day. She is a large woman who usually takes charge, but now she was visibly disturbed, pacing back and forth and muttering about having to cover her head and about the treatment of women in the country. She also had a severe case of the trots and having to squat over the Asian "bomb site" style commodes upset her. Her husband tried to keep her calm and told us that she had suffered similar attacks in the past when she felt she was not in control of the situation.

Eventually, our luggage was processed and we passed through security. I set off the alarm, so I just pointed to my artificial knee, which the agent patted and let me through with my camera in my pocket and my cell phone on my belt. The aircraft was a Fokker 100, a single-aisle aircraft that has two seats on the left of the aisle and three on the right side. It was configured to hold 109 passengers. The flight pushed back early and rolled down the runway on the scheduled departure time at 20:30. It was a smooth one- and one-half hour flight to Shiraz, with a dinner of chicken and rice served en route.

Baggage claim was fast, but it was an over 20-minute ride to the Homa Hotel, Meshkinfam Avenue, Shiraz, and we were not able to get to bed until after midnight.

The Tourist Oath

Friday, November 2, 2007, Shiraz is often called the City of Roses and Nightingales. It is the cradle of Persian civilization and has inspired some of the finest Persian poetry and song. It was the capital of Iran during the Zand Dynasty (1747-1779) and is the southernmost city we visited in Iran.

The Homa Hotel caters to foreign visitors, and on display in the hotel lobby, courtesy of a Canadian travel agency, was the:

TOURIST'S OATH

Thank God that I have found the opportunity to travel and visit other countries and, considering the fact that everyone should play his or her role in achieving peace and friendship in the world, I undertake to travel:

Sincerely, and consider others opinion open-mindedly,

Protect the environment and natural resources during my journey,

Respect all cultures and customs of people whom I come across,

Befriend whom I meet during the journey,

Protect practically and theoretically all agencies, organizations, or people having other opinions and viewpoints.

Encourage others to travel throughout the world peacefully

City of Shiraz Tour

We started the day at the Eram Botanical Garden, which has a beautiful 19th Century Qajar palace with a reflecting pool in front. The palace is now a school of botany, which we were not able to tour. Down the road, we visited the mausoleum of Saadi and the tomb of Shurideh, two of the country's poets. Ali recited several of their poems for us in English from books in glass cases. The site also contains the ancient aqueduct. Water flows into the city from wells in the mountain above the city and is still in use.

The next stop was the mausoleum of Hafez. Ali told us there is a story that every Iranian has at least two books in their house: the

Quran and the Poems of Hafez. Ali read us some of Hafez's poems translated to English from the book he carried.

At lunchtime, Ali picked a Sufi restaurant where we enjoyed the salad bar and delicious lamb kabobs with rice. The flatbread was outstanding, and we were able to see the open kitchen with the large oven that they used to bake the bread. Again, the food was on platters we passed around our table.

After a siesta at the hotel, we toured another garden with a large mansion that is now a military museum. It has beautiful grounds and served as a palace the Shah stayed in when visiting the city. Our next stop was at the Nazzir-El Molk mosque down an alley in a poor section of town. It is one of the oldest most beautifully tiled mosques we visited. It is rarely used, and the caretaker had fun showing us postcards from cities around the world sent him from tourists. He hinted that we should send him a postcard when we get home.

The mosque had unique tiles depicting European buildings, including Christian churches with crosses on their steeples and stained-glass windows, scenes you do not see in pure Arab designed mosques.

The sun had set, but before we returned to the hotel, we stopped at the Quran Gate to the city where we got off our bus and walked through the structure, which is supposed to bring good luck.

Dinner was at another traditional restaurant, where I had fried shrimp and more delicious flatbread. This time we had our own plates, not platters.

Ride to Esfahan

Saturday, November 3, 2007. We departed early in the morning for the full day trip to Esfahan, in a rather cramped van. Our baggage occupied the two back rows of seats. (It is good that three members of our original group had not extended to Iran, or we would have to carry our luggage on the roof of the bus.)

An hour north of Shiraz, we stopped at the magnificent Persepolis complex. It is one of the leading ancient sites in the world, with vast stairways, columns, and stone carvings. Construction started in 518 BC under Darius the Great. It was used for 150 years as a place where kings from all over the world would meet. Although ruined, it still has the lower structure in fair shape since, for centuries, it was covered by sand and was not re-discovered until the 1930s. I was fascinated to visit the site because my mother had a coffee table picture book of the site that I would look at during my visits.

A few miles up the road we stopped at Noqsh-e Rostam, which has four tomb sites carved into the side of a rock mountain. It is difficult to describe the stone reliefs that decorate each tomb. It is like Petra, Jordan, and was built during the same period. They believe the tombs contain Darius I, Artaxerxes I, Xerxes I, and Darius II.

We continued our way north on a four-lane divided highway past granite rock quarries and across desert areas, much like parts of California or Arizona, to Passargad, where we stopped at a restaurant for lunch of traditional stew over rice. The stew had beef, spinach, and beans, individually served. Up the road from the restaurant is the tomb of Cyrus the Great, situated in an open field with a mosque near it that was built using stone from the tomb site.

Persian Caravanserais

Back on the highway we continued north across the same terrain. We had a rest stop at a gas station in a small village. Every 23 km, we passed ruins of a **caravanserai,** which were the motels of ancient times. Twenty-three kilometers was considered the distance that caravans could travel in one day, and these caravanserais were designed to provide rooms for the travelers and their animals, with large courtyards that served as trading places for goods. If "Caravan A" was traveling north with goods needed in the north and stayed at a caravanserai where "Caravan B" was traveling south with goods needed in the south, the travelers would often trade goods and turn around and head home.

After the sunset, Ali had us stop at one of the caravanserais that was being restored to serve as a hotel. It was fun to tour the site as the caretaker turned on lights to show us the rooms under restoration.

We eventually arrived at our hotel in Esfahan, the historical Abbasi Hotel, a 500-year-old caravanserai that has been expanded and modernized to be the top-rated hotel in the city. It is so large my room was a five-minute walk through two large courtyards up a stair, down a stair, and down a long hall. There was no internet in the room, but there was free broadband -available in an area above the lobby.

Esfahan, Iran

Sunday, November 4, 2007, Esfahan is in the middle of the country and is a beautiful, sophisticated city with a look of European tree-lined streets and Persian buildings. In the center of the city is a plaza that is second only to Tiananmen Square in size. Unlike Tiananmen, it boasts large mosques at one end and on a side, -bazaar shops that line the plaza, grass and fountains in the center, and horse-drawn carriages you can ride. The plaza was originally built as a polo ground. We first toured the Ali Qapu palace, reportedly the first high rise in Esfahan (six stories high). It has impressive tile work and some unique features. In the entry room, guards were stationed in the four corners. If they turned to the corner and spoke, their words would bounce off the top of the room and could only be heard by the guard standing in the other corners and not by people in the middle of the room. They let us test this unique acoustics design. The top floor is called the music room, and all the tile design is in the shape of musical instruments.

Next, we visited the Imam mosque, considered one of the most beautiful mosques in the world, with rich blue and yellow colors. Every inch above the lower wall is tile. It is offset 45 degrees from the plaza to be oriented towards Mecca. Under the dome is a spot that allows acoustics to amplify anything spoken to be heard throughout the vast room. During prayer, one person would stand there and relay the Imam's words so they could be heard by the crowd.

We visited the Sheikh Lotfollah mosque across the plaza from the palace, also offset by 45 degrees. It differs from other mosques in that it has no courtyard or minarets. It has underground tunnels that were used by the Shah's woman to hide out and/or exit when religious visitors visited the Shah.

Next, we toured the Chehel Sotun palace, featuring a large terrace facing a long pool (unfortunately empty at the time of our visit) with 20 columns. Gloria suffered another bout of anxiety when her head covering fell to the ground. She muttered and displayed agitation over the head-covering requirement. The misogynistic culture was getting to her.

In the palace are large paintings on the walls depicting the history of battles. Ali pointed out that one of the paintings depicts two women in a lesbian relationship, contrary to the Iranian president's statements that such relationships never existed in the country.

Lunch was at the Hotel Julfa with a nice cream of mushroom and lemon soup and more kabobs.

After lunch, we returned to the hotel. Most stores close for siesta until 16:00. I checked my email and then started on a search to find a yellow hi-lighter to mark the places we had visited in my Lonely Planet travel guides. I had been given two addresses near the hotel and set out to find them. The first store was sold out, and after a long walk, I found that the second one was also sold out. As I returned to the hotel, I saw a group of schoolgirls and figured that they would best know where to find hi-lighters. They had fun attempting to understand my request, and once they did, they produced one from their school bag and insisted I take it, refusing to take any money, So far, I have found Iranians to be the very friendly people my mother had told me in her letters.

Earlier at the plaza, we were approached by many Iranians who wanted to talk to us, all of them stating they were happy to see Americans visiting their country, assuring us that they are peaceful and indicating that their president is touched in the head.

Touring the local area around Esfahan

Monday, November 5, 2007, we started a tour of the local area by driving along the Zayandeh River, admiring the beautiful bridges. We stopped at the Shahrestan Bridge, which is one of the oldest, dating back to the 12th century. It is a footbridge now, and we walked across the bridge and took pictures with the sun behind our back.

Next, we stopped at the Khaju, the most decorated of the bridges. It is also a footbridge, with a small palace in the center where the kings would sit to watch water sports in the river. The bridge also serves as a dam controlling the water in the river and is a popular meeting place for people to just sit, talk, and view the river. The bus met us on the other side, and we were off to the Vank cathedral, an Armenian church with beautiful paintings on the walls inside. Unfortunately, photos are not allowed. There is a museum attached with historical references to the Turkish genocide of the Armenians.

Our last stop before lunch was the Manar Jomban tomb with its shaking minarets. The tomb was built in the 14th century with two not very tall minarets. When someone leans or shakes one of those two minarets, the other minarets shake in unison. The explanation is that the sandstone used to construct them contains feldspar, which dissolves over time, leaving the stone flexible.

Lunch was at a traditional restaurant at the plaza, where Ali ordered various stews. They were served in large bowls on the table, and we could sample each one. Some were tasty, some were strange. I liked the walnut sauce over chicken the best.

After a siesta, we started our tour again, this time to the Jameh mosque, which is the biggest mosque in Iran. It has four iwans around a large courtyard. It was originally built by Seljuks in the

11th century, and was added to by many different religious sects, so it is an example of the various architectures and designs used in mosques. Each iwan is uniquely different and has quite different styles from the other mosques we had visited on this trip.

Following our tour of the mosque, we headed for the Bazar-e Bozorg for shopping. The bazaar stretches from the mosque to the plaza, and we visited many shops. The shops were stalls with just a few people, and each specialized in one type of merchandise.

Back at the hotel, four of us dined at a buffet in the hotel's traditional restaurant. It allowed us to taste items before we had to commit to a meal-sized plate. The salad choices were excellent, and I bulked up on salad and small portions of various eggplant dishes.

Ride to Tehran

Tuesday, November 6, 2007, we checked out of the hotel at 08:30 in our Toyota van with all our luggage. As a result, Gloria and Ed were a little cramped, and Louise and I were in the single side seats. The traffic in the city was light since it was a religious holiday. North of the city, we entered a toll road that would lead us to Kashan, Qom, and then Tehran. The terrain was flat desert with rocky hills in the near distance. Again, it reminded me of parts of California, Nevada, and Utah,

Underground Nuclear Power Complexes

Near the town of Natanz, we started to see artillery emplacements to our west, with only a few 10- by 20-foot buildings to be guarded. Ali told us that we were passing the underground nuclear power facility, and when we asked why it was underground, he told us with a big smile they did not want to disturb the beautiful desert. Eventually, we came upon a complex which was more heavily guarded but had power line towers leading north towards the cities. The site did not look like the nuclear power complexes with tall stacks we have in the US.

Unisex Restroom

We stopped at a rest stop/gas station to buy water and take a rest break. There was one unisex room with a dozen "bomb site" commode stalls with doors. Men, women, and children were flowing in and out of the stalls. It did not appeal to our women.

Kashan, Iran

Eventually, we reached the outskirts of Kashan, where we exited the four-lane highway and entered the old section of the city. Kashan is reportedly the city from which the three wise men started their trek to see Jesus. We stopped to take pictures of the remains of the city wall and an icehouse. In olden times they would create small ponds in the freezing weather, cut the ice and store it packed in sawdust in the buildings.

There is a story that the Arabs tried to capture the city in the 7th century but found the wall impregnable, so the Arab general had his men gather scorpions and throw them over the wall, and the inhabitants surrendered.

The major sites to tour in the city were the traditional houses built in the 1800s by wealthy merchants. The first house we stopped to tour is supposed to be the most beautiful but was closed for the holiday. Across the street, we were able to tour the Khan-e Tabatabei, which has beautiful intricate relief designs carved into stone. The house was designed with a central courtyard with a reflecting (not swimming) pool, and on one end was the "exterior" rooms used for entertaining; the other end had the "interior" rooms where the families (father and sons families) lived. Below their rooms were underground rooms that were cooler in the summer. Off to the side were the servants' quarters.

Around the corner, we toured the Khan-e Abbasin complex, which has six buildings and numerous courtyards. The rooms had beautiful decorations and stained-glass windows. Ali reported that all other sites worth seeing in the city were closed for the holiday, so we boarded the bus and resumed our journey north.

Toll Road Rest Stop

At 13:30, we stopped for lunch at one of the toll road rest areas. It was like a stop on the NJ Turnpike with a large gas station next to a building of restaurants. The parking lot was very crowded, and a uniformed man was directing traffic to parking spots.

Inside there was fast food on the left and sit-down on the right with a long line waiting for tables. The restrooms were large and clean but without western toilets. We elected to order from the fast-food side. Over the counter were pictures of the selection, including hamburgers, fried chicken, and pizza. I ordered fried chicken and a tossed salad. The chicken arrived with coleslaw and French fries. It was quite good, although not the same flavor as KFC. After the meal, we stopped in the ice cream shop, and I had two scoops of delicious coffee ice cream.

Tomb of Ayatollah Khomeini

Back on the road, we by-passed Qom, a scheduled stop to visit the shrine of Fatima, after Ali received word that it was too crowded to get in. We pressed on to the tomb of Ayatollah Khomeini, an impressive site that had a large enough parking lot that, despite the crowds, allowed us to find a spot to take photos. The gold dome over the tomb has been removed and is under restoration. There are two other domes and four gold minarets in the complex. We ran into the first unfriendly Iranians there: a family having a picnic on the grounds did not like Americans visiting the tomb and expressed some negative remakes to our guide. I was surprised, because from the time we had entered the customs building crossing the border, we had been received with very friendly greetings.

Laleh International Hotel, Tehran

We arrived at our hotel at 17:30. It is the former Intercontinental Hotel but was renamed after the revolution as the Laleh International Hotel. It claims five stars, but the pool was dry and the room air conditioning was turned off. Our room was on the sunny side of the building and was 10 to 20 degrees warmer than the hall. We complained, and they sent up a big fan, but even with the window wide open, the room was uncomfortable. Jerry Ray and I ate in the French restaurant on the top floor with a view of the city lights. I had French onion soup and pepper steak, which was tough. For dessert, we had a nice flan.

Wednesday, November 7, 2007, my last night in Iran on the Five Stans plus Iran Tour was the worst. The warm room, noisy fan, and hard mattress combined for a restless night.

Touring Tehran, Iran

Our tour of Tehran started at the carpet museum close to the hotel. There we learned about the styles from the various areas of greater Iran and saw some unique carpets, such as a double-sided carpet, one with world leaders' faces, and a 500-year-old carpet that had ended up in the Rockefeller family and was donated to Iran in the late 1960s.

We boarded our bus and drove past the former American embassy, with large banners on the fence with anti-American statements made by Ayatollah Khomeini, in 1979, such as:

"Today, the United States is the most hated government in the world,"

"Down with USA," and several others I was not able to get a good picture of.

Our next stop was the National Museum, a large building containing items from Persepolis, followed by a stop at the glass and ceramics museum, housed in a beautiful residence style building. The building was built in a western style by a Persian family and eventually used as an embassy. Later, the Shah's wife had the government buy it and turn it into a museum. The building was more interesting than the objects in the museum.

Lunch was at the Luxe Talaee restaurant where we had nice kabobs. After lunch, we drove north to the Sa'd Abad museum complex on the slope of the Alborz Mountains. The complex has many museums, but we only visited the White Palace and Green Palace. The White Palace was the Shah's summer residence and is impressive by its more modern, ornate furnishings, and wall and ceiling decorations.

The Green Palace is at the highest point of the complex, and we had to take a bus to reach it. It was the Shah's father's residence and was built overlooking the former owner of the estate. The original house was converted into the kitchen and storage rooms.

On the way back to the hotel, Ali had the bus drive past the foreign residence compound. It had many two-story homes with garages behind walls, and a small shopping center with several US fast food outlets. It is still the residence for foreigners and is where I believe my mother lived in the early 1970s. It brought back memories of her letters.

Back at the hotel, the group leaving the tour decided to meet for dinner in the coffee shop at 18:00 (I had to check out by 19:30 to leave for my flight).

Ride to the Airport

We finished by 19:10, and I rushed to the room to finish packing and then met Ali in the lobby. He drove me to the airport in his personal car to the new Ayatollah Khomeini International Airport, 30km south of the city. Before we could reach the expressway, we had a nerve-racking drive through the city streets from the hotel. Everyone dares one another at the intersections and refuses to let another car have the right of way.

When we drove past Ayatollah Khomeini's tomb, there was a strong odor, causing Ali to close his window. He told me they raise cows in the area. It smelled like the Omaha stockyards. We joked about it being next to the tomb, and I thought it was a fitting end to my tour of Tehran, Iran. Like Nebraska or California, Iran has a lot of beauty and interesting places, but hold your nose downwind from the stockyards.

I processed out of the country a lot faster than I had processed in. It is a shame that the country is on the "Do Not Travel" list because, outside of Tehran, the people displayed genuine friendship with Americans, and the sites are spectacular. I can fully understand why my mother and stepfather had wanted to return.

CHAPTER 2

IRAQ

In 2007 I started concentrating on visiting every country in the United Nations that I had not visited during my USAF and International Consulting career. In 2008 and early 2009, I took ten trips to "off-the-beaten-path' countries, several with the *Advantage Travel & Tours* "AT&T Family" before a unique trip to Iraq was arranged.

These chapters document my activities, observations, and thoughts on a tour of the Middle East with the group organized by Cathy and Bob Parda's *Adventure Travel & Tours*, Poway, CA. Just like they did for the Iran trip, they designed the tour and made all the reservations, and this time accompanied the group. I had previously traveled with most of the people in the tour group. They included Edna, from Santa Monica, an author and avid environmentalist; Ed, a doctor from Las Vegas, who had paired with Edna to save the single supplement; Bill, a retired school physical educator from Silver Spring. MD, who paired with Edith Ann, from Harrisburg, PA, Neal, a retired Civil Servant from Arlington, VA; Laurie, a retired grade school teacher from Long Island, NY, who has traveled every year since graduating from college and is a prolific photographer; and Bob I from Covina, CA, a high school teacher, retired from the classroom but still tutoring. Like Laurie, Bob has traveled every year since graduating from college and is a prolific photographer. Both Laurie and Bob still used film in their cameras and took time to set the scene before snapping the shutter to save film. They both have been active speakers about their travels in their local areas. We all were on the quest to visit every country in the world and had no fear of being the first group of Americans to tour Iraq since September 2001.

Fly to Istanbul via ORD

Tuesday, October 13, 2009, I had a mid-day flight scheduled on United to connect in Chicago to a Turkish Airlines flight to Bagdad via Istanbul.

I had my bag checked through to Baghdad and had a little delay passing through security. They gave my CPAP machine a secondary check, and I was finally given the OK to proceed to the Red Carpet Club at 11:30.

At noon I walked to the departure gate. The agent had upgraded me to seat 5C, and I boarded.

In Chicago, I had to walk through Terminal C and over to Terminal B to exit security and board the air train to Terminal 5.

When I got to the Turkish Airlines check-in counter, I saw Bob and Cathy Parda checking in. They were straightening out some confusion with our visas. In fact, we were all on one visa, filed with the airline.

We boarded on time at 21:40, and I settled in. I had been upgraded again, and it was nice to have an empty seat next to me. The aircraft was an A-330 and was about 80% full. It had seatback entertainment screens. We took off early on our scheduled push back time of 22:20.

Wednesday, October 14, 2009, the flight arrived in the afternoon at 16:50 35 minutes early for a total time in the air of 10 hrs and 50 minutes.

Local Hotel Stay

Our early arrival made us eligible for a free stay at a local hotel. To get that voucher, we had to stand in a long line to purchase a visa for $20 and then stand in another long line for passport control. After that, we exited the baggage claim area and proceeded to the Turkish Airways hotel desk. While we were waiting for our shuttle bus, Bob Parda read out the ground rules. We are traveling on a Religious Group Visa, which meant that one set of papers would be approved in advance to get the actual visa in-country. He told us to plan for no rest stops along the way, so we will have to hold our bio urges for many hours. Security will be tight entering and exiting the hotel. Edna with two metal knees, and me with my knee, will most likely take time processing the entrance to the hotel.

Eventually, the Turkish Airline agent told us the bus was ready and returned our tickets, and we rode in evening rush hour traffic to the Akgun Istanbul 5-star hotel. I had a nice, although dated, large room where I dumped my bags and proceeded to the hotel restaurant for a light meal. They had a buffet, and as I went looking for a table, I saw Neal, who had traveled with me in 2008 in the South Pacific. I joined him, and he told me that Laurie and Bill had arrived from JFK with him. I ate a large plate of tomatoes, lettuce, cheese, sliced meat, and a mixed salad. At 23:30, I checked out of the room.

Iraqi Security Contractor

As we were waiting for the bus to arrive, I struck up a conversation with a young man who had been on my Chicago flight. His name was Hidel, an Iraqi who grew up in Detroit and served three tours with the US Army. He discharged in January and joined a security contractor and was on his second "home leave." He works 72 days in-country and gets 15 days off. I discussed the use of a laptop in the country, and he told me he has one and that it is no problem. When Bob Parda arrived, I introduced him to Hidel and had him repeat the laptop situation, and we concluded that it was OK for me to take it with me.

Thursday, October 15, 2009, the shuttle bus to the airport left the hotel a few minutes after midnight. I sat in the back row with Hidel in front of Bob Parda and me with Cathy Parda across the aisle. Bob asked Hidel a lot of questions, and we were feeling a lot less anxious over the security in the country. Hidel said he felt the mood of the Iraqi people toward Americans was positive, and the people were upbeat and confident about their future. There are still unsafe areas, but the security forces generally know where they are, and would steer us away from them.

At the Istanbul Airport, we had to go through a security checkpoint to enter the terminal. It was easier than the US. I had to remove my laptop but not my shoes. When my knee set off the alarm, I was given a quick pat-down but no wand. Our group walked to the Turkish check-in counter and discovered that it was closed. Hidel approached us and told us that since we already had boarding passes, we should go directly to passport control. I was surprised that at 00:30 in the morning the concession stands were open. Three passport agents were checking passengers, and we breezed through the check. Once inside the terminal, we dropped our bags at a departure gate area, and Bob Parda held another meeting for the three East Coast members of the group to tell all of us what Hidel had told him on the bus.

I walked around the terminal to look for jewelry for my daughter, Wendy, or my wife Judy, but, finding none, I returned to our waiting area to read my many emails. At 01:40, we gathered our bags and walked to the gate 301.

Along the way, I saw Hidel at a gate and he joined our group walk. Gate 301 was actually a bus to the plane gate and was downstairs. When we got there, we had to go through security again. My bags and I had no trouble. Edna had a lot of trouble with her makeup items and groused that she always checks her bag in the US to avoid such hassles. Hidel had to get a second search because of all the electronic equipment and cables he was carrying.

I was one of the first to board the plane and took my assigned seat 4A. Hidel was in 4C, and soon, a large man took 4B. We were cramped, and Hidel was eyeing an empty seat. Unfortunately, additional buses arrived and the plane filled up. We took off at 03:25 and were served a hot breakfast of scrambled eggs, turkey-ham, and cheese, on toast, chicken sausage, and a grilled tomato.

Iraq from the Air at Night

It was still dark when we crossed the border into Iraq at 05:00. I could see a lot of lights below. At one point, we passed over a well-lighted highway, most likely Mosul, and then it turned weird, no lights at all for miles. Off in the distance, I could see a city, most likely, Erbil, and then the lighted villages returned. There was a row of gas flares heading towards Baghdad, and at the end of the flares and on both sides of the row it was dark until we reached the area north of Baghdad.

Baghdad was a large lighted area after so many miles with no lighted villages. On the outskirts of Baghdad were many farms with plastic covers over their crops. The sun was just starting to appear, and the light reflecting off the plastic gave the impression that the area was flooded with water.

Eight Hours in the Bagdad Terminal

We landed at Baghdad International at sunrise. The airport terminal is surprisingly large, but there were very few planes at the gates or on the ramp. We arrived at a gate at 05:50 and had a rather long walk to immigration and passport control. Bob and Cathy collected our passports and took them to the visa office.

After finding that our visa approval was not on file, and after many phone calls, Cathy discovered that the Ministry of Tourism had the original visa approval and was sending a representative to the airport with it. After two and a half hours, our group was ushered through three baggage and personal security checkpoints to the transit passenger waiting room on the upper floor of the terminal. It was a large room with No Smoking signs in both Arabic and English around the room, but many passengers ignored the signs. We set up camp at the end of the room as far away from the smokers as possible.

I was not getting email messages on my Blackberry, but I was getting Facebook messages. I exchanged messages via Facebook with Judy and Wendy and then connected to the same Blackberry settings Bob Parda was using, and the emails started to flow.

Out the window, I could see C-130 and C-17 military aircraft taking off and landing and, parked by our window, was a Lear Jet with Turkish government markings. We were able to buy food and drinks in the terminal, and I had a form of a burrito with spicy beef in a wrap.

Cathy and Bob had arranged our tour through Geoff Hann of Hinterland Travel in the UK, which had been arranging Iraq tours through the Iraq Ministry of Tourism since March 2009. Geoff had a small group from the UK in-country at the same time, and he was able fill us in. The jet from Turkey had carried the prime minister of Turkey who was being met at the airport for a meeting with the prime minister of Iraq, and the roads to the airport were closed. After the meeting concluded, the roads opened, and the representative from the Ministry of Tourism finally was able to deliver the visa approval form, and our passports were processed. We had been in the terminal for eight hours!

Bus to the City

When we left the terminal, we could understand the difficulty the Ministry of Tourism representative had encountered. There is limited parking by the terminal, and it is only allowed for a select few vans. We had to board one of the vans and be driven to the outskirts of the airport to a large parking lot where we were transferred to the bus we would use during our stay in Iraq. It was a 30-seat bus made in China.

In the right front seat sat Captain Amjad from the VIP Protection Police. He wore civilian attire, but under his shirt carried a handgun. Behind the driver, Ahmad, sat Sergeant Mhson from the VIP Protection Police, also in civvies and packing a handgun. Behind the sergeant sat Saadi, our tour guide from the Ministry of Tourism.

The airport is about 8 miles southwest of the city of Baghdad. It did not take us long to arrive in the bustling metropolitan area of the capital and largest city of Iraq, with over three million inhabitants. The city is divided in half by the Tigris River and connected by several interesting bridges. During the 8th and 9th C, by some accounts, it was the richest city in the world. My first impression was that it looked like many other large cities I had visited in the Middle East and Asia. The roads were wide with wide sidewalks, and the shops were generally open-air fronts. The city could use a good hosing down and fresh paint. There was a sense that it had, at one time, been a more modern city, but had fallen on hard times. We saw no battle damage, but there were vacant buildings and many buildings under construction, some partially finished with no workers or activity around and others with a lot of building activity.

The boulevards had many speed bumps and traffic circles at a major intersection. At some intersections, there were traffic tunnels under the traffic circles to speed the flow on the major highway from the airport. Vehicles on the streets included bicycles, bicycles with attached cargo beds, motorcycles, motorcycles with attached cargo beds, Japanese, German, and American autos, and heavy trucks. At each bridge and traffic circle, there were police with armed Humvees at checkpoints. Most waved us through, but at some, the driver and or our escorts had to show their IDs before we could proceed. We were cautioned not to take pictures where there were soldiers or police in view, which greatly limited our picture taking because they were all over the city. We did not see a single US or multi-national soldier or vehicle. Saadi told us they are only seen when the Iraqi military requests their help, and that had been rare in Baghdad for quite some time.

Hotel Compound

When we arrived at our hotel at 13:40, we found a narrow path with high concrete barriers ringing the hotel complex, and large concrete "Jersey" barriers on the roadside of the path. We had to disembark the bus, remove our luggage, and open it for a search by the guards, and then be patted down by the guards before they would let the bus into the complex.

Two modern-looking high-rise hotels were in the complex: The Palestine, which is where CNN operated from during the early days of hostilities, and the Ishtar Hotel, a former Sheraton hotel where we were staying.

The hotel was large with 17 floors and an open atrium of six floors. It had four elevators, but only two worked. There was a large, beautiful statute of Ishtar, the ancient Assyro-Babylonian goddess of love and fertility in the lobby, but the public rooms were run down and dingy. My room was large and had a balcony with a set of shutters on the balcony to protect the glass from an explosion outside the building. The hotel complex was across the street from the square where Saddam Hussein's statue had been torn down in the first days of hostilities. Across from the square was the blue-domed 14th Ramadan Mosque, often used as a backdrop for TV reports from Baghdad.

First Tour in Bagdad

We boarded our bus again to visit the Kadhimiyra Mosque, but as we drove close, a traffic jam had halted all traffic because it was close to prayer time. Cathy, Bob, Saadi, decided to postpone the visit, and instead, we visited a shrine to one of the Muslim prophets. Traffic was light in the area, but all the signs were in Arabic, and I was not able to get the name of the site. The sun was setting, and Saadi decided to show us the Tigris River up close. The bus stopped at a park that runs along the river, and we were able to walk to the edge in the glow of yellow lights. There were nicely laid out sidewalks curving through the park and several areas to sit among statues of poets. As we returned to the hotel, I noticed that many of the concrete barriers had fine paintings on them. Iraq is coming alive with art and beauty where it can.

Dinner was buffet style in the dimly lit main restaurant. Our group was the only people eating and apparently the only people in the hotel until after dinner when a wedding party flooded the lobby.

I retired after dinner. It had been a long day, and it had been several days since I had slept in a bed.

Ride to Samarra, Iraq

Friday, October 16, 2009, I awoke to my alarm at 05:00 after a solid 8-hour sleep. After a shower (the water was hot and had strong pressure), I rearranged my luggage to take just the carry-on bag to our trip to the Kurdistan area of Iraq.

At 06:30, I went to breakfast where I thought the offering was strange. At dinner, they had bowls of fruit for dessert, but they had no fruit at breakfast. I had a boiled egg, raw tomato, and cheese, with hot tea.

When I returned to my room, Laurie joined me in the elevator (different than the one I had taken down to breakfast), and it was filthy, with cigarette butts all over the floor. The elevators have an ashtray in each one, and someone had knocked this one over. There had been a wedding party in the hotel after I had gone to bed and the party goers had left trash in the elevators and hallways.

At 07:30, I lugged my bags to the lobby and checked my whole baggage and laptop bag with the bellman to hold while we stayed two nights in Erbil. We loaded the bus at 07:45 and drove out of the city. It was Friday, and the traffic was light (Iraq observes the Muslim week (Sunday to Thursday as workdays, Friday and Saturday as the weekend). About ten minutes from the hotel, we stopped at a roadside stand and bought bottled water and exchanged money. Twenty US$ returned 23,000 dinar.

We passed through many checkpoints as we headed north. Each district, village, or city has a checkpoint both entering and leaving. We tasked Bill to count them on his runner's watch. Over the city of Baghdad, there was a large military observation balloon on a tether, and we were told that it was one of many ringing the city with up to 32 cameras covering all areas of the city.

At 09:30, we stopped at another roadside stand where Saadi bought us some bananas, grapes, and figs. We each ate a banana, and several of us ate a fig after we washed it in bottled water. As we approached the outskirts of Samarra, we were met by two police pickup trucks with armed men in the back. They escorted us through the area. Samarra is about 90 miles north of Baghdad and one of the Four Holy Cities of Iraq.

Spiral Minaret Complex

We stopped at the Spiral Minaret Complex, which is part of what some archaeologists believe was the largest (area-wise) ancient city in the world. The 170 ft minaret is part of the Great Mosque, believed to have been built by Caliph Al Mutawakkil in 852. It was the largest mosque built of brick in the world at the time. The mosque itself was nearly 800 ft by 525 ft with walls 30 ft high. The police escorts were very jovial and joined in our picturetaking of this impressive minaret. It was a sight to see in that it is much different than most minarets that are tall towers built like lighthouses. This one has a huge base and tapers to the top with the stairway on the outside spiraling, so the stairs are at a gentle slope.

We visited the mosque restroom, and it was the worst I have ever seen. The facilities were Eastern style holes, and the running water was not working, and a lot of them were full of empty water bottles and thick dust.

On to Kurdistan via Tikrit, Iraq

From Samarra, we drove to Tikrit, Saddam's hometown, and the location of many of his 15 palaces. We drove past several palaces and the mosque where he was buried. The highway splits at Tikrit, and we turned towards Kirkuk and Erbil. The countryside was farmland and desert, much like you see driving from LA to Las Vegas or Palm Springs. At one point, we drove over a high ridge, but for the most part, it was flat desert land with a very straight highway. We passed several areas where new villas were under construction, but few were completed and occupied.

Except for the checkpoints and escort vehicles, we did not get a sense that the country was in a war. People were going about their daily activities: shopping, constructing buildings, and working in the many light manufacturing shops and auto repair shops we saw in the villages. It was just typical third world activities.

At 13:00 we exchanged escort vehicles. As we drove through the hot, dry area, the bus air conditioner blew a fuse, and the driver did not have a replacement. At a small village before Kirkuk, we left the main highway and stopped at an auto parts store to get the proper fuse. When we reached the checkpoint of Kirkuk, the escorts left. We stopped for lunch at Abdullah Rest, the equivalent of a US highway truck stop. Saadi ordered the lunch, and it was a large meal with spiced beef and chicken kabobs on rice with hummus and flatbread.

Kurdistan border Checkpoint

At 16:20 we stopped at the Kurdistan border checkpoint, like the US immigration checkpoints in California, with a large parking lot with covered areas to inspect trucks. We parked and walked to a set of trailers for processing. We were ready to show our passports when the Ministry of Tourism Kurdistan guide (Salih) arrived, and after a discussion, we were released back to the bus while they processed only our driver and guards. It took 25 minutes to process them into Kurdistan. After starting again, we had to stop at another checkpoint, and after a discussion among our guards, guides, and the checkpoint police, it was decided that they needed to see our passports after all. They collected them in the bus and took them to an office and returned in 15 minutes.

Erbil, Capital of Iraqi Kurdistan

My Blackberry stopped receiving when we entered the city of Erbil, because Kurdistan has different cell phone frequencies than Iraq. Erbil is one of the world's oldest continually inhabited cities and was a major stop on the Silk Road. It is the third-largest city in Iraq as well as the capital of the Kurdistan Autonomous Region, which was established in 1970. After the fall of Saddam Hussein in 2003, Kurdistan adopted even greater autonomy and established a flag in place of the Iraqi flag. The Iraqi constitution of 2005 explicitly recognizes the Kurdistan Regional Government and its separate, parallel administration. Historians often associate the city with the 331 B.C. Battle of Gaugamela, where Alexander the Great defeated Darius III of Persia, considered the first time a European army defeated eastern forces.

Hotel Shahan in Central Erbil

Salih told us that there was an international conference in the city and all the western-style hotels were full. By 17:30 we arrived at the Hotel Shahan in central Erbil across from the Citadel. The hotel was in a small shopping mall, and we had to pass by several stores to get to the entrance and walk up a flight of stairs to reception and the dining area. The hotel had no elevator, and I was assigned a room on the second floor at the end of the hall. It was small with two metal beds side by side, a bedside table with a broken cabinet door, an armoire with a broken door, a TV that worked, and a small refrigerator that worked. There was a window that faced a ventilation shaft.

It took me some time to find the light switch to the bathroom because it was behind the TV. The bathroom was all tile with a squat type toilet under the shower. It served as the only drain for the toilet, the shower, and the air conditioner! Fortunately, the shower faucets provided a handle to help me steady my squat. As I was trying to use this contraption, there was a knock on the door, and they wanted to check my refrigerator contents. There was no towel or washcloth, but there was soap and a box of Kleenex. I pulled my pants up and let the clerk in. The bedroom floor was dirty and had a cigarette pack top lying on it. Fortunately, there was an electrical outlet on the wall near the bed, and I was able to hook up my CPAP machine.

Dinner in Erbil

At 18:30 we assembled in the "lobby" and boarded our bus to drive to dinner. The sun had set, and the streets were brightly lit with many modern western-style stores.

A little about Erbil (also known as Arbil, Irbil, Hewler, and Howler): It is the capital of Iraq Kurdistan and is a thriving city with wide boulevards, many stores, car dealerships, and well-maintained buildings. It is considered safe for tourists to walk around and has many fine hotels. To some extent, it reminded me of Hong Kong or Dubai. It was a major contrast to Baghdad. The stores stayed open until 23:00, and there were no checkpoints in the city. They did have a lot of speed bumps on the wide boulevards, which had wide sidewalks, and modern bus stop stands. We passed brightly lit parks with colorful lights and outdoor restaurants. Since it is the bright, safest spot in Iraq, many conventions and meetings are held there, thus the inability to get western-style accommodations for us.

Eventually, the guide found a two-story restaurant that could handle our size group. It was the Istanbul Restaurant, and we were seated on the second floor. The meal started with several dishes of cold vegetables (tomatoes, carrots, and cucumber), then hot chickpea soup, then big baskets of flatbread. Each of us was given a dish of hummus and olives and cucumber. The main entree was spiced beef roll from a shish kabob, BBQ chicken wings, and hunks of white chicken meat from a shish kabob on a bed of rice.

The post-meal tea is served at another table. Everyone moves to a second table while the waiters bus the dinner table. We left at 20:30, and the drive to the hotel was quick. It turned out that after driving us all around the city looking for a restaurant, they picked one right behind our hotel.

The air conditioner had kicked off in my room, but after a bit I was able to get the switch reset and retired to my firm metal cot. The mattress was just a large piece of foam rubber. The hotel ranks as the worst hotel I have ever stayed in!

Tour Nimrud, Iraq

Saturday, October 17, 2009, our schedule was changed. Initially, we were to tour Erbil and then, on the way back to Baghdad, visit Nimrud. After a discussion, Bob, Cathy, and the guides decided to switch and visit Nimrud the first day and tour Erbil the second before driving back to Baghdad. The original schedule had us take a different route back to Bagdad, but because the Iraqi bus driver's license was held at the Kurdistan checkpoint and replaced with a Kurdistan driver's license, we had to return by the route we had taken from Bagdad.

This necessitated an early start. Breakfast was delayed until they got the bread delivered, but they had fresh fruit and boiled eggs and hot tea.

We boarded our bus at 07:00 but had to wait for the Kurdistan guide to arrive. He told us that he had been held up in traffic, which was not believable since it was the equivalent of their Sunday, and traffic was light leaving the city. There was a small park next to the hotel, and it had several people sleeping in it. I guess, despite its appearance of prosperity, the city has its homeless.

At 08:30, we reached the Mosul checkpoint and stopped to pick up an Iraq military escort. The Army Captain spoke English and told us he was serious about our safety. I think he was concerned that if anything happened to us during his escort that his military career would be over.

Our first site was Saint Benham's Monastery (also called Deir al-Jubb - the Cistern Monastery or the Mar Behnam Monastery) on the Nineveh Plain, where Nimrud flourished, dates to the 12th/13th century, a unique place of pilgrimage, in the 4th century AD, an ancient Christian structure. The Monsignor gave us a 40-minute guided tour of the monastery. It was in beautiful condition, and he was proud. Unfortunately, it was heavily damaged by ISIS in 2015.

From the monastery, we drove on to Nimrud to tour the ancient complex of Calah. As we arrived at Calah, we spotted an American patrol on a road down the hill from the complex. It was the first American forces we had seen since arriving in the country.

Nimrud (Calah in the Old Testament) lies on the east bank of the Tigris river 37 km to the southeast of Mosul and was the 2nd capital of the Assyria Empire. It was founded in 883 B.C. and had been a well-settled place for a thousand years before it was built as a center of the kingdom of Shalmaneser I (1273-1244 B.C.). While evidence at Nimrud indicates that people probably lived in its vicinity beginning as long ago as 3000 B.C., the first town-sized population was located there in the 13th century B.C. The capital city of Nimrud was built by the Assyrian king, Ashurnasirpal II, who reigned between 883–859 B.C.

In antiquity, the town was known by the name Kalhu (Calah in the Old Testament). The Arabs called it Nimrud after Nimrod, the mighty biblical hunter, father of Ashur (Assur), the Assyrian hero whose name explains why Assyrians are called Assyrians.

The city has a four-sided wall measuring 8 km tall, and several buildings raised on mud-brick platforms as much as 12 m high above river-level. Some of the buildings are: the temple of Ninurta, the northwestern palace (Assurnasirpal II's) and the southwestern palace (Esarhaddon's), Sargon's palace, and others, notably the ziggurat which looks rather like a conical hill with its remains rising to a height of 17 m. It originally had a square base, probably with a spiral ramp like that of Samarra's spiral minaret (Al-Malweyya), leading to its upper levels.

We entered the palace through a couple of doorways, between impressive statuary showing two hawk-winged lions with human heads in the well-known Assyrian style. These huge sculptures were meant to be the guardians of the city. The buildings inside included the Esida chapel and the temple of Nabu, god of wisdom, arts, and sciences, son of the Babylonian god Marduk, built-in 798 B.C. by the famous Queen Semiramis (Samuramat), mother of Adad-Nirari III (810-782 B.C.).

The World Monuments Fund lists Nimrud as one of its most endangered sites. There have been no funds to maintain the site, and we were some of the few visitors and only Americans to visit in recent years. It is a shame because the hawk winged lions and other murals were impressive, considering their age.

We spent an hour touring the site mostly on our own, taking pictures. The Iraqi army officer escorting us gave us some details on some of the areas of the site. It is a real shame that this ancient site was deteriorating. (Note that ISIS destroyed the site in 2015).

On the way back to Erbil, we stopped to buy a quick lunch. Saadi and Bob Parda bought the spicy beef in a soft bread wrap. Very tasty and not the large meal we had on the previous day at the rest stop.

We dropped our escort at the Tigris River and returned to Erbil. The road to Erbil was through the desert in some areas, but I was surprised at the many new houses under construction. I stopped counting at 100. They were similar concrete and cinderblock two-story homes unfinished in the desert or outskirts of villages.

Minare Park with the Mudhafaria Minaret

When we arrived back in Erbil, we visited the nicely manicured Minare Park with the Mudhafaria Minaret, also known as the Choly Minaret, a 36-meter high column built between 1190 and 1232 during the reign of Muzaffar Al-Din Abu Sa'eed Al-Kawkaboori, the king of Erbil at that time.

The minaret is composed of a high octagonal base and a tall cylindrical shaft, with a balcony located between the base and the shaft.

It is built of baked bricks; the base is decorated with two tiers of niches with pointed arches, two on each of the eight faces that are inscribed in rectangular frames. The balcony parapet is carved with twenty-four small niches; the access door to the minaret steps is on the eastern side of the octagonal base and leads top to the balcony. From there, a small door gives access to steps inside the cylindrical shaft that lead to the second balcony, now collapsed.

The shaft tapers inward and is decorated with several bands of interlocking diagonal Hazar-Baf motifs that are separated with thin bands. Peculiarly splendid "Kufi" calligraphy, which is a type of Arabic handwriting, can be seen, and the names of Muhammad and Mas'oudi Muhammadi, the builders of the Minaret, were inscribed.

Across the road from Minare Park was the Shanidar Park, another beautiful garden park with a large round fort type building. We walked through the gate across a footbridge with an arbor of flowers and up a walk to the building. I was surprised when I entered the building to find a round room art gallery of local artists' paintings. It was very impressive. After viewing the artwork, I exited the room and walked upstairs to the roof of the building and enjoyed a beautiful view of the parks and the city. We spent about an hour visiting the two sites and then we returned to our hotel.

Back at our hotel, we discovered that the hotel staff does not make the bed or clean the rooms but does change the soap. I made my bed with fresh sheets I obtained from a table at the top of the stairs.

Saadi then took us on a tour of the local stores—interesting. We then boarded the bus and went to a diner. It was not as fancy as the restaurant we had dined in the night before, but it was deliciously adequate

After dinner we took another tour of the local shops, and I retired early.

Tour of the Citadel in Erbil, Kurdistan, Iraq

Sunday, October 18, 2009, I arose at 05:00, showered and packed. Breakfast was ready a little faster than the previous day since it was a workday, and they were able to get the fresh bread earlier. We had boiled eggs, sliced cucumber, fresh tomatoes, yogurt, and hot tea.

After breakfast, we boarded the bus and drove up the street to the entry of the Citadel. Even though the site claims that it is the most continuously occupied building in the history of mankind, there were few people in the area except for a troop of military. We were told that some of the houses were occupied, keeping the string going, but we did not see any of the people. Since we were the first people into the site, for the day, we had the run of most of the facility. The military did stop us from visiting some of the back alleys.

We spent about an hour taking pictures of the area. Outside the walls of the Citadel, there was a good view of the city, and at the south gate is a large statue of the 12th-century historian Mubarek Ahmed Sharafaddin. After taking pictures of the scene and the statue, we reentered the Citadel and discovered the shop had now opened. We perused he shop, and I was impressed by an old 1920s era Victor (later known as an RCA Victrola) with an old Nat "King" Cole 78rpm record titled, "I'm Gonna Laugh You Out Of My Life." The store had several other antique items.

When we reassembled and boarded the bus, we exited the Citadel and started on a quest to find postcards and stamps. After Saadi asked several people, we stopped and walked to the post office where we believed that we could buy both. . It turned out they did not sell postcards but directed us to stationery stores a block or two away. After walking about six blocks and visiting many stationery stores, we returned without finding any postcards.

Aborted visit to the Erbil Museum

We boarded the bus to drive to the Erbil Museum. We drove out of town, stopping many times to ask for directions and calling our Kurdistan guide, who was no longer on the bus, for directions to the museum. Our Lonely Planet Guide had the museum marked on the map of Erbil, and we showed the map to Saadi, but no one was able to find it, so we departed for Baghdad. We determined that the Kurdistan guide was one of the most incompetent guides we had encountered in a foreign country. It was sad because we would have liked to see more of Erbil and understand the Kurdistan view of Iraq, which the guide did not provide.

Road back to Bagdad

After stopping at the Kurdistan checkpoint for the driver to get his Iraq license back, we took a different route, more direct and on a better highway, back to Baghdad. Along the way, we stopped briefly to buy spicy beef wraps for lunch and to get gas for the bus.

Iraq has several types of gas dispensing stations. They have the traditional gas station with several pumps on covered islands; they have above-ground tanks with a single hose alongside the roads; roadside bootleggers with bottles of gas (primarily sold to motorcycles and motor scooters); and an interesting sort of portable gas station in a shipping metal container. The latter can then lock up the pumps when there is no one to man them. The containers are painted in bright colors.

On this road, we passed by the banana grove where Abu Mus'ab al-Zarqawi, the top Al Qaeda leader in Iraq, was found and killed by a strike from an RPV. During the long drive, we engaged Saadi in many discussions about how he judged the situation in Iraq and what he thought the mood of other Iraqis was. Saadi expressed an extreme dislike of Saddam Hussein. He initially had done a lot for the country, building a fine network of highways, but soon focused too much of the country's resources and men on the pursuit of war with their neighbors, and had a stubborn resistance to the blockade and sanctions. He, his family, and cronies lived a wealthy life while the country deteriorated around him. Saadi claimed that Iraqis are proud people and don't like to feel they are occupied by coalition troops, but he didn't think the American troops should leave until there has been a stable election and the outside elements that have been generating the bombings subside. He said many of his countrymen like the fact that the Americans provide security: though they are no longer visible, they are ready to assist the Iraqi police and military when needed. Saadi disliked the Iraq voting process that has people voting for parties rather than individuals. The result is that people that they do not want in the Assembly get in because of their party loyalty. Saadi told us that there was a bill to change the election procedure to allow people to vote for individuals rather than a party. He said if the bill is passed, next January's election will have a greater turnout.

One observation our group had is that the Iraqis express a proud independence of their people but do not show respect for their physical country. The country is littered in plastic bags, empty plastic water bottles, cigarette butts, and general trash. It needs a good cleaning, coat of paint, and trash pickup.

When we entered Baghdad, we drove past the Ministry of Finance that was bombed in August 2009. The whole front of the building was gone, and a highway bridge was damaged.

Back in the Ishtar Hotel, I checked into a different room. One of the two elevators that were operational two days earlier had now stopped working. Dinner was the same as we had the previous night at the hotel.

Tour Babylon, Iraq

Monday, October 19, 2009, I awoke to my alarm at 05:30 and went to an early breakfast before our 07:30 departure for Babylon. When we exited the compound, the bus had to maneuver around several concrete barriers, and this time, it scraped one of the barriers along the right side, damaging the whole panel. We learned that the driver would be required to pay for the repairs himself. He was a good driver, and we felt sorry for him.

Traffic at that time of day was heavy in the city and, along the way, we stopped to get an estimate on the damage to the bus. We had not driven south of the city before, and there were a lot of checkpoints along the way. At the edge of the city, we picked up two armed escort police vehicles that led us to the outer gate to Babylon.

The Babylon complex was closed since in 2003, but the site was officially opened again in June 2009, despite some concerns about preservation still in progress. Historians disagree as to the exact site of the magnificent Hanging Gardens, one of the original Seven Wonders of the World, built by King Nebuchadnezzar II for his wife in the 6th C B.C. Though the Hanging Gardens are gone, many of his other sites remain, such as the Summer and Winter Palaces, Street of Processions, Lion of Babylon, and the Ishtar Gate. Babylon is arguably the most famous ancient city, and was the Mesopotamian capital starting with the dynasty of King Hammurabi in the 18th C B.C. (known best for his Code of Common Law).

We were met by the chief archeologist who was happy to see American tourists, and he took us on a lengthy tour of the complex. He had been restoring the site since the 1960s. We walked the Street of Processions and the Summer and Winter Palaces, which have been restored. Our guide showed us walls that he had restored in 1988 and 1989. Outside the restored area were many excavated areas and many areas that still need to be excavated and restored. We walked through some of the excavations and got a sense of the massive effort it will take to completely restore the complex. In an open area, we were able to get close to the famous Lion of Babylon. It took us almost two hours to tour the site, and we could have spent the whole day if we had wanted to tour the un-restored areas.

Saddam's Babylon Palace

Overlooking the complex, Saddam had built a palace which he visited only once during his reign. The palace staff would fix lunch for him every day, and when he did not arrive, they would throw the food in the river. After the tour of the complex, we drove up to the palace. It is a three-story building on an artificially constructed hill overlooking both the Babylon complex and the Tigris River.

The views of both were spectacular. The palace had large rooms with marble floors and wall panels and huge windows, but it had been ransacked by anti-Saddam Iraqis and possibly American troops. All glass was gone, there was graffiti in Arabic on the walls, and a basketball hoop had been installed on the wall in one of the grand halls. There was also some graffiti in English. On the walls of a narrow hallway, "Saddam is not here" was written, and on the opposite wall, "You are here."

Return to Bagdad

From Babylon we drove to Borsippar, an important religious center dedicated to their patron god Nabu. It is the site of the Ezida Temple, built during the time of Hammurabi. The ruins of a 150 ft ziggurat are perhaps the most famous site, but there are also other excavations and the shrine of the Prophet Abraham. We were scheduled to visit Hilla and Kish, but the security team decided they were not safe to visit.

At 13:00 we headed back to Baghdad and, along the way, stopped to buy lunch at a roadside stand. I had spicy beef in pita bread with lettuce and tomatoes. We were told to close the curtains on the bus, and at the stand, only Bob Parda and the guide bought the lunch. When we returned to the highway, the escort vehicle instructed our bus driver to drive fast down the center of the road. They were a little nervous that bad guys may have become aware that we were in the area.

Kadhimiya Shrine and Mosque

At 16:00 we were safely back at the hotel to refresh and start again to visit the Kadhimiya Shrine and Mosque, the second most important shrine in Iraq. It took a long time to maneuver through the traffic and find a place to park the bus near the Shrine and Mosque. We were met by a guide and were ferried in vans to the Mosque. The street leading to it was a ten-block boulevard lined with brightly light lit shops selling everything from food to clothes and hardware. It was a stark contrast to the dark area we had driven through to get to the outer gate of the mosque. The number of people, both along the boulevard, in the shops, and in the mosque, was surprising considering it was a weekday night.

The mosque guide produced a gray hooded garment for the ladies, and we had to surrender our cameras and shoes before we could enter the large square structure. The many people inside the mosque were mostly sitting in small groups and talking. Only a small percentage of people were praying. Our guide appeared to be an important official, and he had a young man in a business suit following us and taking pictures. We were not allowed to enter the shrine area for two important Shiite imams, Musa al-Kadhim and Mohammad al-Jawad, but we could see the two tombs through the doorway.

At one point, the guide directed us to a side door that led to another vast area under construction. He was proud of the area and told us how it would expand the mosque to hold thousands more worshippers. From there, he led us up a flight of stairs to an administration area that had many fine, 3-dimensional wood carvings on the wall. There were several young men wearing aprons in the room. The guide explained that the woodcarvers worked from photographs of the area. Next door was the workshop with an unfinished piece on the bench which we stood by for group photographs.

When we returned to the area outside the mosque, our shoes and cameras were returned, and we stood for more group photos with the guide.

We were ferried back up the boulevard to our bus. I rode on the back seat on the return to the hotel and felt nauseous, either from the bumpy roads or the diesel fumes.

Tour Iraq National Museum, Baghdad, Iraq

Tuesday, October 20, 2009, I awoke at 05:30, and before going down to breakfast, I decided to explore the upper floors of the hotel.

The elevator indicated 17 floors, so I rode it to the top where I found a former nightclub area in disarray. I was able to get out to a terrace which provided spectacular views. East of the hotel, I was able to take a picture of Firdos Square (a traffic circle), where Saddam Hussian's statue used to stand. Beyond the square was the blue-domed 14th Ramadan Mosque that served as a backdrop to many CNN broadcasts. Looking west was a view of a park alongside the Tigris River, and on the other side of the river was the International (Green) Zone. Looking down, I could see that the hotel had a large round pool that appeared to be full and clean, although the cabanas around it were in disrepair.

At breakfast, I learned that I was not the only curious one to visit the 17th floor and that Laurie had found a stairwell that enabled her to get to the roof and even better views.

We boarded the bus at 07:00 and drove to the Iraq National Museum for a visit. Saadi served as our guide. The museum building is quite large and had many rooms and several floors of displays. The displays, for the most part, did not fill the rooms. It was hard to determine how much had been stolen during the first days of the war. Museum docents pointed out displays that had been recovered from countries around the world during the last several years. Just recently, coins from the museum were returned from South America. We were able to take pictures in the museum. During the tour, my nausea returned, and I had to leave the group with one of our guards and seek a men's room, where I tossed my cookies. I felt much better, but I missed some of the tours.

We spent about two hours in the museum and then drove on to the entrance of the International (Green) Zone.

Tour the International (Green) Zone

Getting through security into the zone was time-consuming. Saadi and the Ministry of Tourism had obtained clearance for us to tour the zone, but there was a mix up as to which gate we were supposed to enter.

We finally were met by USAF Captain Fred Saunders, from the American Embassy Economic Development Office, a civilian consultant to the Embassy, and a young Iraqi lady from the office that had grown up in Arizona. Just like the night before, we had to leave our bus and be ferried in vans into the zone.

Our first stop was the Swords of Qadisiyah (Hands of Victory). They are immense and impressive pairs of large hands emerging from the ground, each holding a 140-foot long sword. A small flagpole rises from the point where the swords meet, at a point about 130 feet above the ground. The arms rest on concrete plinths, the form of which make the arms appear to burst up out of the ground. Each plinth holds 2,500 helmets of what Saddam claimed were Iranian soldiers killed during the war between Iraq and Iran.

The Swords mark the two ends of the Zawra Park parade ground. We took pictures and tried to capture each other in a pose that would appear as though we were holding the swords. The direction of the sunlight made it difficult, and I was not able to get in the correct position.

Adjacent to Zawra Park was the Monument to the Unknown Soldier. It is a large area shaped like a small hill with sloping terrace steps leading to an area 820 feet in diameter. Above the flat area is a 137 ft in diameter structure shaped like a warrior's shield. It slopes at a 12-degree angle.

A cube beneath the shield is made of seven layers of metal, said to represent the seven levels of Heaven in the Islamic faith. Inside the layers of metal are sheets of red acrylic, said to represent the blood of the slain Iraqi soldiers. The cube itself is connected to the underground museum by a long shaft with windows that allow light to shine in from above. Inside the museum, visitors can look up at the ceiling and see through the openings leading to the cube above. It is tough to describe.

As our group walked with Captain Saunders, we learned that his primary activity was arranging for the Japanese to invest in the Basra area. He planned on retiring at the end of this tour and returning as a contractor. He was very enthusiastic about the future of Iraq.

We boarded the vans again, and the captain drove us around the zone and along the Tigris River, where we stopped near the American Embassy, the largest American Embassy building in the world. We were told that the Embassy staff was not aware that we were in Iraq and, if they had known days before, the captain could have arranged for us to tour the Embassy. After picture taking of the Embassy from a distance, we exited the zone.

It was a hot day, and it was a little past noon when we exited and waited for our bus to pick us up. We were standing along an Iraqi Army vehicle. They had constructed a shade over their gun mounts and had a cooler of ice-cold water which they shared with us. and posed for pictures.

Tour the Arch of Ctesiphon

Once we boarded the bus, we headed south with two armed police escorts. The escorts helped us get through the traffic and into the town of Salman Pak to see the ruins of the Arch of Ctesiphon. The site of the Arch is 20 miles south of Baghdad. Ctesiphon was one of the great cities of the Persian Empire, and in the 6th Century, it was possibly the largest city in the world. The city had been sacked several times by the Romans during the 2nd Century. Little remains of the legendary White Palace except for the Arch and some surrounding structures. Parts of the arch, which is thought to be the largest brick arch in the world at 80 feet wide and 110 feet tall, still stand. The arch. We were given a rare treat because, 10 days earlier, they had unearthed a statue of a Persian queen in remarkably good shape. The outside of the walls and parts of the arch are all that remained of the once-great city.

A short distance from the arch, Saddam Hussein had built a diorama of the ancient city. The building had been heavily damaged, and the diorama destroyed. The sun was setting as we drove back to Baghdad. It was interesting to see how our escorts protected us. At first, I didn't understand why they would drive at bicyclists and try to force trucks to the side of the road, but then Saadi told us that they were intimidating those bicyclists and other vehicles to attack them rather than our bus.

Last Supper in Iraq

We arrived safely back at our hotel, and dinner was at 19:00. We were joined at the diner by Geoff Hann, from Hinterland Travel, the UK company that arranges tours through the Ministry of Tourism. Geoff has been arranging tours of Iraq since the 1970s and had approval to start back with tours in March 2009. He served as the go-between for the Ministry of Tourism and Advantage Travel & Tours. He was in Baghdad with a group from the UK that had just returned from a tour of the Basra region.

We had an early flight scheduled the next day, so I retired at 20:30.

Fly to Jordan

Wednesday, October 21, 2009, I awoke to my alarm at 03:30 to pack my CPAP machine and other electronic goodies. I spent time rearranging my luggage to support the first two nights in Jordan in my carry-on bag. My activities were slowed by my diarrhea, but I was finished and wheeled my bags to the lobby by 05:35. I was the last to breakfast, but I had eaten an orange, banana, and an apple in my room and did not plan on the hotel breakfast.

We loaded the bus at 06:00 and headed for the airport. The traffic was light, and some of the checkpoints were not manned with Humvees since the city did not start work until 09:00, and the traffic did not start getting heavy until after 07:00.

When we arrived at the parking lot on the outskirts of the airport, we had to unload our bus and bid Saadi, our VIP Protection escorts, and our driver farewell. Sabah, from the Ministry of Tourism's airport office, took over guiding us. He had two minivans, and after attempting to crowd us into them, he changed his mind and arranged for a Greyhound size bus.

As we left the parking lot, we came upon our first checkpoint. A guard checked that we each had a passport and an airline ticket. The bus then drove a short distance and backed into a parking spot where we had to get off and remove our bags, which were lined up in a row, and a dog walked the row sniffing for, I guess, explosives. After reloading the bus, we drove to another checkpoint where we had to get off and walk through a body pat-down area. Back on the bus, we were soon stopped for another passport and ticket check.

At last, we arrived at the terminal and were greeted by a crowd of porters. We were not allowed to push our baggage cart. We had to stand in line outside the terminal entrance, and only a few were allowed in at a time. When my turn came, I entered a room and had to remove my bag from the cart, and have it pass through x-ray while I got another body pat-down. Soon they directed the group I was with to put our bags back on the cart, and I was directed to another door to the terminal where my bags had to go through another x-ray.

Sabah was waiting inside for us to complete this time-consuming process, and he told us that they had called our flight. We regrouped and walked to another terminal with the check-in counters. We again had to send our bags through an x-ray machine and be patted down before we got to the Turkish Airline counter. Bob and Cathy went to the counter to get our whole group checked in. The luggage tags to Amman had to be had written, and it took about 20 minutes to get us all checked in. Our departure fee was $13 each.

From check-in, we went to passport control and the waiting area. It was then 08:15, and we still had an hour before boarding our flight. I sat near the gate and fell asleep, until an agent woke me to tell me they were lining up to board. We had to have another passport check, and the Turkish Airline agent took half our boarding card. Next, we had to have our carry on sent through an x-ray machine and we received a body pat-down. My bag had to be opened because the x-ray saw a pair of scissors in my toilet kit. When they saw that they were blunt nose, they said I could keep them.

I was assigned to seat 11D with Bill in 11E and Bob I in 11F. When the door closed, Bill moved to an aisle seat. The plane pushed back at 09:14, one minute ahead of schedule, and took off at 09:28.

We were served a breakfast of spinach quiche, and a grilled turkey ham and cheese sandwich with cheese and olives. I had tea to drink. The flight arrived in Istanbul on schedule at 12:10.

Reflections

I had safely toured Iraq with the first all American group of tourists. Our focus had been on history and archaeology. We had visited sites and been given tours that US troops have not experienced. The Ministry of Tourism was attempting to rebuild the tourism that flourished in the 1970s. We visited many places that are mentioned in the Bible as the start of the world's civilization. It was an unforgettable adventure that I am glad I was able to experience.

CHAPTER 3

JORDAN

Wednesday, October 21, 2009, I arrived from Baghdad on Turkish Airlines flight 1203 at 12:10. When we entered the terminal, we had to pass through security and be patted down again. We then had a long walk to the transit desk, where we were issued our boarding cards for the flight to Amman. Based on my United Premier Executive status, I was able to get a pass to the Turkish VIP Lounge. They did not honor either Neal's or my Red Carpet Club membership.

Inside the VIP Lounge there were internet terminals. I wrote a lengthy message summarizing the Iraq experience. It was time-consuming because of the Turkish keyboard. I first had difficulty finding the @ sign, and second, the letter "i," which was in a strange location. It appeared to be in the right spot, but tapping it generated a vertical letter like a capital "I," and the spell checker—which I heavily rely on—rejected every word I had typed with an "i" in it and I had to correct each one before I could send the message.

After sending the message, I ate a small lunch of a ham and cheese sandwich. At 17:45 I headed to the gate printed on my boarding pass and noticed on the schedule board that the gate for our flight had been changed.

When I got to the new gate, none of our group was there, so I walked over to the gate on our boarding pass and they were all there, including Barbara, an addition to our group.

Barbara had been scheduled for the Iraq tour, but her mother had an operation that delayed Barbara's departure, so she was joining us for the Jordan, Syria, and Lebanon tour.

We moved to the correct gate, where we had to pass through security again. They questioned my scissors again but let me keep them. I was assigned 5C with no one in 5B and Laurie in 5A. The plane took off at 19:30.

We landed in Amman, Jordan, at 21:15. After obtaining a Jordanian visa and passing through passport control, we retrieved our luggage. We were met by the manager of the tourist agency that arranged for our tours of Jordan, Syria, and Lebanon. He introduced us to our Jordanian guide, Naiem A. Hunetti, a 61-year-old antique store owner and expert in Jordanian archeology.

When everyone had obtained their luggage, we were directed to a bus and a driver (Nomam) who would stay with us throughout our tour of Jordan. It took us almost an hour to drive to the hotel, check-in, and get to our rooms. It was a decent size room and had an outlet next to the bedside table for my CPAP machine. I retired by 23:00.

Ride to Petra

Thursday, October 22, 2009, I awoke to my alarm at 05:00, showered, shaved, and packed my bags. Just before I left for breakfast, I decided to open my window to check the outside temperature and to take some pictures of the city. I had my camera in my right hand and pulled down the window opening lever with my left hand. As I pulled down on the handle, the whole window fell inward on me. Since my hands were both occupied, I could not stop the 3 by 3 feet square double pane window from falling. It hit my body and slid down and landed on my right foot between the top of my arch and the bottom of my toes. I pushed it against the sill with my knees and called the front desk. With a slight limp, I wheeled my bags to the elevator and down to the reception, where I left them while I ate breakfast.

Visit Madaba, Jordan

We departed the hotel at 07:00 for the drive to Petra. Amman was a beautiful city, more modern looking than Baghdad. About an hour south of the city on the biblical King's Highway, we stopped in the city of Madaba, with one of the largest Christian communities in Jordan. It is known as the Byzantine center of master mosaics and for nearby Mount Nebo. We parked in a tourist bus lot and noted that we were not the first group of tourists to arrive in the city that morning. Naiem led us on a walk through the city to St. George's Church, famous for the oldest known mosaic map of the Holy Lands on its floor. We toured the church and were shown a replica of the map. Naiem explained the areas depicted on the map. We spent about 45 minutes touring the church and some of the shops in the city before we boarded our bus for a 15-minute drive west of Madaba to Mount Nebo.

Visit Mount Nebo, Jordan

Mount Nebo is where Moses reportedly saw the Promised Land and then died at the age of 120. From the bus parking lot, there was a long uphill walk to the top. Naiem told us that many churches had been built in the area, some on top of others. It is an active archeological site as they try to restore the churches. There have been earthquakes in the area that have set back some of their efforts. From the top of a restored structure, we could see the Jordan River and the Dead Sea below and all the way to the tall spires in Jerusalem.

We took some pictures of the group at the stone that marks the memorial to Moses and then of the Abu Badd rolling stone used as a fortified door of a Byzantine monastery in the old village of Faisaliyah, once known as Kufer Abu Badd.

Included in the Mount Nebo Archaeological Park was an artist studio with artists producing mosaics. We were able to observe their working. Of course, next to the artists' studio was the tourist shop where you could buy mosaics and other trinkets.

On to Kerak, Jordan

By 10:20 we were back on the road to our next stop to exchange money. Like in Iraq, there was not a formal money exchange office or machine. Instead, there was a man alongside the road selling bottled water and exchanging money.

We drove several hours along the King's Highway, crossing the canyon of Wadi al-Mujib. The walls of the canyon are over 3,000 feet high, and the road down to the river and up the other side was an engineering marvel. This geographic feature was known as Arnon in the Bible, forming a boundary between the Moabites in the south and the Amorites in the north. The road was a sometimes winding road down to the valley and up to a ridge with a view of the city of Al Kerak (called Kir in biblical times). The terrain between Madaba and Al Kerak was rocky and sparsely populated.

The approach to Kerak was impressive. After having driven through the barren, rocky terrain we came upon the city, boasting a large Crusaders Castle on the high point over the city. It appeared to stretch the whole length of the city. We drove down on a winding road from our initial vantage point, across the valley from the city, and then up from the valley through the city to the bus parking lot outside the castle entrance.

The Kerak brochure stated: *Kerak was the stronghold of Raynald of Chatillon, Lord of Oultrejordain. The fortress was built in 1142 by Pagan the Butler, Lord of Montreal. While Raynald ruled, several truces existed between the Christian and Muslim states in the Holy Land, none of which he made any qualms about breaking. The last straw came in 1183 when he organized an expedition around the Red Sea. He captured the town of Aqaba, giving him a base of operations against Islam's holiest city, Mecca. Saladin, the leader of the Muslim forces, could not tolerate this and moved against Raynald's stronghold.*

The Muslims had sought to take Al Kerak for several years, but now they stretched its defenses to the breaking point. At one point, 9 catapults were bombarding the walls and inhabitants within. The Castle resisted the attacks by Saladin's troops in 1183 and 1184, but finally fell after a siege in 1189. The Mamluk ruler Baybars added a tower on the northwest corner in 1263. It was later owned by local families until 1840, when Ibrahim Pasha of Egypt captured the castle and destroyed much of it in the process.

After World War I, Kerak was administered by the British until the Emirate of Transjordan was established in 1921. Kerak is still a predominantly Christian town, with many of today's inhabitants tracing their roots back to the Byzantines.

The castle was impressive inside and out. We toured about eight partially restored buildings and, at the edge, we could see the steep slope that would make an attack difficult. We spent about an hour and a half touring the complex and then walked around the town. Just as before, we were not the only tour bus in the area. At one point, I counted ten buses parked outside the castle.

Petra, Jordan

We continued south on the King's Highway to Petra. The drive took three hours through the terrain, like we experienced driving to Kerak. The sun set early in this part of the world, and it was spectacular as it set below the mountains east of the Jordan River and west of the highway.

We checked into the Movenpick, a 5 Star hotel across the street from the entrance to the Petra complex. My room was a small suite with two queen size beds and a couch area. The internet was expensive, but there was an outlet at the bedside table for my CPAP machine. Dinner was a buffet, and after dinner I walked outside the hotel to an internet café and processed emails.

Friday, October 23, 2009, I rose at 05:00 to shower, shave, and pack. Breakfast was a large buffet, and at 07:00, we gathered in the lobby to start our walking tour of the Petra complex. Mike, from Indianapolis, IN, joined our group. He was on many of my previous tours with Bob and Cathy.

Naiem had planned for Edna to take a donkey-drawn carriage to the Petra Treasury site. We were offered the opportunity to ride a horse or a camel to the site. No one took the offer, and we set out walking with Naiem, who provided a running commentary on the sights in the Siq (a canyon-like cleft in the rock that is the entrance to Petra).

We walked by the area where the horses and donkeys were and were pestered by the horse vendors to ride their horses. Naiem focused on the water supply system. There were aqueducts, pipes, and grooves in the rocks that led rainwater into holding areas. It was a marvel of engineering, but we soon become bored as Naiem kept pointing out each aqueduct. About 20 minutes into the walk, we encountered numerous homes and tombs carved into the hills. We saw the first of the sculptured façades, and in a few minutes, the Triclinium/Obelisk Tomb built by a Nabataean family in the 1st century AD. It was impressive, but we knew that more impressive sights were to come.

Our next site was Wadi al-Mudhling, a natural tectonic gorge formed by flash floods, and then we reached the Siq. The sides start at about 10 feet high, and the path is about 15 feet wide. As you continue, the Siq walls go higher and at points the path narrows. It is easy to understand how the area remained unknown for several generations until it was rediscovered in 1812 by Burckhardt, a Swiss explorer.

After an hour and fifteen-minute walk, we came upon an open area with the magnificent carved façade of what is called the Petra Treasury. It is truly a sight to see. It is a tomb, but early treasure hunters thought that such a magnificent tomb must have been for an important person and that his gold and jewels would have been buried with him. They destroyed some of the figures on the outside thinking they contained valuables, and there are many bullet holes where they attempted to shatter some of the figures. In the end, no valuables were found, but the name "Treasury" stuck.

Its official name is Al-Khazna (Pharaoh's Treasury). It still has the most perfect façade in Petra and is even used in the advertising for Petra. The Treasury is 130 feet high, and the façades were carved from the top down. The lower level is decorated with six Corinthian capitals that are spanned by a frieze of griffins and vases among scrolls. A vegetation goddess is carved in the central temptation. The upper order consists of a central kiosk decorated with the relief of Isis, flanked by dancing Amazons and Victories. The kiosk is crowned by a capital supporting a funerary urn that was supposed to conceal the Pharaoh's treasures, according to local tradition. Although the original function is still a mystery, the Khazna is believed by many archaeologists to be the mausoleum of King Aretas IV (9 BC. – 40 AD) Recently, three Nabataean tombs were uncovered below the Khazna.

We spent about an hour exploring the Khazna and then moved on to see other magnificent sights, smaller tombs carved into the side of the Siq, the theater carved in the side of the walls, and other larger tombs. At the theater, the group split. Bob and Cathy, Neal, and Laurie decided to press on to see the Petra Monastery, a grueling climb that would easily take an hour or more each way.

I elected to stay with Naiem, Bob I, Barbara, Ed H, and Bill. We climbed up the side of the Siq across from the theater and explored tombs and caves. Naiem's favorite was a cave with beautiful colorful rock layers in the walls. Near this cave were several women selling trinkets, a couple of donkeys, and a young girl that took a liking to Bill. We were amazed that the donkeys were up this high, and in one cave two boys were trying to coax a donkey out of the cave.

After seeing Naiem's beautiful cave we descended to the floor of the area near the theater where there were restrooms and drink stands. I stayed with Naiem while he drank tea and then, after I had a soda, I started back by myself at 11:00. I was surprised to see an ambulance drive past because the path we had taken from the hotel was too narrow. The ambulance picked up a tourist and drove away from the way we had come. I had been told that up to a few years ago the caves in Petra had been inhabited, but the government had moved the people out and, on a high ridge to the south, there was a village that they had settled in. I guessed that there must be an exit to the south that could handle vehicle traffic.

It took me an hour to walk back to the hotel. I did not see anyone from the group, so I walked around the town, ate lunch, and visited an internet café. We had our rooms until 14:00, so I returned to my room and freshened up. The weather was hot, and my shirt was soaked from the walk. After a shower and fresh clothes, I packed and checked out of the room.

The group that traveled on to the monastery found the climb difficult and Bob and Cathy rented camels for part of the way.

We boarded the bus at 14:00, drove back to Amman, and checked back into the Imperial Palace Hotel. I noticed they had fixed the window in my room.

Dinner was the usual buffet and, since this stay was to be for two nights, I washed my clothes in the sink and hoped they would all dry by the time we left.

I retired about 23:00. It had been an eventful day. Petra had been on top of my list of places I wanted to visit, along with Angkor Wat and Babylon.

Tour Jerash, Jordan

Saturday, October 24, 2009, I slept until 06:30 and had the buffet breakfast before we started at 08:00. We drove through the city of Amman, first settled around 8500 B.C. during the Neolithic period. It was occupied by the Ammonites, Tiberian Hebrews, Assyrians,

Persians, and then the Greeks. Renamed Philadelphia after the Hellenic ruler of Egypt, Ptolomy II Philadelphius, it remained an important city, and in 106 AD, became part of the Nabotean kingdom under Roman control. Christianity became the dominant religion in 326 and Amman was the seat of the regional bishopric.

Naiem provided a running commentary as we drove north to the city of Jerash (the ancient Gerasa), about 26 miles out of Amman. As we approached Jerash we could see the Ajlun 12th C castle high on a hill overlooking the city. We stopped for a photoshoot of the castle next to an olive grove where several workers were harvesting green olives.

At the Ajlun Castle bus parking area, we visited a small museum that had a model of the castle. The road to the castle was too steep for tour buses so we had to get on a shuttle. It was an unusual shuttle, built on a truck chassis with four rows of seats in the truck bed arranged so the middle two rows were back to back facing a row facing inward.

A group from Japan had arrived before we did, and we waited until the truck returned after shuttling them up to the castle. Once we arrived at the castle, we were met by a man in an ancient warrior costume with a spear, a sword, and a shield. We assumed he was a representative of the Muslim warriors of Saladin.

The castle was built by commander Izz al-Din Usama, a nephew of Saladin, in 1184-1185. The fortress is considered one of the very few built to protect the country against Crusader attacks from Kerak in the south and Bisan in the west. From its situation, the fortress dominated a wide stretch of the northern Jordan Valley and protected the communication routes between south Jordan and Syria.

It was built to contain the progress of the Latin kingdom of Transjordan and as a retort to the castle of Belvoir on the lake of Tiberias. Another major objective of the fortress was to protect the development and control of the iron mines of Ajlun.

The original castle core had four corner towers. Arrow slits were incorporated in the thick walls and it was surrounded by a fosse averaging about 52 feet in width and about 39 to 49 feet in depth. In 1260 AD, the Mongols destroyed sections of the castle, including its battlements. Soon after the victory of the Mamluks over the Mongols at Ain Jalut, Sultan ad-Dhaher Baibars restored the castle and cleared the fosse. Two major destructive earthquakes struck the castle in 1837 and 1927.

We spent about 45 minutes touring and then boarded the shuttle truck for the ride back to our bus. Our next stop was for lunch in Jerash at a tourist restaurant with a small section of trinkets for sale.

Tour of Gerasa

After lunch we started a tour of the ruins of the Greco-Roman city of Gerasa, also referred to as Antioch on the Golden River. It is sometimes misleadingly referred to as the "Pompeii of the Middle East or Asia," referring to its size, extent of excavation, and level of preservation (though it was never buried by a volcano.) Gerasa is considered one of the most important and best-preserved Roman cities in the Near East. It was a city of the Decapolis.

It was the home of Nicomachus of Gerasa (c. 60 – c.120), one of the greatest mathematicians in human history. He is known for Introduction to Arithmetic, The Manual of Harmonics, and The Theology of Numbers, as well as many other books. His most famous book, Introduction to Arithmetic, was written using Arabic numbers and was subsequently translated into Roman numbers. The book remained a standard mathematics textbook for more than a thousand years.

It was a huge complex with the wide boulevards so common in Roman cities, with the foundations of the shops lining the boulevard. In many places the original stone showed grooves worn by carriage wheels over the centuries of traffic. There were still many Roman columns, a large plaza, and cross streets.

One area was a stadium for daily chariot races. We saw the chariots but left the site before the scheduled race. It would have been fun to see a live race, but we had places to go and more sites to see. We spent almost two hours touring the vast complex and then boarded the bus for the return drive to Amman.

Back at the hotel we cleaned up after the dusty walk around the Gerasa ruins and then Bob and Cathy hosted a party in their room to officially welcome Barbara to the group and debrief our tour of Iraq. They plan on offering the Iraq tour to their other customers and wanted our feedback on our experience.

After the buffet dinner I retired to my room and checked on my laundry from the night before. A few of the items needed another night to fully dry. I retired at 23:00.

Tour Amman, Jordan

Sunday, October 25, 2009, I slept until 05:00. My clothes had dried except for the socks, which were still slightly damp. I packed up everything and put the socks in a plastic bag. Breakfast was the usual buffet and we boarded our bus at 07:00 for a drive to the city. Naiem had the driver take us through the high rent district where the embassies are located and the wealthy people reside. Amman is known for the number of white buildings.

The Ministry of Tourism describes the history of the city as follows: Amman is one of the oldest inhabited places in the world. Recent excavations have uncovered homes and towers believed to have been built during the Stone Age. In the 3rd century BC, the city was renamed Philadelphia after the Ptolemaic ruler Philadelphus. The city later came under Seleucid as well as Nabataean rule, until Roman General Pompey annexed Syria and made Philadelphia part of the Decapolis League—a loose alliance of initially ten free city-states under overall allegiance to Rome. Under the influence of the Roman culture, Philadelphia was reconstructed in typically grand Roman style with colonnaded streets, baths, a theatre, and impressive public buildings.

During the Byzantine period, Philadelphia was the seat of a bishop, and several churches were built. The city declined somewhat until the year 635 AD. As Islam spread northwards from the Arabian Peninsula the land became part of its domain. The city reverted to its original Semitic name, Ammon, or Amman.

In 1878, the Ottomans resettled a colony of Circassian emigrants in Amman. In 1900 the city was estimated to have just 2000 residents. Following the breakup of the Ottoman Empire, the state of Transjordan was established. King Abdullah I, founder of the Hashemite kingdom of Jordan, made Amman his capital in 1921. Amman remained a small city until 1948 when the population expanded considerably due to an influx of Palestinian refugees from what is now Israel. Amman has experienced exceptionally rapid development since 1952 under the leadership of two Hashemite kings, Hussein and Abdullah II of Jordan.

In 1970, Amman was the site of major clashes between the Palestine Liberation Organization (PLO) and the Jordanian army. Everything around the Royal Palace sustained heavy damage from shelling. Most of Amman suffered great damage from PLO rockets and the Jordanian army's shells.

The city's population continued to expand at a dizzying pace (fueled by refugees escaping the wartime events in the West Bank and Iraq.) The city received refugees from those countries on many occasions. The first wave of Palestinian refugees arrived from Israel in 1948, a second wave after the Six-Day War in 1967. A third wave of Palestinian and Jordanian and Southeast Asians refugees, working as domestic workers, arrived in Amman from Kuwait after the Gulf War of 1991. The first wave of Iraqi refugees settled in the city after the first Gulf War, with a second wave arriving after the 2003 invasion of Iraq. During the last 10 years, the number of new buildings within the city has increased dramatically, with new districts being founded at a very rapid pace (particularly in West Amman), straining the very scarce water supplies of Jordan as a whole, and exposing Amman to the hazards of rapid expansion in the absence of careful municipal planning.

We drove east of the city center to the Roman Theater. It has 33 rows restored to hold 6,000 people and is an impressive structure, including two small museums. A Bedouin drum and bagpipe band in native costume performed for us.

Our next stop was Citadel Hill and the Jordan Archaeological Museum overlooking the city. The museum was not large, but it contains three statues thought to be the world's oldest examples of sculpture. Outside the museum was the ruin of Umayyad Palace dating back to 720 AD, the Byzantine basilica, and the pillars of the Temple of Hercules (also known as the Great Temple of Amman). The most impressive building of the Citadel is known as Al-Qasr (the Palace) which dates to the Islamic Umayyad period. The domed structure dominates the ruins of the Umayyad palace complex. The area was not as large as Gerasa and we completed our tour before 11:00.

As we headed out of the city, Naiem had the bus stop at a large American style shopping mall. When we entered the mall, the first thing we encountered was a Mrs. Fields cookie shop at the base of escalators leading to many levels. Several of us took the escalators to the top floor where there was an American mall-style food court. I purchased a tuna sandwich at a Subway—just the thing to get my stomach back to normal. Some of the others found a supermarket and bought the ingredients for lunch. When I exited the mall at the scheduled time, I saw Naiem sitting on a bench eating a box lunch from Popeye's.

After the mall we headed out of the city towards the Syrian border. During our drive we engaged Naiem in his views of the Israeli Palestinian problem. He provided an interesting perspective. In Jordan, the Palestinians have been allowed to immigrate and become Jordanian citizens, but not so in Syria and Lebanon. Naiem's opinion was that the Syrians like to stir up trouble in the region by encouraging the Palestinians not to negotiate with the Israelis. He blames the whole situation on the British that ruled the region after World War I and created Israel without a definitive plan for either the Palestinians or the agreement of the other Arab countries. He thinks the British are a shifty bunch, and he pointed out how they conned the US into occupying the Baghdad area of Iraq while they occupied the much safer and less volatile area of Basra.

CHAPTER 4

SYRIA

At the border we bade farewell to Naiem and, after several hours to process across the border, were met by our Syrian guide, Labib. Labib was much younger than Naiem. His father had worked for the Syrian airline, and Labib had also worked there and for British Midland Airways. He was married and had a small child. His English was fair, and he used many UK terms rather than US terminology.

When I entered Syria my BlackBerry no longer received messages and I learned that they also block Facebook and other social networks. A real head in the sand country!

About 30 minutes from the border we stopped at the town of Bosra to tour the 15,000- seat theater. It is unusual for a Roman theater in that it was not built into the side of a hill but rather is free standing in a flat area. The theater was built in the 2nd century AD and had the great acoustics associated with Roman theaters. We spent about a half an hour touring the theater and then set out for the 85-mile ride to Damascus, arriving at the Dedeman Hotel at about 18:00.

The Dedeman hotel was a 5-star hotel; I had a large room with twin queen size beds and an electrical outlet convenient for my CPAP machine. The buffet dinner was outstanding and after some journal entries I retired at 23:00.

Visit Maaloula, Syria

Monday, October 26, 2009, I awoke to my alarm at 05:00, showered, shaved, and packed. The breakfast buffet was one of the better we had experienced, except they did not have a pour- your-own coffee/tea table and we had to wave down a waiter to get a hot drink. Though I drink tea it seemed that I could only get the coffee waiter. Neal drinks coffee and he seemed to get only the tea waiter (we needed to sit at the same table.)

We departed the hotel at 07:00 and drove north. About an hour out we arrived in the city of Maaloula, the "Virgin Village," where Aramaic, the language of Jesus Christ, is still spoken. The city is built on the side of a mountain, and we stopped for picture taking on the outskirts. There was a pickup truck alongside the road full of nuts for sale. Neal had a great time negotiating the purchase of a mixture. We drove into the city and stopped at a typical ancient church. The entrance was a low opening that reminded me of Bethlehem, leading to a beautiful open stone courtyard. From the church we walked to the Convent of Saint Takla, built into the side of the mountain. There was a long flight of stairs to the top and beautiful statues, several brass doors, and a bell tower with an unusual blue cross on top. There were two horizontal members in the cross pointing in four directions. From the Convent there was a trail through a narrow canyon that led to caves dug in the side of the mountain. Three quarters up the mountain was a white statue of the Virgin Mary.

Tour of Palmyra, Syria

All told we spent about 90 minutes in the city and then drove east to Hassa. We started to see more trees than we had seen in Jordan. Both our Jordanian and now our Syrian guide told us their countries had been full of trees but, during the Ottoman period, the Turks cut down the trees to be used as railroad ties and firewood. Though both countries have embarked on a regrowth effort, Syria is ahead of Jordan in getting the trees growing along the highway. A strong wind blows from the Mediterranean across the country causing the trees to grow at a 45-degree angle, leaning toward the east.

About an hour's drive from our last stop we turned off the highway down a farm road to see two beehive-shaped huts. We had seen them in the fields in both Jordan and Syria and now Labib was allowing us to see them up close, even the insides. We were not the only tourist bus visiting this farm, and the inhabitants were dressed in native costumes and posed for photos. I could not tell what kind of farming the people did because the land around their huts was like a desert.

At 13:00 we stopped for picture taking of a group of camels grazing alongside the road. Around 13:30 we entered the outskirts of the city of Palmyra. The highway split where a new road was under construction. To the north of our road was a huge palace under construction. Labib told us that it was for an Arab prince, and when the new road was complete a road would be dedicated to just the palace.

Twenty minutes later we stopped in the center of the city at the Palmyra museum where we toured for thirty minutes.

Palmyra is probably the most important and interesting historical attraction in Syria. Mentioned on ancient tablets as early as the 19th century BC, it was an active trading center and stop along the old Silk Route. The museum described and had relics from the impressive, well-preserved ruins of Queen Zenobia's 3rd C empire. Palmyra was occupied by the Arameans and later, in 64 BC, by the Romans. In 266 AD and after the assassination of her husband, Zenobia claimed the title of Augustus for her infant son Vahaballath. In 272 AD Palmyra capitulated and Zenobia was taken as a prisoner to Rome, which signaled the decline of this once great city.

The museum had artifacts from and/or descriptions of the Temples of Bel, Nebo & Baal Shamin, Great Colonnade (which formed the main thoroughfare of the ancient city), Arch of Triumph, Tetrapyle (four groups of four columns, only one of which is the original granite), Agora (forum), the Theater, Diocletian baths, and the 17th century. AD Ibn Maan Castle.

From the museum we started a tour of the complex. We walked down the Colonnade to the Temple de Bel, the most complete building in the site, then on through the ruins along the Colonnade to the tourist bus stop. From there we then drove to the Elahbel Tower Tomb which we could enter and climb to the top. Along the way we saw several three- to four-story square tombs rising from the rocky desert terrain. Next to the Elahbel Tomb was the Three Brother's Tomb, an underground tomb with beautiful frescoes.

From the tombs we drove back to the ruins and then walked along the Colonnade from the Monumental Arch with its two arches built to mask a 30-degree bend in the Colonnade. As we walked up the Colonnade from the arch, we came upon the Zenobia Baths, containing three parts: Fridgitarium (cold), Tepidarium (warm), and Caldarium (hot). Further along the Colonnade was the Senate, a too-modest building for the ruling body of the city. A vestibule led to a small courtyard with semi-circular tiers of seats. Next, we walked through the Agora, the main place for public discussions and commercial exchanges in the city. Noticeable along the Colonnade columns was the aqueduct water system.

The sun was beginning to set so we boarded the bus and drove up the mountain overlooking the City valley to the citadel so our photographers could catch the sunset light on the ruins below. Unfortunately, a haze prevented the famous rose coloring from being generated. The citadel was a mob scene with several busloads of tourists, and our group was disappointed to miss a scene that our tour books called a must not to miss.

From the citadel we drove to our hotel, the Dedeman Palmyra, another 5-star hotel with a Las Vegas-style lobby. My room was like the one in Damascus, and the buffet was similar. I retired about 22:00

Visits to Hama and Apamea, Syria

Tuesday, October 27, 2009, I awoke at 05:00 to pack, eat an early breakfast, and get some internet time in before our scheduled departure at 07:30. The breakfast buffet offered cereal for the first time on the trip. My appetite had returned, and I ate a little bit more than I had been eating.

I was able to clean up my inbox and respond to some emails before we departed on time. It had rained during the night, and there were pools of water along the side and in some places across the road. The road north took us through farmland where we saw a lot of Gypsy tents. The Gypsies are the migrant farmworkers in Syria, moving from crop to crop picking and planting.

Our first stop was in the beautiful city of Hama with its enormous waterwheels that transition the water in the river up to the high aqueducts that run through the city. Even with the night's rain the wheels were not turning, but we stopped at 09:30 for pictures and a WC visit. The area was beautiful around the waterwheels, and we even found a Chinese market that Cathy visited, only to discover that there were no Chinese people in the market. Mike discovered a stand that sold beer and we stocked up for lunch.

Leaving the city, we drove through more farmland, this time past fields of tobacco with special buildings with ventilation holes to dry the leaves. At 11:30 we reached the ruins of Apamea (2nd C AD), one of the great ancient sites of Syria. It has some similarities to Palmyra, but its structures are gray granite and are set on a high grassy plain. Its colonnade is longer (2km) and has more restored columns than Palmyra, with one area of unique spiral columns. We could see the difference between the carriageway, marked with the scars of chariot wheels cut through the stone, and the pedestrian walkway, lined with the many small shops that fronted on the colonnade. It took us an hour to walk the colonnade and return to the bus.

Ride to Aleppo, Syria

Back on the road we passed through villages where there were funny little pickup trucks with decorations that reminded us of what we'd seen in the Philippines. In some cases, the trucks had a single wheel in the front. They were low to the ground, and many had fake Mercedes grills on them.

At 13:40 we stopped at a truck stop for lunch and a bio break. I had a beef kabob in a bread roll. Heading north we encountered some rain showers and a beautiful rainbow. Our next stop was the red stone ruins of Elba (20th century BC). There has been extensive restoration at the site that lays out the foundation of the city, but no columns and few walls. There were no other tourists there and there was a team working on the excavation. Not much has been written to describe the site, but it was worth the visit and I think it will become better known in the future.

We arrived in the city of Aleppo ahead of schedule at 15:40 and decided to tour some of the sites we had scheduled for the following day. The bus parked near an entrance to an extensive souk network of covered streets.

Labib took us on a tour of the souk, walking at a brisk pace that did not give the vendors time to bother us with their wares. It turned out his motivation was to get us to the Mosque of Abraham the Great (named after Zacharias, father of John the Baptist) before 16:00, which he was able to do. We had to remove our shoes, as usual, and the females were given gray robes with pointed hoods. Their faces showed, making them look like characters from Robin Hood. We could take photographs of the large open area featuring a cabana-like structure in the center. The Mosque has a square minaret which is a little out of the ordinary. We only spent 20 minutes there, and then visited a Serai, the Holiday Inns of the Silk Road. There are many in Iran at set intervals but not that many in Syria. Inside the two-story structure is an open area where the caravans would trade their goods. I noticed that the Swiss Consulate had their offices in this one.

We returned to the bus via the souk, again at a brisk pace with no time to shop for any goods. It took some time to drive to the hotel, as Labib wanted us to see more of the city and we drove past the hotel before we finally came back to check in about 17:30.

My room was like the previous night except that the only electrical outlet near the bed was for the bedside lamp. I went to the reception desk and asked them if they had a power strip. The desk clerk could not understand what I was asking for and asked me if I spoke French. I replied that I did not and tried drawing a picture. Finally, one of the bell boys came over with a 3to1 plug. I returned to my room and found that the device did not work because the European socket is recessed. I returned to reception and got them to follow me to the business office, where I showed them a power cord with three outlets. The IT tech arrived and gave me that power strip. When I returned to my room and tried plugging in the bedside table lamp it would not fit so I returned it to reception.

Back in my room I moved an end table near a wall outlet and plugged in the bedside lamp and used my power strip on the side of the bed for my CPAP machine and other devices. At the desk I connected my laptop and wrote in my journal until it was time to go to dinner.

I took my laptop to dinner and, after eating, went to the business office and connected to the internet and cleaned up my inbox and responded to some emails.

I returned to my room and retired at 21:00.

Tour the Basilica of St. Simeon, Syria

Wednesday, October 28, 2009, I awoke first at 05:00 but, since we were not scheduled to start our touring until 08:30, I decided to sleep until 06:00. At 06:30 I went down to breakfast toting my laptop. I had cereal again with fruit and yogurt. The whole oranges were still green but turned out to be delicious. The rest of the group started to arrive, but I excused myself to go to the lobby and connect to the internet.

I had the usual 40 or so email messages, many repeats of the news line stating that 48 percent of Americans wanted to increase the troop strength in Afghanistan and the World Series was scheduled to start Wednesday night. I answered a few messages and cleaned up my inbox and returned to my room.

We boarded the bus at 08:30 for a 45-minute drive out of the city to Qala'at Samaan, the most famous of what is called the "Dead Cities," to visit the Basilica of St. Simeon, once the largest Christian building in the Middle East. It was built in the 5th CAD after the death of Simeon, a Syrian shepherd who spent 36 years of his life preaching from the top of a massive column around which the Basilica was built. Simeon was the son of a shepherd who first joined the monastery at about the age of 20, around 400 AD. He found the monastery life not ascetic enough and retreated into a cave where he lived in self-imposed severity. Pilgrims on their way to Jerusalem would stop and seek his blessing. He resented the intrusion and built a column on top of which to live. This just increased the flow of people seeking his blessings, so he increased the height of the column until it was 18 meters high. He preached from the column and would shout answers to questions to the men below, but would not address any women, including his mother. He lived there, with a railing and a chain preventing him from falling off in his sleep, until his death.

After Simeon died the column became a holy site, and eventually the Basilica was built over it. A large Baptismal was built adjacent to the Basilica . Many of the walls of both buildings still stand, but the column was reduced to just a large boulder as Pilgrims chipped off pieces.

When our bus arrived at 09:20 there already were at least six large buses of tourists on the site. We headed for the Baptismal building first and then to the Basilica. It was difficult to get pictures without a tourist in the setting. We spent an hour touring the site and then headed back to Aleppo.

The road was well paved except that a lot of speed bumps and ditches across the road had not been properly filled, making for a very bouncy ride. The area is called the "Dead Cities," with ancient, abandoned stone houses and buildings. Syria is full of them, and there is no official explanation of why the cities were abandoned. Speculation is that the trade routes shifted and the people shifted with them. I was amazed at the rock-strewn fields that we passed. There were rock walls all over the place, some even with cement and true square dimensions but with just a field of rocks inside. At one point we saw several dozen 3 to 4 story villas partially constructed with no activity in sight to finish them.

Tour Aleppo, Syria

We returned to the city by 11:00 to visit the Aleppo National Museum. No photos were allowed inside the museum, but some of the most photogenic figures were outside the entrance. They were two-story, wide-eyed characters replicating pillars that supported an 8th or 9th BC temple unearthed in Tell Halaf in northeast Syria. Inside were pieces on display from many of the archeological sites in Syria.

We spent an hour visiting the museum. Our next stop scheduled for the day was the Aleppo Citadel but, on the way, we stopped at a bank to exchange money. The hotel had been reluctant to change money and there had not been the tourist Money Exchange offices at the Basilica or the Museum that one would expect. Along the way we passed the most crowded small bus of school kids you could imagine. It had about four rows of seats and so many 5- to 8-year-old children were crammed in, their faces were pressed against the glass. There were three little boys next to the driver in the front seat. Unfortunately, I was not able to get a good picture of the scene.

At 12:45 we arrived at the Citadel that dominates the Aleppo skyline. It was started in 3rd C BC. We crossed its 30-meter wide moat to enter, passing through massive 12th-century gates. It was built to withstand almost any kind of attack, but to Labib's knowledge it never was attacked. Within the walls, there are still excavations and restorations taking place, but there are many buildings, rooms, several Mosques, a café on the top with beautiful views of the city, and an outdoor theater open to visit. It was hazy during the time we were there so my pictures are not that impressive of the city views. One large Mosque was impressive, with stained glass windows in the dome and a beautifully carved wooden ceiling and chandeliers. We also visited a steam bath with a unique dome to let the steam escape without cooling the bath. Our tour took about one hour.

Across from the entrance was a series of outdoor cafés and, just a long block away, the entrance to the souk we had visited the day before. Several of the group wanted to have lunch, while four of us went shopping with Labib. I had left my razor at one of the hotels and thought it would be easy to purchase another in this large souk. Bob Parda had snapped a strap on his sandals and was in search of a shoe repair shop. We walked through the complete souk and across the main street until we found a stall that sold razors. I got my replacement for less than I would have paid in the states and left the group to return to the bus area. Bob and Cathy continued with Labib to find a shoe repair stall.

Back at the restaurant I found Neal, Barbara, Edna, and Ed eating lunch. I had a Diet Coke and some of Neal's flatbread (he cannot eat bread) and then I walked to the bus. The bus was supposed to leave at 15:00 but I guess the driver had not been told. Eventually he was found and we returned to the hotel, where I was able to write up the day's activities.

A Syrian's View of the Jews

At 19:00 I took my laptop with me to dinner. Dinner was like the previous night's, except that Bob started a political discussion with Labib. At one point I was through eating and planned to leave to connect to the internet, but the discussion about the Holocaust made me want to stay. I asked Labib what Syrians thought about the president of Iran denying that it ever happened. He replied that the Germans planned to exterminate the Arabs after the Jews. Again, I asked him directly about whether Syrians believed that there had been a Holocaust, and he replied that he had never heard of the Holocaust. At this point I excused myself to go to the lobby to connect to the internet. Labib had been telling us that we did not know the truth of the situation in the Middle East because the media is biased, and that he knew more than we did, and yet he never heard of the Jewish Holocaust. Give me a break!! I am glad I was leaving anyway. Later, members of the group asked me if I left because of his answer or because I was planning to leave anyway. If Labib interpreted my leaving as disapproval of his uninformed answer, then I am glad.

I was able to connect and clean up my inbox. Laurie came into the lobby and talked to the manager. The wine steward was overcharging, and she was blowing the whistle on him. I then remembered that I had not paid for my beer and returned to pay. The wine steward charged me 200 pounds, a fair price. I heard later that he was charging as much as 500 pounds before Laurie got the manager involved.

Tour of the Castle of Salah ad-Din, Syria

Thursday, October 29, 2009, I awoke at 05:00 to pack and get some internet time. At 06:30 I had finished packing and lugged my bags to the lobby, and then proceeded to breakfast. I had the usual, cereal, a whole orange, tea, and a roll with jam. After breakfast I signed on the internet, responded to some emails, and cleaned up my inbox.

At 08:00 we boarded the bus and headed towards the coast. About 50 minutes out it started to rain which slowed the driving. Also, the road was over the mountains and was slow in some places.

We stopped at 10:00 for a bio break at a roadside restaurant. It had stopped raining at this point and the driver had the bus washed. We drove another hour to the Castle of Salah ad-Din. It was very remote, and we had to be bused to the castle in a minivan over a very twisted road.

T. E. Lawrence described the castle as follows: "It was the most sensational thing in castle building I have seen." A UNESCO World

Heritage site, the castle is located on a very wooded mountain with steep sides on all sides. . It was built by the Byzantines in the 10th Century and taken over by the Crusaders in the 12th Century. The armies of Saladin captured the castle in 1188.

After the minivan driver let us off, a Syrian TV reporter and cameraman approached us and interviewed Ed and Edna.

We climbed about 80 steps to get to the entrance and then toured the castle for about an hour. Some areas were still intact and others in disrepair, but overall, we got a good sense of the layout of the castle. At the far end of the is a coffee shop which had once served as a summer vacation home for the king's daughters.

Tour Ugarit, Syria

When we left the castle, it was close to 13:00, so many of us ate lunch on the bus as we drove on to Latakia. I finished my nuts and ate an apple and a banana I had picked up at breakfast. The road continued through the mountains and the driver was not able to drive fast. Eventually we entered Latakia, the largest seaport in Syria, the country's third-largest city, and the most westernized city in Syria. We drove through the outskirts on to our next stop at Ugarit.

Ugarit contains ruins of a city that flourished between the 16th and 17th Century BC. It was a busy trade center and is renowned as the birth of the alphabet. Tablets were discovered in Ugarit that indicated the use of an alphabet to define words and describe things. It is known as the "Lost city of Ugarit," founded in the 2nd millennium BC in its present form—a former learning and trading center (once the most important city on the Mediterranean coast and birthplace of the earliest known alphabet.) It was not known until 1928 when an Alawite peasant found an old tomb and unwittingly uncovered the ancient Necropolis. It was an important city on early trade routes dating back as far as the 6th Century BC and contained excavations of a massive royal palace with 90 rooms, private dwellings, and two primary temples dedicated to

Baal and Dagon. Tablets in seven different scripts describing the activities of the time were also found at the site and are in museums in Aleppo and Damascus.

The site is not large and has not been restored but it was interesting. We got down into the ruins off the defined path and had fun getting back to the entry point. Labib led several people in one direction while Bill led others up a hill into what turned out to be a farmer's house and they were told to get out. I was in a middle group that eventually found the entry without alienating the farmer but arrived after Labib's group did.

Latakia, Syria

It was then 14:30, still too early to go to the hotel, so we stopped at a seaside complex of pizza shops. I was determined not to eat any more lunch but found the beer interesting. I had been perspiring on the walk and had rolled up my sleeves and a beer was very appealing. For 75 Syrian pounds ($1.65), I bought a large Danish beer called FAXE which was 10% alcohol. I sat with Bob, Cathy, Mike, Neal, and Barbara. Cathy and Barbara ordered pizza and insisted that the rest of us try a piece. It was tasty, and Cathy kept ordering different varieties, and I bought another beer.

I think the 10% beer insured that we were all having a good time when we boarded the bus for the drive to the hotel.

We checked in to the Afamia Rotana, a 5-star hotel right on the Mediterranean Sea. It had beautiful views of the Latakia harbor. It had an internet cable in the room with a small charge per hour. I had some difficulty getting their login instructions to work so I took my laptop down to the reception for help. When they couldn't follow the instructions either, they called the IT manager who gave me a new set of usernames and passwords to use.

Dinner was the usual buffet that we had been experiencing during the trip. After dinner I logged on to the internet and cleaned up my inbox. The country was going off Daylight Saving Time, so I reset my clocks and retired at 21:00 Standard Time.

Tour Krak des Chevaliers, Syria

Friday, October 30, 2009, several thunderstorms hit the area during the night. The hotel faced the harbor and I had a balcony. The combination of the balcony and the harbor increased the resonance of the thunder, so it woke me up every time. The hotel power failed several times during the night, and when the CPAP machine stopped that also woke me up. It was not a very restful night.

At 05:00 I got up and decided to write some emails. Breakfast was scheduled to start at 07:00 but I wheeled my bags to the lobby at 06:45 and discovered that breakfast was already open. I had cereal and then set up my laptop in the lobby to use some more of my internet time. My hotel bill for two hours of internet and a beer for dinner the night before came to $7.50.

We departed the hotel at 08:00 and drove for two hours to the castle Krak des Chevaliers. During the drive we discussed politics, both US and Syrian. At one point Labib was complaining that he could not get a visa to visit Jerusalem and I told him that it was his country's fault, not the Israelis. All Syria must do is recognize the State of Israel and sign the peace treaty to allow the passage of people between the two countries. He knew I was right and just looked at us with an embarrassed stare conceding that he had lost his argument.

We arrived at the castle around 10:00. It was a picture-book, imposing sight as we drove down from an adjacent ridge. T.E. Lawrence called the castle Krak des Chevaliers the finest castle in the world. It was built 800 years ago and is very well preserved, sitting high on a mountain that has a steep winding road to reach it. The original structures date back to 1031, but it was the Crusader knights around the middle of the 12th century who expanded it into the castle it is today. To a large extent it is the model that theater castles copy, with an outer wall with very steep slanted sides and then a moat and the inner castle. The rooms are huge, and the views of the surrounding terrain would make it difficult for an enemy to launch a surprise attack. After five years of an Islamic siege, the

Crusaders surrendered on the promise of safe passage once they learned that the Holy Land had not been won.

We spent almost two hours touring the castle, our last stop in Syria. It had been an interesting tour and I was glad that I had the opportunity to visit the country and see the antiquities before the revolution and the bitter struggles with ISIS, Turkey, and Kurds. It is such a shame that ISIS destroyed so many places like Palmyra.

CHAPTER 5

LEBANON

Forty-five minutes after we left the castle, we were at the Lebanon border, where we bid goodbye to Labib and picked up a new guide. Her name was Françoise, and she was a professor of architecture at Beirut University. It took two hours for us to process through the border, during which time it rained on and off.

From the border, we drove to Tripoli for a late lunch. It was 15:30 before we started to eat a typical Lebanese meal with hummus and the best salad I had since I left California. While we were eating, there was a heavy rainstorm. By the time we were ready to board the bus, the rain had let up a little, but the sun had set, and we drove through flooded streets to see the sites of Tripoli. We did not see much, and soon headed up the mountains to the ski resort where we were scheduled to stay. It was the Hotel Chbat, a Swiss chalet-style hotel in the Cedars ski area. It was rustic. My room had a single bed and a bunk bed. There was an outlet near the bedside table, so it was easy for me to hook up my CPAP machine and chargers. The bathroom was adequate, but I did have a cockroach in the tub, and there was no shampoo.

They had free Wi-Fi in the lobby, and I tried to connect to the Internet, but the bandwidth was such that I could not delete unwanted messages, so I quit and had a beer with the owner, Mike, and Neal. The owner showed us pictures of the snowfall they typically receive in the area. After several weeks in the Arab desert, it was a little hard to comprehend. Dinner was at 19:00 and included lentil soup and beef plus the salads, hummus, and flatbread. I sat next Françoise, who told us about her teaching and some of the tour groups she has guided. She was passionate about Lebanon and feels sympathetic about the plight of the Palestinian refugees but is adamant that they should not be granted Lebanese citizenship. She is Christian, and the way the Lebanon government is set up, with a division between the various religious sects, granting Palestinians citizenship would upset the delicate balance between sects because of how Muslims are encouraged to have as many children as possible.

After dinner, I wrote in my journal and retired early.

Lebanon Cedars

Saturday, October 31, 2009, my backup alarm woke me at 05:00. I tried sleeping until six, but the sound of rain outside my window precluded me from getting that extra hour. I was the first one with my bags packed and set out in the hall. I tried the Internet again, but the connection was so weak it was frustrating, and I quit and picked up my laptop and headed for breakfast. I had cereal, toast, tea, and an apple.

I helped one of the ladies from the hotel wheel the bags out to the bus. We had a different and larger bus and a new driver. When I went back to get the bag that I carry on the bus, the others boarded, so I ended up in the back row. Françoise told me the front seat right behind the driver was open, so I took it. s. Sometimes Françoise would occupy the seat next to me, but she liked to talk facing the passengers.

Our first site was Lebanon Cedars. We drove up the mountain, stopping along the way for photos of the valley and various churches and village scenes. The driver was a photographer and knew the best stops for Laurie and Bob Ihsen to take photographs. Of course, the rest of us would also pile out of the bus and take many pictures with our digital cameras, while Laurie and Bob were more precise with their film cameras to get just the right shot.

We stopped at a site where there was a cedar overhanging the road that is estimated to be over 160 years old. Across the street and down in a gully was the cedar that served as the model for the Lebanon flag, and a few hundred yards away stood the cedar used as the model on Lebanon money. We were lucky that the rain had stopped at this point.

Visit the Khalil Gibran Museum

We headed back down the mountain and stopped in Bcharre to visit the Khalil Gibran Museum and site of his coffin. I must admit that I had never heard of him. He is the most famous poet and artist from Lebanon. He produced most of his work in the US and France during the first decades of the 20th Century. The museum had copies of his books for sale; the most popular was titled *The Prophet*. There were four floors of his paintings, which were mostly in oil, but he also did many pencil and charcoal works. The pictures were primarily nude bodies in positions that supported his philosophy of life, friendship, marriage, and children. I was impressed and wondered if my father knew him since he was in both France and New York in the same period of the 1920s. Gibran died in 1931 at the age of 49 from emphysema. He requested that his body be returned to his home village in Lebanon. We spent an hour visiting the museum. Unfortunately, they did not allow photographs in the museum.

Byblos, Lebanon

Three hours later, we had descended the mountain for a stop at Byblos (Jbell or Jbail). Byblos is another candidate for the claim of the world's oldest continuously inhabited cities, according to some experts since the 5th millennium BC. It is attractive to archaeologists because of the successive layers of debris resulting from centuries of human habitation. The Phoenician alphabet was developed at Byblos, and the site has yielded almost all the known early Phoenician inscriptions, most of them dating from the 10th century BC.

The site was discovered in 1860 by Ernest Renan during a French survey. Since 1920, it was excavated by the Egyptologist Pierre Montet and then from 1924 by Maurice Dunand for over 60 years, at the request of the Lebanese General Directorate of Antiquities.

The archaeological excavations yielded monuments and objects of great value, illustrating the reputation and the particularity of the city through millennia. There were 16 buildings in the complex. Among them was the "Temple of the Obelisks," so-called because of a considerable amount of obelisk stones found within, and many precious objects were discovered kept in sealed pottery jars and hidden under the floors.

To reach the entrance of the site, the bus had to drive down a boulevard with ruins in the middle. At the end of the boulevard was a U-turn where we were dropped off. From the drop off point, we walked through a souk to the entrance to the ruins. We spent over an hour touring the ruins. The site had spectacular views of the Mediterranean and the city from the highest points in the 12th C. crusader castle.

Jeita Grotto

From Byblos, we drove to the Jeita Grotto. Along the way we decided to stop for a quick lunch. Françoise had told us a story about how popular McDonald's was in her neighborhood and, just then, we passed a McDonald's and voted to stop there. It was in the city of Jounieh, which has been built up with western style malls and gambling casinos. What was interesting about that decision is that very few members of the group would eat at a McDonald's in the US. Half the group even bought a sundae. We saved time by eating on the bus.

The Jeita Grotto is a compound of two separate but interconnected limestone caves spanning an overall length of nearly 5.6 miles. Although the caves appeared to have been inhabited in prehistoric times, the lower cave was not rediscovered until 1836 by Reverend William Thomson; it can only be visited by boat since it contains an underground river that provides fresh drinking water to more than a million Lebanese.

In 1958, Lebanese speleologists discovered the upper galleries 200 feet above the lower cave. That's where we started our tour, in the upper cave, which is famous for its formations, lit by an effective lighting system. The entrance to the cave is reached by cable car or a "Disney-like" train from the tourist bus parking lot. We elected to take the cable car to the entrance, a 380 feet long concrete tunnel into three huge chambers. The first was called White Chamber, the second Red Chamber, due to the color of the formations. White dripstones are pure calcite without defilement; the red color is given by iron oxide (rust) in small amounts. In Lebanon iron oxide has a red color instead of the brown beige color which is common in northern countries because a different chemical reaction caused by the high temperature produces a different kind of iron oxide. The White Chamber was medium-sized but has the most impressive formations of the cave. The Red Chamber was up to 350 feet high, and 98 feet to 160 feet wide. The third chamber is the biggest of all three chambers at a height of more than 390 ft. The longest stalactite in the world is in Jeita's White Chamber; it measures 27 feet long. At the end of the tourist path in the upper cave was a small theater where concerts were occasionally held.

Cameras were not allowed in the grotto which was unfortunate because the scenery was spectacular. Aside from being a Lebanese national symbol and a top tourist destination, the Jeita Grotto plays an important social, economic, and cultural role and is a finalist in the New 7 Wonders of Nature competition.

Beirut, Lebanon

From the grotto we drove into the city of Beirut, devastated by a recent civil war (1975-1991) now beginning to return to its days of glory as the "Paris of the Middle East." It is undergoing a massive restoration. Although references to the city date back to the 15th century BC, and excavations have established thriving civilizations centuries earlier, little of the ancient structures remain.

Françoise led us on a walking tour of what is called the "Downtown Visit" which in her tour book has been divided into 16 Sectors:

Sector 1: The Canaanite Tell. There we saw the Dog's Cemetery, two Greek towers, well-preserved mud-brick walls, the leaning walls, and the Crusader Castle.

Sector 2: We walked through The Martyrs' Square (also known as "Canons Square"), past the Cinema Opera and the Mohammad al Amine Mosque.

Sector 3: The Churches Quarter. Before the Civil War, this area contained many specialized souks. We walked by the Maronite St. Georges Cathedral, the Orthodox St. Georges Cathedral, the Nourieh Chapel, and the Greek Catholic St. Elijah Cathedral.

Sector 4: We walked along Weygand Street past the Al-Nahar building, Samir Kassir Square, and the Amir Assaf Mosque.

Sector 5: We walked along Foch Street past the Abou Bakr Mosque.

Sector 6: We walked past The Souks of Beirut which are now in buildings like western-style shopping malls.

Sector 7: Along Maarad Street we walked past the Al-Omari Mosque, Civil Roman Basilica, and around Star Square.

Sector 8: We walked Riyad el Solh Street, Banks Street and Emir Beshir Street where we saw the Prince Munzer Assaf Mosque.

Sector 9: Walking along Serail Hill we came upon The Roman Bathhouse, a large ruin excavation that stretches for blocks. Above the Bathhouse was the Grand Serail, which is now a government palace with guards who prohibited us from taking photographs of the building. Along the walkway was Omar Onsi Garden, and at the end of the area was the Ottoman Clock Tower

Sector 10: In this sector we saw the remains of the Roman Hippodrome. Then we walked by the Maghen Abraham Synagogue, described in the guidebook as, "one of the most beautiful synagogues in the Orient."

Sector 11: Southwest of Riyad Solh Square we walked by the Garden of Khalil Gibran, the great Lebanese writer and painter whose museum we had visited the day before.

Sector 12: Riyad el Solh Square, named for Riyad el Solh (1894–1951), the first prime minister of Lebanon (1943–1945) after the country's independence. Like all his successors as prime minister of Lebanon, he was a Sunni Muslim. He later served as prime minister again from December 14, 1946, to February 14, 1951. Several months after leaving office, he was assassinated in Amman, Jordan, by a member of the Syrian Nationalist Party. He was known as one of the most important personalities in Lebanon's struggle for independence and as a person able to unify Lebanon's various religious groups in the struggle for independence. In the area we walked past The Grand Theatre and the Maronite Cathedral of Saint George.

Sector 13: Saifi Village is on the edge of the downtown area. A short walk.

Sector 14: Georges Haddad Avenue is also on the edge of the downtown area. Also a short walk.

Sector 15: Fuad Shehab Avenue is also on the edge of the downtown area. Also a short walk.

Sector 16: The Waterfront is also on the edge of the downtown area, another short walk.

Another Fiasco Hotel

At 16:15 we checked into the Lancaster Hotel. My room had twin beds and outlets convenient for my CPAP machine. I attempted to get an Internet connection but needed a user ID and password from the front desk. At the front desk they told me that they did not have the current password and, though they had tried to contact their ISP, they could not get help because it was the weekend. I walked across the street to see if that hotel had an Internet connection. They did not have one either and they could not direct me to an Internet café in the general area.

I returned to the hotel and ran into Mike in the lobby. He had also attempted to find an Internet connection without success. We then headed to the bar only to be told it was closed for a private party, but we could get a drink in the café. When we ordered a beer in the café the waiter told us they did not sell beer, so we left. When I got in their small (Paris style) elevator there was another couple in the elevator. The door closed and the elevator did not move. We pushed all the buttons and it still did not move. I then rang the bell but did not hear anybody outside helping us, so I started banging on the door. The other guy in the elevator started prying the edge of the door and, as I continued to bang on the door, it finally budged so he could pry it open.

When I went down for dinner, I discovered that the restaurant was also closed for the private party and we would be served a sit-down dinner in the café. One of the group ordered a beer and Mike and I were surprised when the waiter who had turned us down earlier took the order. When he came to me, he asked me if I was the one trapped in the elevator and, when I said yes, he told me my beer would be on the house. Mike and I could not get a clear explanation on why we were turned down earlier. The dinner was a delicious fish with lemon sauce.

When we left the café after dinner, we found the lobby full of teenagers and the sound of loud music from the bar and restaurant. I walked up the stairs to my room and retired early.

Walk the Beirut Cornish

Sunday, November 01, 2009, I awoke at 06:00 for a 07:30 scheduled departure. Breakfast was the usual buffet and I had cereal and fruit.

We boarded the bus for a short drive to the famous Beirut Cornish where we exited the bus at the Pigeons' Rock (also known as the Rock of Raouché). Located at Beirut's western-most tip, the two huge rock formations, which stand like gigantic sentinels, form a golden rectangle, a rectangle whose side lengths are in the golden ratio. A distinctive feature of this shape is that when a square section is removed, the remainder is another golden rectangle; that is, with the same proportions as the first. Square removal can be repeated infinitely, which leads to an approximation of the golden or Fibonacci spiral. The rock formation reminded me of Cabo San Lucas except the opening was in a rectangle shape rather than an arch.

From the rocks we walked along the Cornish, the seaside promenade in Beirut, taking pictures of the scenery and observing the joggers, walkers, and bicycle riders. . The Cornish is lined with palm trees and a waterfront boulevard with a magnificent view of the Mediterranean and the summits of Mount Lebanon to the east. It had rained during the night and it was overcast so our pictures were not as good as we would have liked, and before we caught up to our bus at the American University it started to rain.

The rain was light and as we drove out of the city Françoise had the bus drive through some of the areas we had not walked through the previous afternoon. One stark reminder of the civil war is the Holiday Inn. This 30-story building stands vacant with large holes in its side from rocket fire during the civil war. A Japanese company has purchased the building, but they have not started to tear it down or remodel it.

Tour Baalbek, Bekaa Valley, Lebanon

We drove north to the city of Jounieh and then headed across the mountains into the Bekaa Valley. We stopped for a break in Zahlé before driving up the valley. In the valley we passed several checkpoints that were manned by Hezbollah solders. Both our guide and driver had positive things to say about the Hezbollah leadership which they see as caring for the Palestinian refugees more than their elected leaders in Palestine. But, like the Syrians, they do not allow Palestinians to immigrate, become citizens, or be granted licenses as professionals (lawyers, doctors, architects, etc.) to practice outside the refugee camps. The problem in Lebanon is the delicate balance between religious groups. The Palestinians tend to have large families and, if they were granted citizenship, would soon become the dominant group in the country.

One thing that caught my attention as we drove through the small towns was the advertising for Dutch Boy paint. It was almost as prevalent as ads for Coca Cola. When I told Françoise that my father had painted the Dutch Boy for their advertising and Painter's Magazine, and that I had often posed for his paintings, she was impressed because Dutch Boy paint was so popular in the country. I had also seen ads for it in Syria but they were not as prevalent as in the Bekaa Valley.

By 10:30 we had reached the city of Baalbek (Baalbek, Heliopolis, or the "Sun City" of the ancient world), one of the largest and best preserved ancient Roman sites (and the finest in the Middle East). it is the most important archeological site in Lebanon. The Greeks and Romans dedicated the city to the God of the Sun, father of all gods. It was conquered by Alexander the Great and later by Roman emperors; it was frequently visited by the likes of Pompey, Julius Caesar, and Hadrian. Despite the destruction caused by a series of earthquakes and invasions by Arabs and Tamerlane, it has been restored to much of its original splendor.

Our first stop was at what is advertised as the largest stone in the world. There is a quarry at the southern entrance of Baalbek where the stones used in the temples were cut. A huge block, considered the largest hewn stone in the world, still sits where it was cut almost 2,000 years ago. Called the "Stone of the Pregnant Woman," it is 21.5m x 4.8m x 4.2meters in size and weighs an estimated 1,000 tons. The stone quarry was used as the city dump up until 1991 when a Lebanese solider decided to clean up the area. After he retired from the Army, he worked full time to remove the trash, get the city to establish a trash collection service, and use a new dump area. When people would still dump their trash in the quarry he would sift through trash, find something that would lead him to the individual, and then confront the individual and ask them to stop dumping in the quarry. As a result, he has a nice, well-kept area around the stone and a small tourist shop.

We stopped for a bio and photo break before driving to the Roman ruins. We spent several hours touring the site. Françoise went into detail in explaining the architecture of the site. The first survey and restoration work at Baalbek was begun by the German Archaeological Mission in 1898. In 1922, French scholars undertook extensive research and restoration of the temples, work which was continued by the Lebanese Directorate General of Antiquities.

Baalbek's temples were built on an ancient tell that goes back at least to the end of the third millennium .BC. Little is known about the site during this period, but there is evidence that during the 1st millennium BC an enclosed court was built on the ancient tell. An altar was set in the center of this court in the tradition of the Biblical Semitic high places.

During the Hellenistic period (333-64 BC) the Greeks identified the god of Baalbek with the sun god and the city was called Heliopolis or City of the Sun. At this time, the ancient, enclosed court was enlarged, and a podium was erected on its western side to support a temple of classical form. Although the temple was never built, some huge construction from the Hellenistic project can still be seen. The Romans placed the present Great Court of the Temple of Jupiter over the ancient court.

We were left off across the street from the small circular structure known as the Temple of Venus, estimated to have been built in the mid-3rd Century. In front of the Temple of Venus were the ruins of the Muse Temple. The north and northeast side of the ruins were pillars of the Portico. After picture taking of this complex, we walked to the main entrance

Our tour group entered the complex via the Propylaea and entered the Hexagonal Court. The Propylaea and the Hexagonal Court of the Jupiter temple were added in the 3rd Century under the Severan Dynasty (193-235 AD) and work was presumably completed in the mid-3rd Century. From the Hexagonal Court we entered the Great Court Complex of the Temple of Jupiter, with its porticos, exedra, altars, and basins, which were built in the 2nd century AD. The view was breathtaking as I could picture in my mind what it would have been like in its heyday.

In the center of the court was the Tower and, farther along, the Sacrificial Altar and the court were ringed by columns. Straight ahead was the Temple of Jupiter. The temple was begun in the last quarter of the 1st century BC and was nearing completion in the final years of Nero's reign (37-68 AD). The Temple measures 288x157 feet and stands on a podium 42 feet above the surrounding terrain and 22 feet above the courtyard, reached by a monumental stairway.

When Christianity was declared an official religion of the Roman Empire in 313 AD, Byzantine Emperor Constantine officially closed the Baalbek temples. At the end of the 4th Century, the Emperor Theodosius tore down the altars of Jupiter's Great Court and built a basilica using the temple's stones and architectural elements. The remnants of the three apses of this basilica, originally oriented to the west, were seen in the upper part of the stairway of the Temple of Jupiter. After the Arab conquest in 636, the temples were transformed into a fortress.

On the south side of the temple stood the six large Corinthian Columns which are often used as the signature picture for Baalbek. Originally the temple was surrounded by 54 external columns, but most of them now lie in fragments on the ground. The six standing columns are joined by an entablature decorated with a frieze of bulls' and lions' heads connected by garlands. The podium is built with some of the largest stone blocks ever hewn. On the west side of the podium is the "Trilithon," a celebrated group of three enormous stones weighing about 800 tons each.

During construction, it was decided to furnish the temple with a monumental extension of the podium which, according to Phoenician tradition, had to consist of no more than three layers of stone. This decision initiated the cutting, transporting, and lifting of the largest and heaviest stones of all times. Not only was it to have a wall of 42 feet in height, composed of three ranges of stones, but in the interest of appearance the middle blocks were to be made of a length four times their height. Adding to this was a depth equal to the height of the stones that had to be of a volume of up to 1312 cubic feet per block, corresponding to a weight of almost 1000 tons. Technically, the builders of Baalbek proved that they could do it, since three such blocks of the middle layer are in place, but in terms of time they failed—and the podium remained incomplete. Nevertheless, so awe-inspiring were those blocks to all beholders that ever after Baalbek was known primarily as the site of the three stones, the trilithon.

From the temple we toured the Arabic Citadel and Mosque ruins and then climbed down to a lower level. After a group picture with the Corinthian Columns in the background we toured the Bacchus Temple, and then we entered a long exit tunnel with a small museum which some of us toured before we boarded our bus.

It was after noon and we were a little exhausted and hungry from the lengthy tour of the complex. Françoise had a treat in store for lunch. We were driven to the Monte Alberto hotel and resort in Zahlé, with a spectacular setting overlooking beautiful Wadi Zahlé and the Berdawni River. There, we had a large lunch consisting of Lebanese foods, several different flavors of hummus, flat bread, and kabobs.

Ride to Aanjar

From Zahlé we drove to Aanjar, home to a large Armenian Apostolic community (our driver was a proud Armenian from the area). It had started to rain but we stopped at Umayyad walled-city ruins dating back to the 8th Century. A few of us with rain gear joined Françoise for a tour of the ruins. She again gave us a detailed description of the site and its architectural and engineering details.

Aanjar is completely different from the other archaeological sites in Lebanon. The other historical sites in the country have different epochs and civilizations which were superimposed one on top of each other. Aanjar is exclusively one period and the Umayyad is a relative newcomer, going back to the early 8th Century AD. It also stands uniquely as the only historic example of an inland commercial center. The city benefited from its strategic position on intersecting trade routes leading to Damascus, Homs, Baalbek, and to the south. This almost perfect quadrilateral of ruins lies amid some of the richest agricultural land in Lebanon. It is only a short distance from gushing springs and one of the important sources of the Litani River. The name "Aanjar" comes from the Arabic Ain Gerrah, "the source of Gerrah," the name of an ancient stronghold founded in the era prior to Hellenistic times. Aanjar has a special beauty. Its slender columns and fragile arches stand in contrast to the massive bulk of the nearby Anti-Lebanon Mountains - an eerie background for Aanjar's extensive ruins and the memories of its short but energetic moment in history.

We spent about an hour touring the site in the rain before we boarded our bus for the short drive to the Syrian border where we bid goodbye to Françoise and were reunited with Labib. It took us one hour to process across the border.

The sun had set and the hour and a half drive to Damascus was in the dark. We checked into the Dedeman Hotel again and had the buffet dinner. My room was like the one I had formerly. I had lost BlackBerry service again when we entered Syria and now was able to send a short message on the Internet, then retired at 23:00.

Tour Damascus, Syria

Monday, November 02, 2009, I arose at 07:00 for the last full day of the tour. Breakfast was the usual except we had difficulty getting tea or coffee. The restaurant was crowded with lots of waiters and supervisors, but they were more concerned about busing the tables than serving the guests. The supervisors seemed preoccupied with the display of food. Cathy was the last one to arrive for breakfast and it took over 10 minutes for her to get coffee after I requested it for her from several waiters and two supervisors.

We boarded the bus at 08:30 in a light rain. Our first stop was the National Museum and it was tricky to get the bus to the entrance. Our guide had expected it to be open at 08:30 but found that it did not open until 09:00. Bob Parda, Neal, and I walked in the garden in the rain to take pictures of some of the objects outside the museum. At 09:00, several busloads of tourists crowded the front entrance. When all our group assembled our guide had to vary his tour of the museum to have us visit rooms without another guide talking to a group.

It was an interesting museum to visit at the end of our days in Syria because it contained artifacts from the many sites we had visited and that made them easier to relate to their origin. As an example, the museum entrance was relocated from Palmyra. We saw artifacts from Bosra, Maaloula, Apamea, Basilica of St Simeon, Palmyra, and Ugarit.

Damascus is a metropolis of 4 million people and the chief manufacturing and trading center of Syria. It is said to be the world's oldest inhabited capital. Written history mentions the city in the 15th C BC, but recent excavations date the site to more than one thousand years before that time. The city has been conquered and settled by numerous civilizations throughout the ages and has one of the richest histories of any city in the world. Israel's King David, the Assyrians, Nebuchadnezzar, the Persians, and Alexander the Great were early victors in battles there. By the time of Christ, Damascus had become an important Roman city. It adopted Christianity in the 4th C. AD only to be converted to Islam during the 7th C with many of the early churches changed into mosques. Subsequent "visitors" included the Abbasids, Seljuk Turks, Crusaders, Mongols, Mamluks, Ottomans, Germans, and French.

We spent almost two hours in the museum. When we left the building, the rain had let up and those that had skipped taking pictures before were able to take pictures at that point although it was still overcast.

Ten minutes down the road we left the bus again to enter the Hand Craft Market with the adjacent Takiyya as-Suleimaniyya Mosque. The market was in a large square area and it only took twenty minutes to see the whole area plus take pictures of the Mosque.

We boarded the bus and drove 15 minutes in very heavy slow-moving traffic to the Souk al-Hamidiyya adjacent to the Damascus Citadel, the only Citadel in Syria that was not located on a high hill or mountain. We disembarked in light rain. The streets of the souk are covered but there were holes in the covering, so though we did not get rained on the street was wet. The main street is 2km long and I walked not only the main street but up some of the cross streets. We were scheduled to rendezvous at the end of the street by the Western Temple Gate. I arrived early with Neal, Bill, Barbara, and Mike. Neal needed a WC and we had fun trying to get directions to one from a vendor. He did not understand my pronunciation of toilet and we went through several sign languages before he said, "Oh, toilet!" and told us where to head. We found the WC and they wanted us to pay before we entered, I guess to make sure we would pay.

At noon, the group (minus Edna, who stayed on the bus), were back together and our guide led us to ticket office of the huge Umayyad Mosque. It was raining a little harder and adjacent to the ticket office was a building that contains the tomb of Saladin, the leader of many Muslim battles. The sign over the entrance calls it "The Tomb of the Conqueror." I elected not to go in since I could see the tomb from outside and photos were not allowed, and I would have to have taken off my shoes.

After those that elected to enter the tomb had finished, we all entered the mosque. We could take pictures in the courtyard but were not supposed to take them inside; however, many tour groups were taking pictures, and no one was stopping them. The Umayyad Mosque was built in the 8th C on the site of the Roman Temple of Jupiter. The structure, which took more than 1000 craftsmen over ten years to build, is unique in that it started as a pagan temple and was then a Christian church before it was converted to a mosque. The highlight of the mosque is the tomb of John the Baptist (known as the Prophet Yahia to Muslims), and adjacent to his tomb is a baptism urn dating back to the period in which the site was a church. Another highlight is the Minaret of Jesus Christ where they believe he will appear on Judgment Day.

From the mosque we walked to the Azem Palace built in 1749, whose rooms display the traditional life of a wealthy Damascus family during the Ottoman Period. Each room had mannequins dressed in traditional clothing in poses that displayed the traditional activities in the palace during that period. Examples were the bride's room with the bride and her mother and mother-in-law getting ready for the wedding. Other rooms displayed kids in a school room, men watching an early movie, women's dresses, etc. We spent an hour touring the Palace and then, in heavier rain, walked down the Biblical Straight Street with the remains of a Roman Arch and what is described as the Christian Quarter.

By now the rain was very heavy and we decided to return to the bus and the hotel. It took us 25 minutes to get to the bus. My North Face rain jacket served me well and, although my pant legs were soaked, my shirt was dry. I had no umbrella, just a cap and the hood of the jacket. In the heavy rain and traffic, it took us over an hour to get to the hotel. Our bus driver was magnificent navigating around parked cars and down narrow streets to reach our hotel from the back side. It was amazing that he did not scratch the side of the bus.

I returned to my room and washed the dirt off my shoes and trousers. The power in my room along the wall with the TV and computer kept flickering on and off and I had to call maintenance. They did not do anything in the room but after they left the power settled down.

I was able to login to the Internet and clean up my inbox and read the New York Times and LA Times. Then I wrote in my journal before our farewell party in Bob and Cathy's room at 18:45.

Everyone that had beer, wine, or nuts brought them to Bob and Cathy's room for the farewell celebration. Bob asked us for a critique of the "Exploratory Tour" that they might incorporate in a regular offering. He told us again that we were handpicked to assist them in exploring the region because we had all traveled with them in the past and they knew what kind of trouble we would create for them (lol). Generally, everyone liked the tour. We discussed the guides and felt that for the most part they were a little too detailed at some sites; several of the group would have preferred an overview and then gone on their own to take pictures and tour.

The party broke up at 20:00 and we proceeded to dinner. I had hummus, salad, a piece of lamb, and a small piece of beef. After dinner I returned to my room and took a nap until 22:40, then showered, shaved, packed, and browsed the Internet one last time.

Fly Home

Tuesday November 03, 2009, I checked out of the hotel at 00:15 and we departed for the airport at 00:30. It was a 25-minute drive without the traffic jams of the day before. The Damascus airport is set up like other foreign airports with a security check point before you can enter the departure check-in hall. When our group lined up to pass through the security gate, we were told we were too early for our flight. Labib and Cathy discussed the situation with the security guard and he finally let us in.

Labib had determined that check in counters 16 to 19 would be used by Turkish Air to check in our flight so we lined up there. There were agents at each counter, but a lot of discussion was taking place and Labib told us they could not get the computers to work at that bank of counters. Although we were first in line at these counters, we lost that advantage when the agents decided to switch to counters 10 to 15, a 90 degree turn from the first counters. This enabled the people behind us to get in line first and, of course, the first people at each counter had problems causing us to have a long wait. When my turn came the agent had trouble checking me in even though she had already checked in Bob and Cathy. The problematic rule was that they could only check our bags to the first US destination. A supervisor finally took over and, though he only issued a boarding pass as far as Istanbul, my bag was checked through to ORD.

Labib collected our passports and got them processed through Passport Control. We then had to line up for the departure gate security check. It was easy, and although they did have me open my laptop bag, when they saw a laptop, I did not have to remove it and they passed me into the gate waiting area.

I initially sat near the door to the bus, but the seat was broken, so Neal and I moved to a spot next to Edna and Ed. When the buses arrived and we started to line up to board, Edna left her cane at the seat and I tripped over it and then tried to get it to her. Mission accomplished, but it cost me a spot on the bus and Bob I., Neal, and I had to wait for a second bus. Instead a catering truck arrived and a passenger in a wheelchair was loaded on the truck and driven to our plane. We finally boarded the second bus and rode to the plane where we got off and people started climbing the stairs. I was about to get on the stairs when the people on the stairs started descending. They were not allowing them to board the plane until they got the wheelchair passenger seated via the galley door, and they did not want a crowd on the stairs. We waited on the ramp with a cold (46° F) wind blowing across the ramp for about 15 minutes before they let us board.

I was seated in 21C and seats A and B were occupied when I arrived, but there was space for my bags in the overhead. Another bus arrived and I could not believe the luggage people were carrying on and trying to stuff in the overhead bins. It was really a screwed up scene that delayed our departure until 4:15, 40 minutes late.

At 05:00 they served a "breakfast" which consisted of two slices of cucumber, a slice of tomato, two small wedges of cheese, a roll and a small (1 in sq.) cake. They gave us a small cup of water with a sealed cover which exploded when it was opened at altitude. The man next to me sprayed my leg and I sprayed the woman across the aisle from me. After they picked up the trays, they dimmed the cabin lights and I slept for about an hour.

We landed in Istanbul at 06:07 and spent 23 minutes on the ramp before they allowed us to deplane. We crowded on two buses and waited until all the passengers and their luggage had deplaned before they drove us to the terminal. By the time we entered the terminal it was after 07:00– we had been on the ground for almost an hour! Once in the terminal our group proceeded to the transit desk for our next flight's boarding pass. The agent that processed me put a block on the seat next to me. I was assigned a middle aisle seat (12D). Then the fun began. After getting their boarding passes, US bound passengers had to be interviewed by a security agent. When I got to the interview, the agent already knew that I had been to Iraq and asked me the standard questions: had I packed my own bag? Had anybody given me something to take to the US? Did I have any sharp objects in my carry-on? He put a sticker on the outside of my passport and then I had to go to another line where they checked my passport and affixed another sticker on my passport, then I got in the transit security line and was checked again.

At long last, I was able to get into the departure hall and proceed to the Turkish Airline VIP Lounge. Neal was already there and was trying to log-in at the terminal I had used when I waited for my flight to Amman. I told him about the problem with the letter 'i' and the man next to him showed him how to generate the '@' symbol. Once he got in, he found that FaceBook was blocked.

I tried to get an internet connection for my laptop but ran into the same problem I had experienced before. The procedure is to enter your cell phone number and they SMS a password to your phone. I never received the SMS message, so I decided to forego the internet and concentrate on writing in my journal.

At 10:00 I ate some soup and a sandwich at the lounge food bar and then strolled to the departure gate. I had to process through security again to get to the waiting area. They pulled my bag again to check the scissors again. This time they confiscated them. I told them that they were TSA certified with the blunt length, but the security guard said that he was following Chicago's requirements. I was unable to convince him that I had passed through TSA checks with the scissors many times. So, without the scissors, I boarded the plane. I was seated in 12D, a middle aisle seat with two empty seats to my right. We took off at 12:10 for an almost 11-hour flight. The passenger behind me moved to an empty seat to her right so I felt comfortable reclining my seat as far as it would go and slept about six hours.

We arrived at our gate in Chicago 15 minutes late. When I had my passport check, the agent noticed the Iraq stamp on my customs declaration and was amazed when I told him that we were there as tourists. He asked me who arranged the tour and I pointed out Bob and Cathy. He just shook his head and said he would rather stay in Chicago.

My bag had been tagged as Star Alliance Priority, so it came off the carousel soon after I got there, and I bid Bob and Cathy and Bob Ihsen farewell and proceeded to the baggage transfer desk. On the United schedule board, I noticed that there was a flight to LA earlier than my reservation, so I asked the agent to book me on the earlier flight. She tagged my bag for the earlier flight but told me that the best she could do was put me on standby.

The baggage transfer to the LA flight went quickly, and I then took the train to the United domestic terminal where I had to go through security again. When I was patted down, I asked the agent about the rules on scissors and he told me that if the blade is less than four inches (which mine was) it is legal. Oh well, security is not the same all over the world.

I walked down the escalator and through the tunnel to the "C" concourse and the Red Carpet Club. There I called Judy and reported that I was back in the US and alerted her that I might need the car service earlier. Then I called Verizon and cancelled my Global BlackBerry Service. I checked the gate for the earlier flight, and it was at the very end of the concourse. I walked down to the gate and did not see my name on the standby list, but when I asked the agent, she handed me a ticket. She had already paged me. I called Judy and we confirmed the time for the car service. We boarded and pushed back on schedule at 18:20. I was seated in 8D, an economy plus row. Next to me was a woman who had just flown in from Paris. Though this flight was not as long as from Istanbul, it was still long enough to give us both no trouble dozing off.

The flight arrived at the LAX gate one minute ahead of schedule at 20:40. At the baggage carousel I was met by the car service driver who lives in my neighborhood. He was happy that I was able to get on an earlier flight since I was his last customer of the day. I was home before 22:00—my Middle East odyssey was over without any major incidents.

I had just completed an unforgettable, unique trip of a lifetime as a tourist. Many Americans travel to Iraq, Jordan, Syria, or Lebanon as journalists, in the military, for work, or for government business, but few experience the number of places we visited with local guides. Not only was I was blessed to have this experience, but also to travel with so many friends from our AT & T Family.

CHAPTER 6

NORTH KOREA

I continued my world travel, taking 18 trips before taking the definitely "Do Not Travel" trip to North Korea. Like the trips described in Chapters 1 to 5, it was arranged by Cathy and Bob Parda, *Advantage Travel & Tours*. The trip started in South Korea and this chapter documents just the North Korea portion of the trip

Start in Beijing

Sunday, September 2, 2012, leaving a tour of Jeju Island, Korea, our Advantage Travel & Tours group flew to Beijing to obtain our visas for the Democratic People's Republic of Korea (DPRK) which we call North Korea. Our group of eleven, led by Cathy and Bob Parda, included Lynn (my roommate on many prior trips), a retired schoolteacher from WV; Linda and Terry from Washington, D.C. (Terry is British, and both he and Linda had traveled with me before); Edna, Bill, and Edith Ann from many previous trips; and two newcomers, Mary, Lynn's high school girlfriend (they had just reconnected at a high school reunion); and Carla.

From Jeju Island, we flew to Pusan, South Korea, and changed planes for our flight to Beijing. At the Beijing airport, we had to wait for Carla to arrive from Chicago. David, our guide, did not have a printed sign welcoming Advantage Travel at the customs exit. However, when Cathy and I left customs we found David holding a sign for Cathy. Since Carla was new to the group, she did not know what we looked like, nor did we know what she looked like, so the wait was a little longer than planned. She had not keyed on the sign for Cathy and had exited customs and wandered around the terminal. Eventually, she spotted our group of American tourists sitting together, and she introduced herself to the group.

The ride to the hotel took almost two hours in the Beijing traffic during the evening rush hour. We were booked into the Crown Plaza Beijing hotel in the center of the city. It was a 5 Star hotel, but only had free Wi-Fi in the lobby. The room was exceptionally good, and there was an outlet near the bed for my CPAP. The bedside console had a separate switch for floor outlets, so I was able to control the lights and still have power for my CPAP.

Dinner was on our own. After catching up on my email in the lobby, I set out to find someplace to eat. As I wandered the streets near the hotel, I saw Lynn and Mary ordering in a McDonald's and decided to join them.

Tour of Beijing

Monday, September 3, 2012, while Cathy and Bob obtained our North Korean visas, David took the rest of the group on a tour of Beijing. We started at 09:00 and drove to the "798 Art Zone" located in the Dashanzi area, northeast of central Beijing. It was the site of state-owned factories, including Factory 798, which originally produced electronics. Beginning in 2002, artists and cultural organizations began to divide, rent out, and re-make the factory spaces, gradually developing them into galleries, art centers, artists' studios, design companies, restaurants, and bars.

When Judy and I toured Beijing in 2007 with OAT, they did not take us there, so I enjoyed the new experience, and hope that my daughter, Robin, can visit it someday to see the many sculptures and art galleries. Some of the sculptures were large and quite impressive. Robin has been working in the art industry since 1996.

There was a lot of slow walking around the complex, and Edna was unhappy because the guide did not understand that she cannot walk a lot. From there, we drove to the Olympic Center and had to walk to the "Birdcage" stadium. Edna paid for a tram to give her a ride around the exterior while the rest of the group walked to the top, where we were able to see the most amazing group of performers hanging from cables practicing for a big show that evening. From the top of the Birdcage, we had great views of the surrounding area. Across a plaza was the practice track, still in excellent condition.

From the Birdcage, we walked across a very wide plaza to the "Water Cube," which contains the swimming pools. There were many tourists in the plaza and in the stadium and Water Cube. Overlooking the complex was a large building shaped like a lion with IBM on the top.

The Water Cube is also called the Magic Water Place and the Holy Palace of Swimming. Twenty-four world records and 66 Olympic records were set during the 2008 Games. We had a little difficulty finding open doors to get into the seating area next to the pools, but eventually did. In addition to the swimming pool, there was another pool for diving and a water park for kids. A display of a London bus and telephone booth was set up near the gift shop.

Our bus was parked next to the National Jade Hotel where we were scheduled to have lunch. The hotel was across from the center, so we had a long walk back to eat lunch.

The lunch had a lot of Chinese dishes, not any spicy ones. Everyone liked it. But then I had a strange experience at the hotel toilets. I was the first one to make the trek up the stairs and down a dark hall to a wide-open doorway, where I found the doors to the Men and Women's room doors open. Next to the large open doorway was a sign with a figure of a man in black on the left and a figure of a woman in red on the right, so I went in the room on the left and into a stall. When I emerged from the stall, the ladies from the group were standing at the sink. I had somehow entered the women's room. We had a little laugh, and I was kidded at lunch.

After lunch, we had a long drive back to Tiananmen Square, where our bus stopped at the National Theater for a tour. It is an impressive building in the shape of a large egg. Edna stayed on the bus, and we walked to the theater and discovered it closed for an event. We then walked to Tiananmen Square and back. The square had changed since I was last there in 2007. There is a long wall in the middle with a large screen that displays a panoramic vision of China in English. The wall of the Forbidden Palace facing the square was draped in cloth, which I think was to cover some renovation work. Without the wall as a background, the groups of tourists that I observed in 2007 having their pictures taken with the wall in the background were not in the square, and it was not as crowded as before.

We had to walk back to the National Theater to board our bus. We were back at the hotel at 15:30 and had our North Korea briefing at 17:30. Bob gave us a briefing on the do's and don'ts in North Korea, and we were dismissed to eat dinner on our own.

I lugged my laptop down to the lobby and caught up on my emails and messages. After a while, I got hungry and set out in another direction from the night before to get a quick bit to eat. This time I came upon a large shopping mall and noticed a sign for a Subway, which I soon found and had my quick dinner. On my way out of the building, I passed a Pizza Hut and saw several of our group eating there. They were the ones that asked for forks at each meal, so I guess they were not accustomed to Asian food.

Air Koryo

Tuesday, September 4, 2012, we had a good breakfast at the Crown Plaza and got ready for our flight to Pyongyang on Air Koryo in a Russian Tu-204-100B aircraft. The tour guide taking us to the airport suggested we remove all luggage tags from our bags so as not to flag us as Americans. We found out later that only about 100 Americans visit North Korea every year.

The flight left on time and the aircraft was clean and in good condition. There were drop-down TV monitors, but the seats had no headset plugs, and the sound of the TV was broadcast over speakers above each row. The show was a musical performance. The flight was full, and we discovered later that a group of Italian Parliamentarians were on board. They sat in first class and their staff in the front seats of coach class.

Arrival in Pyongyang

We landed in Pyongyang and had to wait to exit while the dignitaries were greeted on the ramp and driven away.

When we picked up our luggage, we had to pass it through x-ray, and at that point I had to hand over my cell phone. The agents gave me the 3rd degree on my laptop but let me keep it. Our assigned guide for the duration of our stay in the country was Mr. Kim, a young man who spoke excellent English. He was assisted by Ginny, a young intern who had just graduated from university. Our bus and bus driver were assigned to us for the duration of the tour.

Pyongyang Arch of Triumph

On the drive to the hotel, we found the streets to be very wide with few cars and people on the sidewalks. We saw very few trucks. There were rows of five-story buildings along the route and the grounds around the buildings clean. As we entered the center of the city, we stopped at the Arch of Triumph, which celebrates the end of the twenty years of Japanese occupation in 1945. It is modeled after the Arch in Paris but does not have the traffic Paris has. After taking our photos, we continued through the city, past massive buildings with wide plazas, devoid of any crowds. As we passed the sports complex, we saw many school children in the plaza.

When we reached a bridge over a river, we exited onto an island in the middle of the river and drove to a 47-story hotel at the tip of the island.

The hotel is a 5 star and was busy with tourists. Bob and Cathy invited me down for a draft beer in a pub off the lobby. For dinner, we left the hotel and drove to a restaurant in the city. It was dark, and there were few streetlights, very few neon signs, and few cars on the streets. The restaurant was well lit and the food delicious—especially if you like kimchee flavoring. The beer was good.

The Gift House

Wednesday, September 5, 2012, we were asked to wear ties for the special places were where scheduled to visit. Our first stop was the newly opened Gift House, not to be confused with Kim Il's International Friendship Exhibition Hall. This site has 11,000 gifts, 8,000 of which, from 155 countries around the world, were on display. The International Friendship Exhibition Hall reportedly contains 90,000 gifts. It was not clear if the new Gift House contains new gifts or gifts transferred from the International Friendship Exhibition Hall.

We were told we were the first Americans to visit the new hall. No cameras were allowed inside, and we had to wear covers over our shoes. The first room contained a large statue of Kim Jong Il, the "Great Leader," which we had to bow to before entering the exhibit rooms. The gifts were impressive, including several Remington sculptures presented by the Korean American Business Association. Since we were dressed up with ties on, we took group pictures outside the building.

Grand Peoples Study House

From the Gift House, we drove to the Mansudae Fountain Park and visited the Grand Peoples Study House, a huge marble library. The library contains large rooms with adjustable desks, and people can check out books from computers lining the hall and read at the desks. Other rooms contain classrooms where students can take extracurricular classes or obtain extra study on the subjects they are studying. We observed classrooms teaching Russian and English. Every room had pictures of the "Great Leader" and the "Supreme Leader" on the walls. At the top of the building, we had great views of the city. Down below, we observed wedding couples having their pictures taken in Mansudae Park.

Mansudae Grand Monument

Leaving the building, we walked through the park to the Mansudae Grand Monument on Mansu Hill boasting two 65-foot high statues in bronze of the "Great Leader" and the "Supreme Leader." We paid our respects, and Cathy laid flowers below the statues. On each side of the statues are monuments of the struggle with Japan on one side and the Korean War on the other side. It was a beautiful clear day, and the views of the city and monuments were outstanding.

Chollima Statue

Mansu Hill also features the 150-foot high Chollima statue, completed in 1961. It was built to honor the heroism and invincible fighting spirit of the Korean people like the legendary winged horse Chollima that is said to cover a thousand li (or 250,000 miles) in a day. Mounted on the winged horse is a worker holding high the "Red Letter" of the Central Committee of the Workers' Party of Korea, and a young peasant woman holding a sheaf of rice.

After the Korean War, the country was devastated, and the Korean people had to rebuild everything, starting from ashes. To expedite the construction, President Kim Il-sung devised the slogan, "rush as the speed of Chollima." It is said that ten steps were needed when others took one, and one hundred needed when others took only ten. Every building and monument we visited, we were told, was built in an exaggerated short time because the workers followed the speed of Chollima.

The next stop was lunch. This time each person had a pot over a Sterno can heat flame to cook meat and vegetables. Again, there were dishes of vegetables and sauces around the pot.

Heavy Industry Exhibit Hall

After lunch, we drove to the Heavy Industry Exhibit Hall in the Three Revolutions Exhibition Park. The park is like the Washington DC Mall with exhibit halls lining the edge of the park. Inside the hall we saw diorama displays of mines and power plants, North Korean automobiles and motorcycles, plus other heavy machinery. They were clearly proud of their computer-controlled milling machine.

Mass Gymnastic Games and Arirang Festival

We returned to our hotel and shed our ties, had dinner, and prepared for the Mass Gymnastic Games and Arirang Festival. We arrived at the Pyongyang May Day Stadium, one of the biggest sports arenas in the world, to find the parking lot full of tour buses, soldiers, and students practicing their routines. The show was held four times a week in 2012, from August 1 to October 10. We made our way through the crowd to the beautiful stadium and were ushered to our seats in the VIP section, about ten rows up on the 50-yard line in US football stadium speak. Our seats were standard business conference seats with armrests, facing a long green velvet top table. Below us was a similar row seating the Italian Parliamentarians who rode in on our flight from Beijing. The end zone seats were empty, and we were told not to take pictures in that direction since they are often filled by the military. The area from the end zone to about the 30-yard line was full of spectators in standard stadium seating. When I tried to look behind me, an usher told me not to turn around and to look straight ahead. I did see that the stadium had three decks. Across the field sat 20,000 students each with a book of 170 color cards that they used to make beautiful pictures like we saw at the Beijing Olympics in 2008.

Fifteen minutes before the 20:00 show start, a column of performers carrying blue flags trotted into the arena and lined the back and sides. Above the card flippers, a sign displayed 1912 – 100 – 2012, and below a signboard displayed the time and the performance in Korean. Right on time, the show started with a colorful display of precision marchers, which soon blended into displays of gymnastics, dance, acrobatics, and dramatic performance, accompanied by music and other effects. The impressive effects included high wire acrobatics, light shows, and fireworks. In the background was the ever-changing mosaic of colorful scenes

Our assistant guide, Ginny, told us that the students start practice in January after school, and each student practices just one routine. She was in the Games two years ago dressed as a soldier beating a drum. She politicked for two years to be accepted for the position. Eighty thousand students participate every year.

Arirang is a Korean folk song. The song supports an old Korean fable about a boy and girl from a poor village. They are in love, but the boy leaves to fight with the rebels, and the landlord makes passes at the girl. The boy returns and observes the girl with the landlord, so leaves again. The Mass Games performances loosely followed the story with happy, fighting, and sad scenes, and ended on a happy note. Some Western observers describe the performance as Communist propaganda. Still, I found it a well-executed display of precision talent based on the same theme of boy and girl fall in love, boy goes to war and returns to find girl associated with another man, that is the basis of so many operas and plays.

After the show, we encountered a mob scene in the parking lot with our bus hemmed in by other buses, but our driver was able to weave the bus out skillfully and back to the hotel.

Tour Sariwon, North Korea

Thursday, September 6, 2012, after breakfast we boarded our bus and drove 40 miles south to the city of Sariwon, the capital of

North Hwanghae province. There we got out of the bus and walked along Sariwon Folk Street, a beautifully landscaped area below a mountain called Folk Village. We exited our bus just as a group of school children walked by all dressed in white shirts with red bandanas. The boys had black slacks and the girls mostly in black skirts or slacks, though I did see some girls in other colored slacks.

Sariwon is known to produce the country's tastiest Makgeolli, a popular Korean alcoholic beverage, a milky, off-white, and lightly sparkling rice wine with a slight viscosity and a somewhat sweet, tangy, bitter, and astringent taste. Kim had a bottle, and we all tasted a bit. It tasted a little like sparkling sake.

The Folk Village had an ancient gate with two ponds on either side. One pond had a concrete boat in the center. On the opposite side of the walkway past the gate was a recreation center with beautiful mosaic murals, and inside game rooms with Yut-nori, the Korean form of checkers and chess boards, on the floor. The games pieces, colored sticks and tokens shaped like bottle tops, were in a cabinet. Yut-Nori is played by throwing the sticks in the air, and the way they land indicates how many places you can move your token. Outside the building were concrete tables with the game pattern on top surrounded by concrete stools. In the back of the building was the larger of the two ponds. Boats of kids were rowing around in the pond. Giant sculptures of animals, including elephants and tigers, ringed the area.

Back through the gate, we visited a compound that had a series of maps in colorful mosaic tiles on walls that describe Korea's cultural ruins and historical relics. Also, in the compound, we visited the Provincial History Museum, various pavilions, and houses in the style of the Ancient- and Middle-era of Korea.

From the Folk Village, we visited the base of Mt. Jongbang, where we were entertained by a musical group practicing in an open pagoda perched on the side of the mountain. The director sat in back, and as the singers performed, he critiqued them. It was an interesting scene and performance.

Songbul Buddhist Temple

Back on the bus, we rode up the mountain to Songbul Buddhist Temple.

Founded in 848, Songbul Temple encompasses some of the oldest wooden buildings in the country. Rebuilt in 1374, the pavilion sits on a raised stone platform and features delicate paintings, cow-tongue eaves, and doors with carved flower grilles. A Koryo period five-story stone pagoda stands in front of it. Ungjin Shrine, rebuilt in 1327, is one of the oldest wooden buildings in North Korea. The long, spacious hall sits on a raised platform, and is a paradigm of Koryo architecture. One of the unusual features of the temple is the small figures of heads that bordered each side of three Buddhas. The Japanese destroyed the heads, but they have been recreated.

Arch of Reunification

We rode back to the city and, on the way, stopped for photos at the Arch of Reunification, or Monument to Three Charters for National Reunification. Erected in 2001, the Arch is situated on the Tongil expressway, which leads straight from Pyongyang to Panmunjom and, eventually, Seoul. The three principles (formalized by Kim Il-sung during a meeting with the South in 1972) are independence, peaceful reunification, and national unity. The monument depicts two Korean women in traditional dress, with their arms stretched out, trying to embrace one another and shout "long live reunification." Each woman represents the idea that the North and South are the same nation living in the same territory with the same mind but are unfortunately divided. The upper part of the tower body depicts letters reading "three charters," a map of one Korea, and magnolia designs. Both sides of each platform display group sculptures based on the themes of the three principles of national reunification, the proposal for founding a federal republic, and the concept of Korean national unity. Both sides also have the slogan. "Long Live Reunified Korea."

Mansudae Art Studio

After another great Korean lunch (for a man who usually just eats a salad for lunch, these meals were not helping my waistline), we rode to the Mansudae Art Studio. The studio is where bronze castings, sculptures, and paintings of the Great Leader and Supreme Leader are crafted, plus other artwork. We visited the studio of one of the full-time landscape artists. In the courtyard stood the 18-foot tall statue of the Kims riding side by side on horseback for Pyongyang's first public sculpture of the late leader. It was cast before Kim Jong Il died, intended to be unveiled d on his 70th birthday. During Kim Jong Il's reign, he resisted any proposals to erect bronze statues of himself. Now they are being cast to stand alongside his father

Mangyongdae Children's Palace

From the studio, we rode to the Mangyongdae Children's Palace. Dedicated in 1989, it is a large marble multi-story building that includes escalators from the ground floor of a large round center of the building to the first floor. Ringing the wide-open area were classrooms where students attend extracurricular classes. We observed music instrument, needlepoint, calligraphy, and painting classes. There was a gift shop where the students' projects are on sale.

After we toured the building, we were ushered into an auditorium where the students gave us an impressive performance of their talents in musical instruments, singing, dancing, jumping rope, and performing gymnastics. We were impressed!

Rungna People's Pleasure Ground

Our dinner that night was in a private room in a fancy restaurant. Delicious! When we returned to the hotel, we were offered the opportunity to visit the Rungna People's Pleasure Ground, a new amusement park in the capital, and the location of the first public sighting of Kim Jong-un's wife. Only Bob and I accepted the offer.

The Rungna People's Pleasure Ground is located near the Arch of Triumph and was surprisingly crowded for a weeknight. We were given the VIP treatment and could buck the lines on any ride of our choosing, but first we toured the grounds. We were intrigued by the snack bar where American style hamburgers, hotdogs, corn dogs, onion rings, French fries, and chocolate chip cookies were on sale. The trash bins were just like you would find in an American fast-food restaurant.

The first ride Bob and I selected was a twisting roller-coaster. We were ushered to the head of the line and climbed a ladder with our hands holding two arms. A cage was then closed on us. The device tilted, so we were parallel to the ground when it started. We went rolling through 360 degrees in our cage. At the same time, we were looping along and up and down on the roller-coaster. I survived without losing my dinner. Next, we picked the vertical drop ride. We again were seated ahead of the crowd, and our seats were raised 12 stories high and sat there for forty seconds, admiring the view of the Arch and the city before we dropped and were eventually braked to a gentle stop to let our body parts realign. When I left my seat, Kim pointed out that our seats had a red star, which indicated that these were seats that Kim Jong-un and his wife had sat in when they rode.

After that ride, we decided to call it a night and returned to our hotel.

Visit the DMZ

Friday, September 7, 2012, we checked out of the hotel and rode south to the DMZ. There was a steady stream of tour buses on the highway, and about an hour and a half out, we stopped along with other buses at a rest stop that crossed over the highway. Vendors had set up tables selling tourist items, coffee, and snacks. Kim told us we had a scheduled time to tour the DMZ, but we could take pictures of the countryside along the highway. We saw a lot of rice fields, and soon passed through Kaesong and then stopped at Panmunjom. There were about twenty buses in two columns in front of our bus. We walked to the Panmun souvenir shop, which was packed with tourists. Eventually, it was our turn for Kim to give us a briefing on the DMZ and the buildings we would see. It was the first time since we entered the country that we saw maps that had the dividing line drawn. Before this point, all maps showed the whole country with no mark indicating two countries.

On the wall was a map and a depiction of the buildings we would see. On each side of the DMZ line stood a three-story building set back from the line, and between those buildings there was a row of seven one-story buildings with the line running through the middle of each one. Three of the buildings were painted blue (the shade of the UN flag blue), and the others were white. After Kim's briefing, our bus arrived, and we boarded it for a short ride through tank traps to the complex. We were directed to stand on the steps of the three-story building and await our turn to enter the middle blue building. There we were given five minutes to cross back and forth freely in the room, sit at the table, shake hands with fellow travelers on the other side of the table, and take pictures.

Next, we rode to the building where the Armistice was signed on July 27, 1953. Again, we sat and shook hands across the table where a copy of the Armistice Agreement resided in a plexiglass box. Since this building is in North Korea, it also serves as a museum featuring extensive displays of the war on its walls. Included in the displays were pictures of the capture of the USS Pueblo and the Navy EC-121 that the DPRK shot down.

From the Armistice building, we rode into Kaesong where we were greeted by a very wide boulevard leading to a bronze statue of Kim Il-sung. We stopped for the renowned Kaesong cuisine which is served in over a dozen brass cups of various sauces, hardboiled egg, soups, casseroles, and vegetables. Our utensils were a brass spoon with a long handle and brass chopsticks. Each cup had a brass lid. The food was delicious.

After lunch we toured the area, and some of us walked up to the base of Kim Il Sung's statue. We then visited the Koryo Museum, which has replicas of the Koryo king's tombs. The museum resides in the city's old Confucian academy. We toured an art gallery and visited the Sonjuk Bridge, site of the murder of loyal official Jong Mong-Ju in 1392. We rode to the Nam Gate and stopped to walk around and take pictures. We also stopped at a Kaesong Folk Hotel were Kim was able to find a store that sold Coke Zero, the first diet soda we had come across in the country. Edith Ann stocked up for the rest of the trip.

Visit Hyonjongrung Royal Tomb

We then rode to Hyonjongrung Royal Tomb (also called the Tomb of King Kongmin), nominated for World Heritage status. It is one of the best-preserved royal tombs in North Korea, still in its original state, having avoided extensive "restoration" under the Communist government.

Kim told us the following story:

A local tale relates how the mountain opposite that on which the tombs sit got its name: When Kongmin's wife died, he hired geomancers to find a perfect location for which to place her tomb. Becoming upset when everyone failed to please him, he ordered that the next one to try would be given anything they desired if they succeeded; however, if they failed him, he would kill them on the spot. When one young geomancer told him to review a spot outside Kaesong, Kongmin secretly told his advisors that if he waved his handkerchief, they should execute the geomancer.

While the geomancer took the King's subjects to the spot where the tomb is now located, Kongmin climbed the one opposite to review the site. When he reached the top of the mountain, exhausted, he dabbed his brow and surveyed the area. Delightedly, he found it to be perfect and prepared to congratulate the young man personally. However, upon climbing down the mountain, he found that the man had been executed; the subjects had seen him wipe his brow and thought that he had wanted the man executed. Hearing of his foolishness, the King exclaimed: "Oh, my!" His subjects then named the mountain "Oh, my" as a memorial to the story.

Pyongyang Koryo Hotel

We returned to Pyongyang and checked in to the Pyongyang Koryo Hotel. Built in 1985 in the center of the city, it has two towers with an orange-bronze exterior and a revolving restaurant on the top of each tower. It is. Dinner that evening was in a local restaurant with a propane grill in the center of the table for four of us to cook our meat, and again there were small dishes of sauces and vegetables. My room was a small suite with a bedroom, an anteroom, and a small alcove with two window seats and a small table.

Saturday, September 8, 2012, breakfast was in a large room on the 3rd floor of tower two, which was the 2nd floor of tower 1, where our rooms were. Got that? Two towers with different numbering systems! Several of our group rode down to the lobby and crossed over to the tower 2 elevators and rode up to the 3rd floor, only to discover that if they had gotten off on the second floor in tower 1, they would be on the same level. To further confuse us, they charged for coffee and tea. It had been free in the first hotel.

City Tour

The weather had finally turned on us, and a light rain was falling. Our first stop was the bookstore. Buses could not park near the store, so we had to walk two blocks in the light rain. The store was not big, and another tour group was already there, making it very crowded. The others soon left, and I bought some books on the history of the Korean War from the DPRK viewpoint.

Our next stop was a ride in the Metro. It was not a long walk from the bus drop off to the Metro entrance. It is one of, if not the deepest, Metro lines in the world, 360 feet below ground. It seemed like one of the longest escalators I have ever ridden. The station had beautiful murals and sculptures, but the cars were not beautiful. They were clean but plain, with a 1950s style design. Since it was Saturday, there was not a rush of workers. The patrons did not look at us but just went about their business. We only rode to the next stop, which had an interesting set of chandeliers that looked like fireworks bursts.

USS Pueblo

Our bus was waiting for us at the Metro stop and drove us to the USS Pueblo, DPRK's major trophy. The ship is fitted just as it was when it was captured in January 1968. The ship was an American Electronic and Signal Intelligence (ELINT and SIGINT) banner-class technical research ship which was boarded and captured by North Korean forces. The DPRK claimed it was in their territorial waters; however reported positions showed that it was outside the 12-mile range of the coast but could have been within 12 miles of a small island. The crew was eventually released in December 1968, after the United States admitted that the ship had intruded into North Korean territory, apologized for the action, and pledged to cease any future such action. A female DPRK naval officer guided us through the ship. The ELINT and SIGINT equipment was still as it was in 1968.

When the Pueblo incident happened, I had recently been assigned to a top-secret position at the USAF Strategic Air Command headquarters in a joint service unit. The Navy officers in my unit were surprised that the crew had not destroyed the "spy" equipment on board. The incident was followed in April 1969 with the DPRK shooting down a US Navy EC-121.

Chongsan-Ri Collective Farm

After the tour of the ship, we rode out of the city to visit the Chongsan-Ri Collective Farm. Along the way, we stopped for lunch at a park next to a reservoir. The lunch was served in an outdoor pavilion where we sat on mats, and the food was cooked on small charcoal-fired grills. The entrance to the pavilion was through a decorative arch gate, across a short bridge to a small island with a pretty structure. Then to another bridge to the pavilion. It was very picturesque, but not comfortable in the cold rainy weather. Fortunately, the food was good.

At the Collective Farm, the rain had stopped, and we saw corn kernels spread on the concrete to dry. Overlooking the farm's plaza was a statue of the "Great Leader" surrounded by farmers. He reportedly visited this farm many times. In some books it is referred to as the Chongsan-Ri Revolutionary Monument and Museum. I found it interesting that we could take pictures around the site, because Google Earth shows a Surface to Air Missile (SAM) site not far (about 2,000 feet) from the areas we toured on top of a hill overlooking the farm.

We toured the farm and visited one of the farmers, who showed us his mother-in-law, his twin babies, and his modest house. It was clean and neat. The yard around the house was planted with vegetables, and the roof had watermelon growing on it. In the back, his wife was harvesting lettuce.

A short walk from the farmer's house, we entered a tomato hothouse. It was a very neat farm.

Kangso Three Tombs

Back on the bus, we rode to the Kangso Three Tombs, registered as a World Cultural Heritage site in 2004. They were charging US $150 to enter the tomb to see the drawing on the wall that we had seen replicated earlier in the week during the tour in Kaesong, so we passed on the fee.

A Night in the Bus on the way to Ryonggang Hot Springs

The rain had stopped, so Kim decided to have the driver take country roads to the Ryonggang Hot Spring Hotel where we were scheduled to spend the night. The roads were not paved, and the going was slow, but we saw a lot of the small villages and farmland along the way. About forty-five minutes after we left the tombs, we encountered a washed-out bridge from a typhoon that had passed through the previous week. The river was shallow, and the locals were piling rocks across the river so people, vehicles, and bicycles could ford the river.

The bus driver turned around, and we back drove back to the last fork in the road and started up the other road, which led to an Army base. A lengthy discussion took place with a guard at the gate, and then an officer was summoned, and more discussion took place. Finally, the bus was turned around, and we returned to the washed-out bridge.

We got off the bus at the edge of the river to lighten the load, and it was able to get across. We had to walk across stones where, in some spots, about two inches of water was flowing over them. About twenty-five minutes later, we encountered a washout of the road in a gully, and the bus bottomed out. It was a city bus, extremely low to the ground. Kim got out and directed the driver to steer the best course but the bus ground into rocks that bent an arm on the door, making it impossible to open. The driver crawled out the window and was able to use a tire tool to bend the arm back so he and Kim could enter the bus. The same thing happened twice more, and then we reached a stretch of road with deep ruts filled with water, and the bus came to a stop with the wheels spinning.

We exited the bus, and with the assistance of a couple of local farmers started to pile stones under the wheels. It was now three hours since we left the tombs, and we were not having any luck. Kim and the driver went into the village down the hill from our bus and returned with several shovels and a local farmer who started to dig out the mud and fill in rocks in front of the right rear tire. The main problem appeared to be that the undercarriage of the bus was hung-up on the crown of the road.

With the driver and Kim's attention focused on digging the bus out, we were able to wander around the village without a guide. The people paid little attention to us. The houses were one story, and gardens grew on the roof. I was surprised that, so far from the main highway, there was a checkpoint just over the hill from where we were stuck. They guard paid no attention to our walking around, taking pictures.

The sun set and we boarded the bus and snacked on power bars and other snacks that Carla and Cathy had and then tried to sleep. I had a pinched nerve in my leg, which caused a lot of pain and prevented me from falling asleep. Soon a group of about a dozen men arrived wearing yellow hard hats, and Ginny told us they were engineers from a local mine. They were able to jack the frame up and pile enough rocks under the tires so we were able to move forward. They told the driver that there was more bad road ahead, so he turned the bus around and we retreated the way we came, having the same problems at the washed-out points and the washed-out bridge. The bent arm on the door was removed to stop it from allowing the door to open.

Engine Problems

Once past the washed-out bridge, the engine emitted a warning tone. We stopped, and the driver discovered a big pool of oil leaking from the engine. He got a pail and caught a lot of it. After a while, he and Kim were able to stop the leak. So, he drove until the warning tone came on again. By then it was after midnight, but people were walking along the road. The driver stopped the bus, and Kim got in a conversation with one of the men walking along the road. Soon the three of them disappeared. They were gone a long time as we tried to sleep on the bus. Around two in the morning, a large truck appeared, heading straight for us, blinking his lights and blowing his horn. He stopped just a few feet in front and started yelling. I guess he wanted us to move. Ginny engaged him in a heated discussion and finally got the point across that we had a broken engine. Then an Army truck came up behind us, blowing his horn until the driver from the truck in front was able to calm him down. The Army truck then was able to squeeze past our bus.

Kim and the driver returned and repaired the leak, and we were able to continue to the hotel. We found out later that the leak was a cracked oil pipe, and they had gone into a village and got some epoxy cement that they applied to close the leak.

Ryonggang Hot Spring Hotel

Sunday, September 9, 2012, we finally arrived at the Ryonggang Hot Spring Hotel after 05:00. We were greeted by boxes of Korean food in Styrofoam containers, but we were not in the mood or that hungry to eat 12-hour old Korean food. Each room had a large deep tub with, in addition to the standard faucets for filling the tub or taking a shower, a faucet that delivered hot spring water. Staff informed us the hot spring water would not be turned on until 07:00. Breakfast was scheduled for 09:00. I got a couple of hours' sleep, then took a hot salty spring bath, showered, packed my bags, and left the room for breakfast on time.

Visit to Nampo, Korea

Ryonggang Hot Springs is on the outskirts of Nampo, the west coast seaport. After breakfast, we drove to the West Sea Barrage, which is located 10 miles from Nampo. The barrage, or dike, stretches for 5 miles across the Taedong River estuary, separating the saltwater from the freshwater.

Completed on June 24, 1986, after five years of construction by soldiers of the Korean People's Army, the barrage has three locks capable of handling 2,000 to 50,000-ton ships, 36 sluice gates, a swing bridge, a railway, and a highway. The barrage provides water for irrigation, industrial uses, and drinking. Before the construction of the barrage, the river was subject to tidal changes all the way to Pyongyang, and it was salty. Now the river is freshwater and stable in Pyongyang.

The main dam also has three fish ladders to permit the movement of fish between the fresh and saltwater. There is also a hydrologic and oceanographic research center. An 82- mile-long

West Sea Barrage-Sinchon-Kangryong-Ongjin waterway has also been completed to provide much-needed irrigation water to tens of thousands of acres of farmland and reclaimed tideland.

We stopped at an observation center where we were able to take photos of the barrage. A model of the complex was on display and there were pictures on the walls. Kim informed us that former US President Jimmy Carter visited the site during his June 1994 visit to North Korea.

Leaving the complex, we rode through the city of Nampo and past a 65-foot bronze statue of Kim Il-sung with a cap and long coat. The shape of this statue and the type of attire made this a little different than the other bronze statues we had seen around the country. Back on the highway to Pyongyang, we stopped at the Pyongyang Golf Course for lunch. The exit for the golf course was not marked on the highway, and the road leading to the clubhouse was not paved. It seemed like they were hiding its existence from the public. The greens and fairways were lined by dense woods. The clubhouse was at the top of a hill overlooking little of the course. We noticed that the caddies were young pretty women. (I wonder if Tiger Woods has played the course).

The lunch was roasted clams—very unusual but delicious. I had to assist the non-New Englanders in our group to open their clams. We noticed that the bus was still leaking oil. I wondered what the "big wigs" who were members of the club thought when they saw a large oil stain in the club parking area.

Pyongyang Circus Theater

Back on the highway, we made a mad dash to reach the Pyongyang Circus Theater for the 15:00 performance. What a show we were treated to! After the Mass Games and the children's performance, I thought we had seen the best talent in North Korea, but I was wrong.

The show is like Cirque de Soleil. It started with ice skaters, skating in precision maneuvers, performing gymnastic routines, and then having a bear and two baboons skating through tricks like jumping rope, jumping through hoops, shooting basketballs through a hoop, and performing other tricks. We were not allowed to take photos. I discovered after I returned to the US that PETA has taped the show and has been critical of the treatment of animals.

The ice-skating act ended with doves performing tricks. Having trained dogs during my life, I saw the animals performing like obedience dogs, rewarded with food after every stunt. The doves were something else. How they are trained to fly in a performance and return to the skater mystified me.

The ice was covered, and roller skaters performed as did dogs, as I have seen in Las Vegas. Next were performers, including young kids jumping rope inside a jumping rope, inside jumping rope! There also were jugglers, acrobats, and gymnasts.

Visit Mangyongdae, the birthplace of Kim Il-sung

After the Circus, we were greeted by a different bus and driver. Our bus was in the shop to replace the cracked oil pipe. We rode on the new bus to Mangyongdae, the birthplace of Kim Il-sung. His birth house is located only 7 miles away from the center of Pyongyang, and his grandparents apparently lived there until the 1950s.

This rural house shows how Kim Il-sung spent his childhood years with family members and has photos of this period of his life; thus, it is an important scenic spot in North Korea. The humble, restored thatched house is now surrounded by well-trimmed bushes, neatly mowed yards, and an entrance more like that of a palace. The mudded wall house is divided into a barn and several living rooms. Several objects used by the "Great Leader" and his family during their lives remain.

DPRK 64th Anniversary Dance Party

From Mangyongdae, we rode back to the center of the city to see the massive dance party held in Pyongyang's central square to celebrate the 64th anniversary of the founding of the DPRK on

September 9, 1948. Hundreds of students and others danced to music blaring from the top of the steps overlooking the square. Several of the tourists we crossed paths with during the week were also observing the dancing and, in some instances, were taking part. It was an impressive sight. But I noticed that the Korean men seemed happy and were smiling as they danced, but the women did not smile and seemed serious about correctly executing the dance steps. When I mentioned this observation to Ginny, she told me Korean women are trained not to show emotion.

From the square, we rode to back to the Pyongyang Koryo Hotel and I checked back into the same room I was in two nights ago. At 19:00, we left for the same restaurant we had eaten in on Thursday night. Again, we were seated in a private room. At the end of the dinner, we were treated to a surprise birthday cake for Carla and Terry, who both had birthdays on the 9th.

Kumsusan Memorial Palace

Monday, September 10, 2012, we rode to the Kumsusan Memorial Palace and walked up 530 steps to the Revolutionary Martyrs' Cemetery, located on Mount Taesong overlooking the city. Flanking the steps were large white sculptures of revolutionary fighters. The cemetery is the final resting place of Koreans who died fighting the Japanese during their occupation of the Korean peninsula. Each martyr's headstone was topped with a bronze bust of the martyr. At the top of the cemetery were the busts of Kim Jong-suk, Kim Il-sung's first wife and Kim Jong-il's mother. Behind their graves was a large reddish monument in the shape of a DPRK party flag with a large fan shape white structure that provides the impression of a sunburst behind the flag.

Visit the Chongrungsa Buddhist Temple

The next stop was a visit to the Tomb of King Tongmyong and the Chongrŭngsa Buddhist Temple. We were met by the resident monk, who explained the history of the site. From there, we rode back to the city and visited the Monument to Victory in the Fatherland Liberation War. The sculptures reflect the different battles of the war, one for the soldiers (The Battle of Taejon Liberation), one for the air force (Defending the Sky of the Country), one for the families of soldiers (Home Front's Support for the Front), one for the women, one for army artillery (Defenders of Height 1211), one for the navy (Defending the Territorial Waters), one for the tanks, one for machine gunners, and finally the Victory Sculpture as the centerpiece.

Visit the Chollima movie studios

After we toured the Monument to Victory in the Fatherland Liberation War, we returned to our hotel for lunch and then visited the Chollima movie studios. Inside the gate to the studio, we passed a large bronze statue of Kim Il-sung, surrounded by actors and directors in a courtyard. In the back lot, we toured mock-up sets of various countries and periods. The first stop was the ancient Korean village, where one of the buildings contained costumes we could try on and have our picture taken. Next was a street with more modern looking buildings, past that street was a thatched roof village on a side street, and then a Chinese street. At the end of the street, we were welcomed by one of the actors who was on a break with a group of support personnel. We walked on past a European house and an English Pub.

Handicrafts Exhibition Hall

The next tour was the Handicrafts Exhibition Hall, which featured embroidery, a favorite activity of Kim Il-sung's wife. There we saw young women producing beautiful embroidery pictures and saw similar pictures hung on the walls throughout the building.

Juche Tower

The next stop was the Juche Tower. It is located directly across the Taedong River from Kim Il-sung Square and is a tapering, four-sided, 560-foot tall monument built of one stone for each day of Kim Il-sung's life, and is topped with a giant red flame, illuminated at night. It is taller than the Washington Monument—upon which it is supposedly modeled—by merely a few feet. The tower serves as a chance for the North to begin educating visitors not just on the greatness of Kim Il-sung, but also on Kim Il-sungism, as Juche is sometimes called.

This "leading light of world philosophy" extolls the virtues of the independent North Korean way of socialism. By stressing strength through independence and self-reliance, it thought the people of the North could be inoculated against the evil material temptations of the outside world. "We may be poor, but at least we have our dignity. Unlike those money-grubbing sellouts in the South."

The tower offers excellent views of the city and surrounding area. We had an interesting guide who spoke excellent English and tried to explain Juche to us.

We took numerous pictures of the city, and then we rode back down to the base where we took pictures of the sculptures surrounding the tower.

Founding of the North Korean Worker's Party

We boarded the bus and rode on to the 164-foot -high monument to the founding of the North Korean Worker's Party (WPK). It is a three fisted monument: one fist holds a hammer, one holds a sickle, and a third fist holds a brush (to symbolize the success of intellectuals). We walked to the center of the monument, where there is a ring with the inscription on the outside that said: "Long live the Workers' Party of Korea which organizes and guides all victories for the Korean people!" Carved in relief in the inside of the circular band are three large sculptures showing the historical root of the WPK; the might of the single-minded unity of the leader, party, and masses; and the fighting feature of the Korean people to carry out the human cause of independence.

Relax Tour

Kim decided to move the mood away from the heavy propaganda of the last two monuments and had the bus stop at the Pyongyang Gold Lane bowling alley and pool hall where we could see the locals relaxing.

We stopped at the Rakwon department store. On the first floor, there was a supermarket selling food and other daily requirements, while electronics and clothes were found on the second floor. It was not very well stocked, and I do not think anyone in our group purchased anything. The hotels had similar merchandise in their shops, so the souvenirs had already been purchased.

The Last Supper

The next stop was for our last dinner in North Korea. We were scheduled to eat at the Diplomatic Club, an exclusive restaurant, but found that it was closed in observance of the DPRK Founding Day. As it had fallen on a Sunday, Monday was being observed as the holiday. Instead, we went to a pizza and spaghetti restaurant.

That was an interesting experience. We sat at one long table and ordered from a menu with pictures of the various pizzas and other dishes, loosely translated into English. Bill wanted a pepperoni pizza, but what he got was a pizza with sliced green peppers. He turned it down, and I had a piece, and I'm told my face turned bright red when I ate the hot spice seeds of the pepper.

The place also had karaoke, and we were able to hear Ginny play the piano. She played several tunes, including "You are the Sunshine of My Life," and finished with an excellent version of "Danny Boy." It was a fitting end to our adventure.

Summary of Our Tour

In summary: Our English-speaking guide estimated only about 100 Americans visit the country per year. However, a lot of tourists from China and other countries visit each year which is why we saw so many tourist buses.

I did not see any starving people, but we only traveled in the area between Pyongyang and the DMZ. We were supposed to visit the mountains to the northeast, but due to the typhoon, there was too much damage and many roads were washed out. The vehicle traffic was light except for the buses at the tourist attractions. I did not see very many trucks moving goods to or from the villages. We did not see any farmers markets, so I am not sure where the people obtain their food. Even in Pyongyang we did not see a lot of people, even on the Metro. The people we did see did not show curiosity and did not look at us or attempt to talk to us. The guides had a good command of the English language and had a good knowledge of the sites we were being shown. We saw a lot of men and women in Army uniforms, but they often were doing work like construction and clean-up. Our guides did not preach or spout a "party line"—they just gave us facts (lots of technical facts like size, the number of times one of the leaders visited a site, and the time it took to construct a site). There was no attempt to convince us that they lived in a superior system. All explanations and maps (except at the DMZ) referred to one country, with South Korea having a different type of government. The books I read that were published in North Korea referred to the southern provinces as puppets of the "Imperialist US," but that was not emphasized by the guides. At no time did I see any hostility toward Americans or any Westerners.

Fly back to Beijing

Tuesday, September 11, 2012, we got up early and checked out of the hotel for the ride to the airport. My cell phone was returned, and we departed at 09:15 on the same plane that we had flown in from

Beijing. The group broke up in Beijing. Edna and Carla returned to the states while Lynn, Mary, Terry, Linda, and I spent the night in Beijing and flew to Mongolia the next morning.

CHAPTER 7

SOUTH SUDAN

My short visit to South Sudan was part of a "Horn of Africa Adventure" arranged by Bob and Cathy Parda's *Advantage Travel & Tours*. It was a small group. We had all traveled together to many places in the world for over five years, with a goal to visit all the countries in the world. This trip was to provide various members of our AT&T Family the opportunity to visit South Sudan.

South Sudan is the newest country in the United Nations after splitting from Sudan. It was not an easy split, and at the time of our visit was not considered a very safe place for tourists.

Bob and Cathy were not on this portion of the adventure and asked me to be the group leader. Included in the visit to South Sudan were Lynn, Neal, Laurie, Linda, and Terry. The week before, our colleagues from the Family, Edna, Mike, and Bob Ihsen, had visited South Sudan while we toured Somaliland, a country they did not need to visit.

After our tour of Somaliland, we spent a night in Addis Ababa to avoid a long layover between flights.

Monday, November 5, 2012, I woke early and walked around the hotel grounds to loosen a cramp I had in my leg from the hours I had spent the four previous days in a crowded SUV riding around Somaliland. The pool was full at 06:00 with lap swimmers, and the gym was busy at that time of the morning. The main dining room did not open for breakfast until 07:30, and we had to leave for the airport by 08:15. Our Ethiopian agent, Befekadu, was there to help us check out and leave on time.

The airport check-in process was a little less hectic than it had been for our flight to Somaliland four days earlier. It helped that we had a South Sudan visa in our passport, so check-in was routine. I was able to find the Ethiopian Airlines lounge this time and waited there where I could check my email before departure. When the lounge agent called the flight, I arrived at the gate to discover the gate agent could not unlock the door to the stairway to the ramp. It was a little comical, but after trying many keys on a large ring, he was able to open the door, and we walked down the stairs and across the ramp to our aircraft. I had a window seat in the back of the plane and was able to take pictures of the South Sudan countryside before we landed at Juba, the capital of South Sudan.

Juba is located between the island of Gondokoro and Rejaf (the capital of the Lado enclave). We were warned that photography is forbidden in most of the city due to a recent attempted assassination of the president. When we pulled up to the terminal it started to rain, and by the time Laurie and I departed the plane, the rain had turned into a downpour, and we were soaked. The other members of our group had dashed to the terminal before the downpour.

I was surprised that we did not have a tour guide with a sign waiting for us. One of the young ladies from the plane asked me if I had the name of the guide, and when I told her it was George Ghines, she replied that he is well known and reliable. There was a tourist desk, and I asked them to call George, but they got an 'out of service' message. I then arranged to get a cab to take us to the Quality Hotel.

When I returned to our group, I found Linda in an altercation with a security officer. She had taken a picture of airport terminal, and the officer wanted to confiscate her camera. She was apologizing and told him she would delete the picture. Terry was there, and we were able to calm down the situation. Linda deleted the picture and was able to keep her camera.

A policeman had arrived, and I took the opportunity to ask him if he knew George, and he replied that he did and left, presumably to call him. When the taxi van arrived, the policeman had not returned, so we piled in and rode to the hotel. The hotel reception staff were expecting us, and he told us that our Guide had been there and dropped off our names for registration. We went to our assigned rooms and the reception clerk called George. A short time later, a man who introduced himself as George's colleague, Travis, arrived. He told us that when the other group (Edna, Bob, and Mike) came earlier in the week, their plane did not arrive until 16:00. He claimed he called the airline and was told our flight would also arrive at 16:00, so he was waiting to meet us at that time. George was out of the country, which is why his phone indicated it was out of service. I had paid US$50 for the cab, which Travis said he would refund.

As a result of the heavy rain, the roads were very muddy (Juba has only two paved streets), and Travis decided not to take us on the scheduled tour of the city. He instead planned to take us to dinner at 19:00 and then take us on the city tour at 08:00 in the morning.

The rain had stopped, so the group (minus Lynn) walked to the center of the city. Neal, Laurie, and I toured the market in the mud. When we returned to the hotel, we watched the sun set over a Nile (beer) at the hotel.

Laurie had haggled with a street vendor over the price of a bracelet during our walk back to the hotel. She wanted it, but they would not take US dollars. As we sat drinking our beers, her desire for the bracelet still strong, she realized the hotel reception could exchange enough dollars to enable her to make the purchase. We had another round of beers while Laurie obtained the local currency and walked back to town to purchase the bracelet.

When Travis picked us up to drive us to dinner, he gave us some background on the country. While there have been several reports of violence in the country, they have been centered in the northern and eastern border regions. South Sudan is still a bit of the "Wild West," but with reasonable caution, it was safe to tour the city. Juba is like most large African cities. Everything is imported, and the over-abundance of NGO and oil workers had caused prices to skyrocket. There was an ongoing road improvement program, but the city still has mostly unpaved streets that make for slow travel. Infrastructure improvements have slowed since there is serious consideration being given to moving the capital to a new location. In the past year, the city has rapidly transitioned from a "tent and container quarters city" to a city of over 200 hotels.

Dinner was at Notos Restaurant, which is the same building where former President Theodore Roosevelt and his son Kermit spent a night in 1910 with the members of the Smithsonian African Expedition. Notos is an old warehouse converted to a five-star restaurant with multi-ethnic cuisine. The stone building represents a typical structure of the first Greek settlers, who established Juba at that time. As per Mr. Roosevelt's memoirs, they spent a night at a Greek merchant's house. The rehabilitation of the building started in 2008. The inauguration of the remodeled Notos in 2010coincided with the centennial of the visit of the Roosevelts.

It turned out that George was the owner of the restaurant, and Travis was the general manager. George was a native of the city. His parents had come from Greece and had run restaurants, eventually purchasing and restoring the Notos.

The dinner menu was impressive, and I had a tasty poached tilapia in lemon sauce. Travis permitted us to take pictures of the place and even took a picture of our group, but when Linda took some pictures in the bar area, one of the patrons objected, thinking he was in the background. Linda just could not win in this country. Travis defused the situation, and overall, we had a delightful time.

The hotel provided free internet, and I was able to check my email before retiring.

Area Tour of Juba

Tuesday, November 6, 2012, breakfast was rather good in the hotel restaurant, and Travis arrived as promised at 08:00 to take us on the tour of the area. He canceled the tour of the ancient volcano because the road would still be very muddy. He told us to be very stealthy with the picture taking, a warning which drove Laurie nuts because her large film camera and telephoto lens would be very visible to people we drove past.

We started out crossing the river past the Belgian cemetery of King Leopold's soldiers, now so overgrown that we could not determine that it was a cemetery, and then out into the country to Equatoria (Rejaf Payam), the first capital of the region. The capital eventually moved to Juba on the Nile River. In Equatoria there was a large brick church, a school, and some thatched-roof huts, and not much else in the village. Travis let me place my compact camera on the dash and take pictures as we rode without appearing to point the camera at people or places that would upset the locals. Laurie was very jealous.

We rode back to Juba on the dirt highway, which Travis told us was the main highway to Kenya. When we crossed the river in Juba, Travis turned off and stopped at the De Vinci Restaurant and Bar on the river's edge. We were able to take pictures of the river and the restaurant. We had coffee on the deck overlooking the dock. Due to the rain, the water was very dirty and wild. There was a small Arts & Crafts market at the restaurant.

We returned to the hotel to get our bags and check out. Travis deposited us at the airport to take a 13:30 flight back to Addis

Ababa. At Addis Ababa, we bid Laurie farewell since she would be leaving the group to fly back to her home in New York.

It was a quick trip, but informative to understand the controversy and political situation that created the split from Sudan.

CHAPTER 8

CUBA

Cuba has been on my bucket list for decades. It was the last country in the Americas for me to visit. I jumped at the opportunity to legally visit when Debbie, my travel agent at Cruise Specialists, sent me a brochure earlier in the year advertising the *Tauck Cuba People to People Cultural Exchange* tour. Tauck's after-Thanksgiving 9-day tour fit nicely in my schedule, falling after my Horn of Africa Trip and before Judy's December 11th birthday, so I signed up.

Tauck Tours is headquartered in my hometown area of Connecticut, and I had visited their headquarters during a trip to visit my daughter in New Jersey earlier in the year after I had signed up for the tour. That provided me with details on what to expect that exceeded the information in their tour brochure.

Monday, November 26, 2012, I flew to Miami via Houston to join the *Tauck Cuba People to People Cultural Exchange* tour.

Tour Briefing

Tuesday, November 27, 2012, I was scheduled to meet with the Tauck Tour Group at the Hilton Miami Airport Hotel at 18:00. I arrived at 15:00 and checked-in at the Tauck hospitality desk. The Tauck director, Ulla Salafrio, informed me that there would be 25 people in my tour group. It was a larger group than I have been used to on a land tour.

At 17:45, I went to the Cove meeting room for the mandatory briefing. Ulla and a couple from Phoenix, Arizona, Mary & Dennis Schumer, were the only ones there, but the bar was open and snacks laid out. Ulla handed me an envelope with the information and paperwork we would need on the trip. Panic set in when I reviewed the paperwork and discovered that it had my 2-year old passport numbers on the Cuban visa, a passport that was currently with UTS obtaining visas for my January trip to Africa. I only had my 10-year passport, but happily Ulla told me she could fix it after the briefing.

The others arrived, and we sat at a U-shaped table. Ulla handed out everyone's envelopes and had us introduce ourselves to the group. Six were from California, four from Pennsylvania, and the others were couples from Arizona, Florida, Hawaii, New Jersey, South Carolina, and Massachusetts, and one woman from Vermont.

Ulla then had us review the paperwork and complete the arrival forms for Cuba. She then took my visa and used a sharp felt tip pen to write the correct passport number over the incorrect number. On the health form we had to list the countries we had visited in the last 15 days. I thought Djibouti, Ethiopia, North Sudan, and Germany would fall in that period, , but when I realized the form would be dated the 28th and I had left those countries on the 10th, I left the entry blank.

After the meeting I talked to several of the people in the group, then retired since we had to be checked out by 05:00 in the morning.

Fly to Havana

Wednesday, November 28, 2012, I awoke at 03:30 to shower, shave, and pack. At 05:00, a porter picked up my bag, and I went down to breakfast. It was a quick breakfast since we had to be on the bus by 05:15.

It was a short ride to the airport, but the flight check-in was a long multistep process. First, we lined up behind a desk that checked our paperwork, then we went to the check-in counter and had our luggage weighed, including our carry on, and then we told them our body weight. They also checked our paperwork and issued a boarding pass with the luggage tag fixed on the back. After that, we had to go to another station and pay a $33 fee. From there, we passed through immigration and then security, and finally could go to the gate. The security check had the full-body scan, but they still did a quick pat-down after the body scan.

The airline was Sky King, a charter airline founded in Sacramento, CA, in the early 1990s, but after bankruptcy it moved its headquarters to Florida, where they mainly fly to Cuban cities. The plane we flew on was a B-737-400 painted all white. The seats were comfortable.

The flight took ninety minutes and arrived at the scheduled time of 09:00 at the Havana airport. There was no sky bridge at the airport, so we had to walk to arrival terminal. There we passed through immigration, where they took our pictures and took half of the visa. Next, we passed through a security checkpoint where my artificial knee set off the alarm and had to be checked with a wand from a security agent. I had to go to another desk for another paperwork check. Following the check, we were ushered into the VIP lounge, where we gave an agent our luggage tags. She retrieved our luggage and took it to be x-rayed. The VIP lounge had free sandwiches and drinks (rum, beer, Coke, and juice). When everyone's luggage had been x-rayed, we were led outside to retrieve our luggage and board a bus.

Museum of the Revolution

On the bus, we were told that it was too early to check-in at the hotel, so we rode to the Museum of the Revolution and then to Revolution Square.

The airport parking lot had been full of new Korean and Japanese made cars, but at the museum and the square, we saw a lot of 1950-era cars. I got some good pictures. The old cars still in excellent shape were used as taxis. There were a lot of old Russian cars, and a lot of old American made cars not in shape to be taxis, but still on the road.

The Museum of the Revolution was an interesting mixture of indoor and outdoor displays of the rise of Castro and the demise of Batista. The museum is housed in what was the Presidential Palace of all Cuban presidents from Mario García Menocal to Fulgencio Batista. It became the Museum of the Revolution during the years following the Cuban Revolution. The museum was designed by Cuban architect Carlos Maruri and Belgian architect Paul Belau and was inaugurated in 1920 by President Mario García Menocal. It remained the Presidential Palace until 1959. The building has neo-classical elements and was decorated by Tiffany & Co. of New York.

The museum has the pockmarks of the bullets shot during the March 13, 1957, attack by a group of university students who stormed the Presidential Palace intending to execute dictator Batista. The assault failed, and most of the young attackers got killed. The Palace has three floors. On the first floor, we toured a chapel, hall of mirrors with a beautiful painting on the ceiling, the flag hall, President's office (where we were shown the closet stairway Batista used to hide from the students), and Council Ministers' office. On the second floor, we saw a display of the Liberation War period. The Che Memorial was on the third floor.

To the right side of the lobby was a mural that Isabel warned us we might find offensive. It had large cartoon caricatures: of Batista saying: "Thanks, you cretin, for helping us TO MAKE THE REVOLUTION."

Ronald Regan, in a cowboy outfit, saying: "Thanks, you cretin, for helping us TO STRENGTHEN THE REVOLUTION."

George Bush Sr. dressed as Caesar, saying: "Thanks, you cretin, for helping us TO CONSOLIDATE OUR REVOLUTION."

George W. Bush with a Nazi helmet, saying: "Thanks, you cretin, for helping us TO MAKE SOCIALISM IRREVOCABLE."

Behind the building was the Granma Memorial, a large glass enclosure that housed the "Granma," the yacht that took Fidel Castro and his revolutionaries from Mexico to Cuba for the Revolution. Around the "Granma" was a SA-2 Guideline surface-to-air missile of the type that shot down a U.S. Lockheed U-2 during the Cuban Missile Crisis. The engine of the U-2 airplane was displayed. There was also a Pontiac used to carry weapons, a Willy's Jeep, a Toyota Jeep, a tank, and a Hawker Sea Fury F50 fighter aircraft used in the revolution. Near the museum was an SU-100 Soviet tank destroyer. Also, on display was the remains of the B-26 bomber which was shot down during the Bay of Pigs invasion in 1961.

Across the street, we saw a nice lineup of vintage convertible taxis, including two Model A Ford replicas, and a 1932 Ford with rumble seat. Outside the front of the museum were the remains of the old city wall of Havana.

Revolution Square

We rode from the museum to Revolution Square, one of the largest city squares in the world. The square is dominated by the José Martí Memorial, which features a 358 ft. tall tower and a 59 ft. statue of Martí. The National Library, many government ministries, and other buildings are in and around the Plaza. Located behind the memorial are the closely guarded offices of former President Fidel Castro. Opposite the memorial on the far side of the square is the famous Che Guevara image with his well-known slogan of "Hasta la Victoria Siempre" (Ever onward to victory!) that identifies the Ministry of the Interior building and an image of Fidel Castro on another building.

Next to where the tour buses parked was a street bordering the square lined with many beautiful 1950-era taxi convertibles and a few "Coconut Taxis." The "Coconut Taxis" are three-wheel motor scooters with round yellow shells that resemble a coconut. I took more pictures of the cars than the monuments and statues.

Melia Habana hotel

It was then time to check in to the Melia Habana hotel. But first, we had lunch at the La Scala Restaurant in the hotel. Lunch was a salad and pizza, and I finally got to my room at 15:00. It was a 5-star hotel, and I had free Wi-Fi in the room.

Cuba-U.S. Relationship Lecture

At 16:30, we met in a hotel conference room to attend a presentation about the Cuba-U.S. relationship by Ph.D. Camilo Garcia Lopez-Trigo, a graduate of the Institute of International Relations in Havana in 1991 and a former Cuban diplomat. Camilo had lived in New York City when he was assigned to the Cuban delegation to the United Nations.

He told us of the implementation of the Monroe Doctrine in 1823 by John Quincy Adams, Monroe's Secretary of State. In 1848 the U.S. attempted to buy Cuba from the Spanish. The U.S. became involved in Cuba's second war of independence in, 1898 when the USS Maine was blown up in Havana harbor. After Spain surrendered, the U.S. was granted control of Cuba. The U.S. military governor of Cuba drafted a constitution that included an amendment by U.S. Senator Platt that guaranteed America's right to intervene in Cuban domestic affairs. It also forced Cuba to lease in perpetuity to the U.S. a naval base at Guantanamo Bay and required the Cuban government to: "maintain a low public debt; refrain from signing any treaty impairing its obligation to the United States; to grant to the United States the right of intervention to protect life, liberty, and property; validate the acts of the military government; and, if requested, provide long-term naval leases.

In 1902, following the elections of 1901, Cuba was proclaimed an independent republic under the official protection of the U.S. During the next three decades the relationship was rocky, with many interventions by U.S. military and business interests that eventually lead to the "Sergeants' Revolt" and the overthrow of the government by Batista in 1933. Batista backed several presidents and served several terms as president himself. When he ran again in 1952, he did not win, but he simply decided to take over in a bloodless coup. On July 26, 1953, Fidel and Raul Castro led a group of revolutionaries in an attack on Moncada Barracks, and the Cuban Revolution began. They were captured and imprisoned but were released in 1955 and fled to Mexico. They returned in 1956 and forced Bastia to flee in 1959.

A U.S. embargo on Cuba began in 1960, prohibiting all exports to Cuba. In response, Cuba strengthened trade relations with the Soviet Union, and the following year the U.S. ended all diplomatic relations with Cuba and closed the embassy in Havana in January 1961. In April, a group of Cuban exiles invaded Playa Giron on the Bay of Pigs. The Soviet Union began to install missiles in Cuba in 1962. Despite Castro's desire to fire them at the U.S., Soviet Premier Nikita Khrushchev agreed to remove them after he negotiated with President Kennedy.

During the next thirty years, there were several programs to allow Cubans to leave for the U.S. The Cuban economy limped along with Soviet aid until the collapse of the Soviet Union in 1991.

In 1992 the U.S. implemented the Torricelli act, which forbade foreign subsidiaries of U.S. companies from dealing with Cuba, prohibited any ship that has docked in Cuban harbors from entering U.S. ports for 180 days, and called for a termination of aid to any country that assists Cuba. The act did not bring down the Castro regime, so in 1996 the U.S. Congress passed the Helms-Burton Act that allows the USA to penalize foreign companies that invest in Cuban properties seized after the Revolution. The Helms-Burton

Act also deprived the U.S. President of any discretionary power to end any aspect of the embargo. The bill permits Americans with claims to property confiscated by the Cuban government to sue for damages from foreign corporations or individuals that traffic in such property. The U.S. also denies entry to the executives and major shareholders, as well as their immediate families, of firms found to be trafficking in confiscated property. The legislation also restricts U.S. aid to independent states of the former Soviet Union if they assist intelligence facilities in Cuba, but also provides waivers for humanitarian aid or aid to promote market reforms and democratization. It reaffirms the embargo under the Trading with the Enemy Act. The act has severely hurt the Cuban economy, but the regime is still in power. President Obama eased travel restrictions to Cuba in 2011, allowing for more educational, religious, and cultural programs.

Camilo also told us about the "Cuban Five," which is a very emotional issue in Cuba. The five men were Cuban intelligence agents caught spying on Miami's Cuban exile community. The men were sent to South Florida in the wake of several terrorist bombings in Havana masterminded by anti-communist militant. The five were convicted in Miami of conspiracy to commit espionage, conspiracy to commit murder, acting as an agent of a foreign government, and other illegal activities in the United States.

In the Q & A after his talk, Camilo told us that because of the Helms-Burton Act; there are limited things a President can do to ease the tensions between the countries. It would require an act of Congress to change the provisions of the Helms-Burton Act, which severely restricts the Cuban economy and interaction between the countries. Cubans do not understand why the anti-Castro lobby is still so effective since the Cubans that fled in the 1960s are dead or past the age of retirement.

I left the meeting wondering what the Miami based anti-Castro lobby expected to achieve. Their property has been lost for so many years that, in many cases, they would not have anything to return to. I went to sleep, wondering if it had been worth the effort to attempt to bring down the Castro regime.

Art in Cuba

Thursday, November 29, 2012, my first morning in Cuba. After two nights of less than eight hours of sleep I slept until 07:00. We had a choice of two restaurants in the hotel to eat breakfast. I selected the VIP Bar on the 9th floor, which was just one flight of stairs from my 8th-floor room. It was pretty much a standard hotel buffet breakfast bar. I was not impressed with the texture of the bacon and the fact there were no whole oranges, but I filled up and returned to my room to check my email and get ready for a 09:30 departure.

Our first stop was the home and studio of José Fuster, one of the most celebrated artists in Cuba. I was not prepared for the sight as the bus drove close to his studio. The houses had walls along the sidewalk and a large arch over the gateway covered in colorful bits of tile. Even the street names were in colorful tile. When we arrived at his studio, we were greeted by the sight of many arches, geometric shapes, and figures of people all covered in colorful tile. Fuster's son met us at the entrance to the three-story studio. I noted that there were two late-model Japanese cars in the yard. The son told us that over a dozen men assist in the creation of the displays. I counted at that moment at least four men on the various floors applying cement to walls and railings and embedding pieces of tile. Another man was breaking the tile in different colors into pieces that others would apply.

I walked upstairs to visit a room where the tile was created. Many 6x6 tiles had colorful scenes, and some were hanging on a wall for sale. In another room were Fuster's oil paintings and one of the etchings. He is called a visual artist with the paintings along the style of some of Picasso's and tile in a style like Antoni Gaudi in Barcelona. After touring the three floors of his studio and taking dozens of pictures, I wandered around the neighborhood.

158 | ED REYNOLDS

Across the street was another artist's home with a display of wooden VW Beatles and figures of musicians. His house had a fence decorated by Fuster, as did all the houses in a two-block area. Many had the house walls decorated in Fuster's style.

Our next stop was the Institute Superior de Arte (ISA). The Institute is an impressive set of domed brick buildings built on the grounds of a former country club's golf course. The ISA teaches college-level classes in art, theater, dance, and music. The ISA guide told us that it is highly selective and, as an example, only 15 students were selected from 400 applicants this year. We toured the various art classrooms and workshops which covered a wide range of specialties, from paint in various styles and mediums to ceramic and metal sculptures.

I was impressed in some areas, but overall, it impressed me that the artists are morbid, tortured, unhappy souls. There were no displays of landscapes. Many works were colorful, but many were dark, bloody, and gloomy.

From ISA, we went to lunch at Don Cangrejo's, a seafood restaurant on the coast. We were greeted in the yard in front of the restaurant by a large ceramic tile crab. There was a light rain, so we had to eat inside. I could see that they usually set up tables overlooking the sea wall.

The meal was delicious. It started with a family-style dish of crab balls, olives, cheese, and fried fish fingers. The main course was a medley of clams, calamari, fish, shrimp, mussels, crab, lettuce, tomatoes, cabbage, and beets. Drinks were a rum mojito and wine or beer. Dessert was a scoop of peach ice cream with a nickel size crème brûlée.

During our lunch, a jazz band with an outstanding female singer performed. She sang several Nat King Cole songs, "Mack the Knife," and "When the Saints Come Marching In." Al and Suzanne Frederick danced to one of the songs, and then Judy Zon and Mary Kopa did the Mummers Philadelphia New Year's Parade dance to "Saints."

After lunch, we visited Casa de la Cultura in the Plaza de la Revolution. There are many neighborhood cultural centers around the city where people of all ages can take extracurricular classes in art, music, dancing, and theater. We visited a ceramics lab and a knitting class and then were treated to a special performance in the theater. The performance started with a young girl around eight years old singing a ballad, then a group of younger girls doing ballet, and then an older man singing a ballad, followed by a younger man singing a salsa tune with a couple dancing in the back of him, and ending with six couples dancing what they called a casino dance (they jitterbugged and changed partners in a circle similar to square dancing, but in more of a circular pattern).

After the performance, we visited the Center's art gallery. They had some beautiful pieces on display. I thought they were better than in the ISA. We returned to the hotel and left for dinner at 18:30.

Dinner was at the La Moraleja restaurant, which is not government-owned. I had a delicious Greek salad, braised lamb, and ice cream for dessert. We were sitting at three tables with a single family occupying one of the tables. The wine was flowing freely, and they started telling family stories in louder and louder voices, drowning out cross-table conversations at the other tables. It dampened the spirit of the dinner. Isabel, the Tauck director, was sitting at our table, and when we could converse, she had some interesting stories to tell us. She has worked for several different tour agencies, including Grand Circle and OAT. She mainly works the Panama Canal and Costa Rica ecology tours.

The service was slow at the restaurant, and it was close to 22:00 before we returned to the hotel, and since we had an early departure scheduled for the next day, I went right to bed without updating my journal.

Visit a Pinar del Rio

Friday, November 30, 2012, we rode out in the country southwest of Havana on a four-lane highway to the city of Pinar del Rio.

Along the way, we stopped at the Las Barrigonas rest stop. There were several buses already there and more arrived following us. Las Barrigonas was a brick shelter with clean restrooms and arts and crafts for sale. Near the building was a farm with several pigs, a cow, and a donkey hooked to a cart. As we were returning to our bus, the farmers rode off in the donkey lead cart.

When we arrived in Pinar del Rio, I noticed that the taxis were not the 1950s era cars but were three-wheeled bicycles with a double size seat over the rear axle and a roof over the driver and passenger.

We toured a cigar factory set up for visitors. N Photos were not allowed; I guess because it showed the way they handled each step: selecting the crushed tobacco, forming it in the size of the cigar, compressing it, and then wrapping it with the outer leaf.

Viñales Valley Viewpoint

From Pinar del Rio, we rode north, stopping on the way at Hotel Horizontes Los Jazmines, one of the most renowned hotels in Cuba. Its bus parking lot has a stunning view of the Viñales Valley UNESCO site. The valley is surrounded by limestone mountains with spectacular cliffs full of indentations and caves. The parking area was full of tour buses of Europeans. There were several tables with arts and crafts displayed and a saddled ox. Doug Kish from our group climbed on for us to take his picture.

Benito Camejo's Tobacco Farm

Leaving the vista, we rode past the village of Viñales to a tobacco farm. As we drove into the farm, we saw a turkey slowly wandering around the yard. In the back of two white farmhouses, there were two oxen hooked to a cart and a group of on farmworkers on a break.

When we got off the bus, we were ushered into a tobacco barn for a presentation by the farmer, Benito Camejo, who was out of Central Casting. A handsome man with a bushy mustache (for those of you who know my neighbor, Gary Wales, who restores and shows Bentleys, you'll appreciate that he reminded me of a young version of Gary. You can also see his picture if you Google his name). As he sat talking to us, he rolled a cigar and lit it up. Benito then led us to his house for a cup of either Cuban coffee or rum or a mixture of both. I was the first to have just the rum, and he took a liking to me and led me to his garage to see his 1953 Chevrolet. It still has the original engine, but the carburetor has been swapped out so it could burn diesel, which is significantly cheaper and, as I understand, easier to get. I learned that most of the old cars have converted to diesel because gasoline is about $7 a gallon. H also showed us his tobacco crop and told us how he transplants the seedlings from a wet area next to the river to fields next to his house. He also showed us his coffee bushes and fig tree.

Stop at a tobacco processing plant

From the farm, we headed back towards Viñales and stopped at El Estanco II, a tobacco processing plant where they remove the stems, grade and size the leaves, then ferment the leaves and bundle them up for shipment to a cigar factory. We were given a briefing on the process. I found the process of fermenting the tobacco leaves fascinating. A thermometer is stuck into a compressed bale of tobacco and monitored until the temperature no longer increases and the leaves no longer feel slightly sticky to the touch. Another interesting fact is how they bundle up the removed stems and use them to control insect pests.

We ate lunch at Palenque de Los Cimarrones in a valley out of town between mountains full of caves. The restaurant was a symmetric structure of open log cabins joined by halls, with roofs made of leaves taken from the royal palm tree and displayed as in an ancient African village. The restrooms were in round structures with murals on their sides. We were serenaded at lunch by a trio of singing guitarists. The lunch was family style. It was Susan Hendricks' birthday, and somehow the guides were able to have a birthday cake baked and served for the occasion. After lunch, I decided to walk through the cave.

Near the entrance were two life-size figures of a slave fighting a runaway slave hunter, representing how runaway slaves used to hide in the caves. At the entrance were a couple of local performers. One of them was a fire eater, and he entertained me. The limestone cave was narrow in many spots and had deep crevices branching off the path. There were also carvings in the limestone of snakes and rats. At the other end of the cave was a stage for band concerts and a bar constructed of limestone. Outside was an old sugar cane press, which I noticed was manufactured in Buffalo, NY. I walked back towards the restaurant, but the bus had started to leave and picked me up on the way.

Tour Viñales

We returned to Viñales and spent an hour walking around the town. It was set up for tourists, and several of the European tours were already there. It had showered as we approached the center of the city, but soon the covers were removed from tables of arts and crafts. In the city center, there was a beautiful little church, and a statue of José Martí dated 1895. After we toured the town, we boarded our bus for a two-hour ride back to our hotel.

Hotel Dining Rooms

Dinner that night was on our own in one of the six restaurants in the hotel. Our choices were:
• Sabor do Brasil
• Miramar (Buffet)
• Vedado Restaurant (where we ate breakfast)
• El Bosque de la Habana (Lobby bar)
• La Scala (Italian restaurant)
• Bella Cubana (Fusion Asian restaurant)

I chose the Miramar, where one of my choices was pork cut from a full roast pig. After a rather quick dinner, I returned to my room and caught up on my email before retiring.

Literary Arts in Cuba

Saturday, December 01, 2012, after a breakfast of a fried egg, a link sausage, and two Danish rolls, we met for a presentation on the life of Ernest Hemingway and his relationship with Cuba. We were supposed to visit Hemingway's home, but they were filming a movie on his life, so the home was closed to visitors. Sharon Stone was scheduled to be in the movie and was staying at our hotel, although I never saw her.

Havana Club Rum Museum

We left the hotel with the intention of visiting Hemingway's old haunts in Old Havana, but it was raining, so the guide changed our schedule and dropped us off at the Havana Club Rum Museum. At the museum, we were assigned an English-speaking guide who took us on a tour of the museum. She explained the differences between the white and dark rum and the distilling and aging process. One of the rooms had a detailed model of a sugar mill, including a model railroad with model trains. It was very impressive. She then led us through the distilling vats and aging barrels. After the tour, we had a sample of the seven-year-old dark rum and saw a $1,200 bottle of rum in a glass display case.

Cojimar, Cuba

We boarded the bus and rode out of town to Cojimar, the small fishing village east of Havana, where Hemingway fished and found the inspiration for his novel, "The Old Man and the Sea." His house is in the area but set back from the road, so we did not even drive by. The rain appeared to be letting up when we arrived at the old fort on the sea wall across from a bust of Hemingway. We got out of the bus to take pictures, but the rain increased, and we quickly got back on.

Next, we stopped at the La Terraza de Cojimar restaurant, where they had a table roped off in a corner with a view of the sea that was Hemingway's favorite table, where he dined with Gregorio Fuentes, captain of Hemingway's yacht, Pilar. It was in this restaurant that Hemingway met Cojimar's fisherman. The restaurant's walls were covered with pictures of Hemingway and paintings of the sea and fishermen. It was very colorful.

On the drive back to Havana, we stopped for lunch at Divino's restaurant. The restaurant was already decorated for Christmas, and we were greeted at the door by a giant statue of Santa Claus. I had salad and fish for lunch. When we left the restaurant, the rain had stopped, and I was able to take some pictures of a beautiful four-door 1931 Ford sedan.

Walking Tour of Old Havana

Back in the city, we got off the bus at san Francisco Plaza and started our walking tour of Old Havana. The first stop was the old fort of La Real Fuerza. We then walked up the narrow streets to Hotel Ambos Mundos, where Ernest Hemingway stayed and wrote many of his short stories. We took an elevator to the top floor where we were served a mojito and enjoyed great views of the city. The open rooftop bar had pretty art decorated panels on the walls.

After a crowd of European tourists left the area, we were able to visit Hemingway's room, which has been set up as he used it when he stayed there. A typewriter with pages from a short story is in a display case on the standup desk he used when he wrote. The closet had one of his suits and a tie hanging behind a glass door. A model of his yacht, Pilar, was on display on top of a bookcase. A case displayed cards, poker chips, dice, and a small roulette wheel.

On our way out of the lobby, we found it was full of European guests checking in and out with their luggage. We were then on our own to explore Old Town Havana. I walked up the narrow streets and visited several shops. Of interest was the restored Johnson Drug Store with a display from floor to ceiling of ceramic jars used to contain drugs. Along the way, I walked through a large open market with arts, crafts, and clothes for sale.

At the end of the walk was another Hemingway hangout, the Floridita Bar, home of the original daiquiri. Inside was a spot where Hemingway liked to sit, and there were pictures on the wall of him with famous people such as Errol Flynn, Castro, and Mafia dons.

We returned to the hotel before 17:00 and had a rest before leaving for at 19:00 to dine at El Tocororo, a privately owned restaurant until recently only open to foreigners. It had plaques on the wall from various tour groups and a great jazz band. Dinner was delicious.

After dinner, we rode to the Tropicana night club, where we took in the show. It was spectacular, with dancing, singing, many costume changes, and lots of colorful lights. It ranks with the best Las Vegas shows.

It was a great way to spend Saturday night in Havana.

Tour Colón Cemetery

Sunday, December 02, 2012, the subject for the day was spirituality in Cuba. Our first visit was a tour of the Colón Cemetery, founded in 1876. Named for Christopher Columbus, the 140-acre cemetery was noted for its many elaborately sculpted memorials. It is estimated that the cemetery has more than 500 major mausoleums, chapels, and family vaults. The entrance featured a massive stone gate called the "Gate of Peace" in the form of the Arc de Triomphe, with three arches over openings. We were met by a guide who showed us around the cemetery describing the many large mausoleums, chapels, and family vaults. He pointed out several notable people's graves, the Chapel of Constante Ribalaigua, a friend of Ernest Hemingway and founder of the Floridita, the famous Hemingway bar in Old Havana. Ribalaigua is credited with having invented the famous daiquiri drink. The most impressive gravesite was the 75-foot high monument to the firefighters who lost their lives in the great fire of May 17, 1890. We were impressed by the clean condition and massive size of the sites, many dating back to the late 1800s and early 1900s. It indicated that there was once great wealth and taste for the arts in the history of the nation.

We toured the chapel in the center of the cemetery between funerals, which go on all day, and then visited the popular grave of La Milagrosa (The Miraculous One). The story goes that when Amelia Goyri de la Hoz died in childbirth in 1901, she was buried with her stillborn daughter placed at her feet. When the tomb was opened a few years later, the baby was found in her arms. Amelia is now considered the protector of pregnant women and newborn children. Pilgrims paying homage must not turn their backs to the tomb upon leaving. We saw many women visiting the grave and laying flowers on the tomb in just the few minutes we were there.

The cemetery has more than 800,000 graves and 1 million interments. Space is currently at a premium and, after three years, remains are removed from their tombs, boxed, and placed in a storage building. The cemetery ranks right up with the most impressive in the world, such as the ones in Paris and Buenos Aires.

Visit to Muraleando Mercado de San José

Our next visit was to the area called Muraleando Mercado de San José. Muraleando means mural-making and, what started as art classes taught in the street because there was no local room to teach, the classes grew into a community beautification project where trashed areas were cleaned up, metal sculptures installed, and murals painted on the walls. Even Charles Schulz's estate has contributed by allowing pictures of Snoopy to be painted on the walls. The community gained permission from the government to turn an old concrete water tank into an art studio. In front of the tank, they built a covered stage where we were entertained with the talents of the local musicians and a 'rap' artist.

The music became a group dance where the locals had us dance with them. It was great fun and was followed by a showing and selling of their artwork. Of course, I had to buy a small print of a painting by the young lady that had asked me to dance.

Arts and Crafts Market

From the community center, we boarded our bus and rode to arts and crafts market that occupies the old warehouse space along the seaport docks. There I was able to purchase a few small art objects for the grandkids. We then rode to the San Francisco Square, where we had the official group photo taken in the archway of the cathedral.

We had lunch at Cafe de Oriente on the square. It was exquisite, and we had the whole top floor, with a jazz trio serenading us. I had a delicious seafood lunch, and afterwards we had the choice of staying in Old Havana or returning to the hotel. I choose to return to the hotel to catch up on my email and journal.

Bellas Artes Museum

At 17:30, we departed to the Bellas Artes Museum to attend a musical performance by six local music teachers called the Groupo Vocal Elé. They sang many songs in Spanish and English. Their rendition of "Summertime" was outstanding.

Following this surprise event, we rode to Casa Espanola for dinner. The meal was a traditional Cuban meal with beans and a potato quiche.

It had been another memorable day on my visit to Cuba.

The "Green Tiles" House

Monday, December 03, 2012, education in Cuba was the subject of the day.

On our many trips back and forth to and from the hotel we would pass by a beautiful old three-story mansion on a corner which Isabel called the "Green Tiles" house. Well, we finally stopped and visited the house. The house had been owned by a wealthy lady with a lot of land holdings in the country. After the Revolution, she had to give the state all her holdings but could keep one house in which to live. She chose this beautiful house with a large lot and water fountains and reflecting pools in the backyard. When she died, the house passed to her niece as her only living heir in the country. When the niece died, she had no heirs, and the property was turned over to the state.

The government restored the house to its former glory, and it was then used by the Havana Revitalization Works as an office, reception, and briefing room. We were led up to the third floor past beautifully decorated rooms to a large room where we were given a presentation on "Restoring the Memory - Approach to Cuban Architecture and Havana Revitalization Works." The presenter was a female architect from the Havana Revitalization Works. She traced the history of architecture in Cuba through its history, the influence of wars, the renaissance influences in the fortress, the Spanish-Arab influences in houses, the colonial period, the cathedrals, convents, neoclassic buildings, and the period from 1902 to 1958 which included the 'Capital' building, is a replica of the U.S. Capitol, and the casinos and hotels. She then described the damage to the buildings caused by strong storms over the years.

That background led to the establishment of the Revitalization Works—Cultural and Touristic Infrastructure. She talked about and showed us before and after pictures of the projects her department has undertaken and some of the artists that perform the work, including the National School of Arts, the Mills Farm in central Havana, and the Green Tiles house. In the Q&A following her presentation, she talked about the funding which comes from tourist fees and how the U.S. embargo hampers the funding by reducing the tourist trade.

After the presentation, we were given a tour of the house. Fabulous!

Hotel National

We then rode to the famous Hotel National. The New York architectural firm of McKim, Mead, and White designed the hotel, which features a mix of styles. It opened in 1930, when Cuba was a prime travel destination for Americans, and the hotel has had many famous and distinguished guests.

The hotel was built on the site of the Santa Clara Battery, which dates to 1797. Part of the battery has been preserved in the hotel's gardens, including two large coastal guns dating from the late 19th Century. There is a small museum featuring the 1962 Cuban missile crisis. During the crisis, Fidel Castro and Che Guevara set up their headquarters in the hotel to prepare the defense of Havana from an aerial attack. The Hotel Nacional de Cuba is a World Heritage Site and a National Monument, and it was inscribed in the World Memory Register.

At one end of the long ornate lobby, I entered the 'Hall of Fame,' which has a panorama of the famous guests that have stayed in or visited the hotel. On the walls are large collages of famous people's photos grouped by decade. In addition, there were individual photos of famous people and even a full-size bronze statue of Nat King Cole. At the other end of the lobby was a bar which also had pictures on the wall of luminaries. Our side in the back gave us a beautiful view of the harbor.

I didn't visit them, but many rooms that have been occupied by the famous have been zealously conserved, and several declared historic, including the rooms for Nat King Cole, Compay Segundo, Ava Gardner and Frank Sinatra, Fred Astaire, María Felix, Johnny Weissmuller, the Mafia boss, Bola de Nieve, Tyrone Power, Gary Cooper, Agustín Lara, Jorge Negrete, Mario Moreno, Stan Musial, Pablo Casals, and Errol Flynn. On display in each room were photographs and biographical profiles of their celebrated former occupants.

Out front, as I waited for the bus to arrive, I saw a beautiful 1957 red Chevrolet convertible pull up to pick up a passenger. It was in outstanding condition!

Cuban Folkloric Dance

Our next visit was to an art museum, where we entered from the side into a long room with a band set up at one end. We sat on folding chairs on each side of the room. We were introduced to Cuban Folkloric Dance. The group was a family of three men and three women. They danced what I considered a very wild gyration, and I did not think the movements were in sync with the rhythm of the music. They looked like they were on drugs. I was not impressed. At one point, they performed a mating ritual where the female danced with a skirt which she would raise, teasing the male, who would flick his handkerchief at the raised dress. If she did not like him, she would drop her skirt; if she liked him, she would encourage him to get closer.

During the dance, the female dancer tried to get Buck, sitting next to me, to dance the man part. He declined and told her to pick me. I gyrated with the handkerchief and turned my back to her and flicked it between my legs. I felt silly since I still did not sense the correlation between her movements and the rhythm of the music. Chris came to my rescue and took the handkerchief and enabled me to sit down.

After the mating dance, we paired up and danced a sort of a square dance where we danced up and down and then in a round. Finally, it was mercifully over, and we left for lunch.

El Aljibe Restaurant

Lunch was at the El Aljibe Restaurant, an open-sided thatched-roof building. It was a good lunch, and it was a popular place full of tour groups, including a group from the Hemingway movie crew. (No star actors included).

Santovenia Senior Home

After lunch, we visited the Santovenia Senior Home, a Catholic run home since 1886. We toured the various areas of the home. One wing held males, and another wing just females, and across the rear were small apartments for couples. In the middle was the chapel. We were shown the common facilities like the physical therapy room. Our host was one of the women living with her husband, and we visited her small apartment, which had a patio and a garden in back.

Farewell Dinner

We returned to the hotel and prepared for our farewell dinner. At 18:30, we gathered in the hotel lobby to board the bus but were told the bus had broken down. Isabel then told us she had ordered taxis to take us to the Saratoga Hotel for dinner. I was elated and boarded a 1957 blue Ford convertible with Cecile and Judy. The driver took our picture, and then Isabel jumped in the front seat. She confessed that the bus was not disabled, and the surprise was to give us a ride in the old cars we had been drooling over all week. The driver told me he had replaced the Ford engine with a Hyundai diesel and that almost all the taxis had diesel engine replacements. We had fun on the way to dinner, passing some of our colleagues, or being passed ourselves.

Our farewell dinner was at the rooftop of the Saratoga Hotel in the center of the city. It was a clear night, and we had spectacular views of the city. I sat with Dennis and Mary and Isabel. It was a delicious meal and a fitting end to our visit to Cuba.

Back in the room, I read an email that informed me that my youngest daughter, Robin, was going to arrive in Miami to attend the Art Basel Miami Beach art fair at the same time I was scheduled to arrive.

Return to the United States

Tuesday, December 04, 2012, I arose early to pack and have my luggage ready for pick up before I went to eat breakfast. We departed for the airport at 08:00 for a 25-minute ride. Check-in was a little confusing because another large group was checking in at the same time. I was motioned to be first in line at one of the counters, but the agent had not set up his system, so it took me a little longer than those in the other line. I was assigned a window seat. Immigration and security went fast. Some of the group carrying pictures in a tube had to show the contents. Once inside the departure hall, a man with a Tauck sign directed us to the VIP room overlooking the hall. We gathered in the room and waited until one of our group noticed people lining up at our assigned gate. I hustled down to the hall, and the line started growing to be the length of the hall. I managed to get in near the front with several of the members of our group.

The flight on a World Atlantic B-737 charter took off on time and landed ten minutes early at Miami International. I hurried off the plane to try and get through immigration and customs to meet Robin when she landed. I do not know the layout of Miami International, but I think we parked as far away from passport control as possible. I walked as fast as I could, passing by everyone from my plane, finally arriving at the passport control hall just to find it full of passengers from other flights. It took me forty minutes to pass through. My bag was just coming off the carousel, and then I had a ten-minute wait to process through customs. Robin had landed and was trying to contact me, but cell phones are not allowed in the area. Finally, I was able to talk to her, and we agreed to meet at the Hertz rental building.

We met all right and used her iPad to direct us to her small hotel in Miami Beach on 18th Street. She checked in, and I found a parking lot. We then had one of her staff join us for lunch. They had meetings to attend, so I left them and drove to a Residence Inn in Coconut Grove to spend the night.

Summary

Since the 1950s, Cuba has been a fascination for my family. I have a cousin who worked as executive secretary for the Cuban Airlines New York office. When Fidel Castro became premier of Cuba in 1959, I had an uncle who was an outspoken supporter of Castro.

My brother, Bob, used to love to discuss support of Castro and his initial revolution.

As a USAF navigator stationed in Bermuda during the Cuban Missile Crisis, I flew recon missions tracking Soviet cargo ships with missiles on their decks. For all these reasons I have always wanted to visit and tour the island.

When I worked in Canada, I was jealous of my coworkers who would vacation on Cuban beaches. I also had American friends that snuck into the country from Mexico. I wanted to do it the legal way and have an enjoyable tour. Tauck provided that, and I highly recommend the tour for everyone.

CHAPTER 9

MALI

In January 2013, I scheduled my first tours with *Universal Travel System* (UTS). Klaus Billep, CEO of UTS, advertised two West Africa tours that could be scheduled together for one long 36-day tour led by a personal guide familiar with the countries. West Africa Tour #1 traveled to Mauritania, Senegal, Cape Verde, Gambia, Guinea Bissau, Guinea, Sierra Leone, Liberia, and Ivory Coast. West Africa Tour #2 started in Mali, then went to Burkina Faso, and finished in Niger. Klaus assigned one of the best tour guides in the business, Herb Gobels, a German who had been working with Klaus and one other German guide since the 1950s.

A brief history of Mali.

Present-day Mali was once part of three West African empires that controlled trans-Saharan trade: the Ghana Empire (for which Ghana is named), the Mali Empire (for which Mali is named), and the Songhai Empire. During its golden age, there was a flourishing of mathematics, astronomy, literature, and art. At its peak in 1300 AD, the Mali Empire covered an area about twice the size of modern-day France and stretched to the west coast of Africa. In the late 19th century, during the Scramble for Africa, France seized control of Mali, making it a part of French Sudan. French Sudan (then known as the Sudanese Republic) joined with Senegal in 1959, achieving independence in 1960 as the Mali Federation. Shortly after that, following Senegal's withdrawal from the federation, the Sudanese Republic declared itself the independent Republic of Mali. After a long period of one-party rule, a coup in 1991 led to the writing of a new constitution and the establishment of Mali as a democratic, multi-party state.

Alpha Oumar Konaré was elected president in the country's first democratic election in 1992. He was succeeded in 2002 by Amadou Toumani Touré, a former army lieutenant-colonel who ruled until a coup was launched in 2012 by a group of young officers angry at the military's failure to stop Islamist insurgents. In response to continuing territorial gains, the French military launched Opération Serval in January 2013, after Herb and I started our trip to Mali.

I was reading the *New York Times* and other news outlets on my cell phone as we traveled east across West Africa and became concerned about our ability to tour Mali. On January 16, France decided to commit forces to help southern Mali retake territory in the north and oust Islamic militants. Herb and I were in communications with Klaus, and he informed us that our trip to Timbuktu was canceled. The militants were invading south towards Bamako, and he would keep us informed of the situation and adjust our schedule.

Abidjan, Ivory Coast

Wednesday, January 23, 2013, we flew into Abidjan, Ivory Coast, from Monrovia, Liberia, for the last stop on UTS West Africa Tour #1. We arrived at night and checked into the Hotel Novotel.

Thursday, January 24, 2013, Herb took us on a tour of Abidjan, Ivory Coast.

Friday, January 25, 2013, a change in my trip's schedule, which provided me with an extra day in Côte d'Ivoire, turned out to be a blessing in disguise. UTS West Africa Tour #1 had ended the day before. My fellow travelers on the tour, Lee and Connie, flew back to the United States. I was supposed to fly to Algiers but was unable to obtain an Algerian visa, so I stayed in Côte d'Ivoire with Herb Gobels before flying to Bamako, Mali, to start the UTS West Africa Tour #2 .

Herb arranged for a driver to take us on an all-day tour to Yamoussoukro, the capital of Côte d'Ivoire, 153 miles northwest of Abidjan. We left the hotel at 09:00 on a smooth four-lane divided highway. The scenery was mostly forest, some areas of open fields, a few villages, and little evidence of farmland. Over an hour out of the city, the highway was diverted to one side as repairs were performed on the other side. Then the divided paved highway ended, and we rode past the construction of the continuation of the divided highway. Finally, we reverted to a single road that contained a lot of potholes. The road has a lot of heavy trucks, and large and medium-size bus traffic since it is one of the roads between landlocked Mali and a seaport.

The few villages we passed always had at least one bus stopped to discharge and pick up passengers, surrounded by locals attempting to sell their goods to the passengers. Women with trays of food (bread, bananas, peanuts, and pineapple) balanced on their heads and young men with wooden bowls and mallets, and sometimes dead rabbits. It was always a chaotic sight, with numerous close calls as people ran across the road as we drove by. Some places the crowds were so large that we had to crawl at slow speed to get through.

Eventually, we reached the city. It has a fascinating history. It was the village of Félix Houphouët-Boigny, the "father" of Côte d'Ivoire independence and its first president. He built a capital for the new country, much like Brasilia, but no country moved their embassy there, and the government agencies were not moved from Abidjan.

As we entered the city, we were riding on an eight-lane street with few vehicles. On the horizon, I saw several impressive buildings. Our first stop was at the Presidential Hotel. A beautiful 5-star, 14 story high building with a 360°-view restaurant on the fourteenth floor. We used the toilet and took pictures of the exterior and interior, which still had Christmas decorations. In the back was a beautiful lagoon-style pool with an oriental bridge across the middle leading to the 18-hole golf course.

In the front parking lot were numerous vans from various beer and soda manufacturers attending a conference in the hotel. It was a very colorful scene with the red Coca Cola vans next to blue, yellow, or green beer vans and orange Fanta vans.

One of the most spectacular sights I have seen

From the hotel, we drove to one of the most spectacular sights I will ever see—Basilica of Our Lady of Peace of Yamoussoukro, *Basilique de Notre Dame de la Paix*. The basilica was constructed between 1985 and 1989 at the cost of $300 million. The design of the dome and encircled plaza were inspired by those of the Basilica of Saint Peter in the Vatican City, although it is not an outright replica. The cornerstone was laid on August 10, 1985, and it was consecrated on September 10, 1990, by Pope John Paul II.

Guinness World Records lists it as the largest church in the world, having surpassed the previous record-holder, St. Peter's Basilica, upon completion. It has an area of 322,917 sq. ft. and is 518 ft. high. However, it also includes a rectory and a villa (counted in the overall area), which are not strictly part of the church. It can accommodate 18,000 worshippers in air-conditioned pews, compared to 60,000 for St. Peter's.

While designing it after the Vatican Basilica, Lebanese architect Pierre Fakhoury constructed the dome to be slightly lower than the Basilica of Saint Peter but ornamented with a larger cross on top. The basilica is constructed with marble imported from Italy and is furnished with 75,000 sq. ft. of contemporary stained glass from France.

Columns are plentiful throughout the basilica but are not uniform in style; the smaller columns are there for structural reasons, while the bigger ones are decoration and contain elevators, rainwater evacuation from the roof, and other building mechanical devices. There is enough space to seat 7,000 people in the nave, with standing room for an additional 11,000 people. Apart from the basilica are two identical buildings, one serving as the rectory and the other as a private papal villa. The papal villa is reserved for papal visits, though the only one that has occurred was when the basilica was consecrated.

We had an English-speaking guide who gave us a thorough tour of the facility. He showed us the air-conditioned pews, the acoustics, the various statues around the edges of the pews, and explained the marvelous stained-glass windows. He took us to the roof in a round elevator in one of the columns. There we had an excellent view of the French gardens and a panoramic view of the city.

From the basilica, we rode to the presidential palace. We were not allowed to tour, but we were able to take pictures from across the moat that used to contain crocodiles. The next stop was another impressive building of the Foundation Houphouët-Boigny, similar in function to a US president's library.

We had then seen the four significant buildings in the capital. As we rode between the buildings, the streets were very wide, with many streets on either side leading to future development. It was a little eerie. Our last stop was another pit stop at the Presidential Hotel. This time we rode to the 14th-floor restaurant and walked around, getting one last view of the city.

The ride back appeared to be faster, and we were in the hotel by 17:30. It was a very memorable day!

Saturday, January 26, 2013, was a day that I did not think would come. I made it to Mali! Yes, it was a country at war, and our tour of the country had been canceled, but I had a non-refundable ticket from Abidjan to Bamako, so I used it. The local tour guide changed our hotel from a 5-star downtown to a 3-star in the suburbs, which is off the main highway and not well advertised. I had a little challenge to even find a hotel sign for a picture of the hotel name. It is also in the embassy area with well-guarded streets.

My day had started routinely in the Novotel Abidjan. I took the 09:45 hotel shuttle to the airport only to find that I could not check in until the afternoon. My ticket had listed the flight as departing at 14:10, but the airport had it listed as 14:50. The Abidjan airport has one large hall when you enter and then an arrivals hall and a departure hall. I had to wait in the large hall with no seats and no air conditioning for over two hours. The only time I cooled off was when I used my Star Alliance Gold card to beg the Ethiopian Airline office to use one of their computers to print my ticket, which had been emailed to me a couple of days earlier.

At noon they let me in the departure hall, where I found that Mauritania Airlines had not yet set up the check-in counter, but at least the hall was air-conditioned and had chairs. They started checking passengers in at 12:50, and immigration passport control was a breeze, but security was a little tighter than I had been experiencing in other West African countries. They searched my carry-on and almost everyone else's in line.

The departure gate area ran the full length of the building. At one end was a bar and restaurant up a flight of stairs. I went up and discovered that they had free Wi-Fi, so I checked my email and had a sandwich. After I finished, I wandered down to my assigned gate and saw out the window a ramp of French military planes. There were several C-130s and a KC-135. Soon one of the C-130s taxied out and took off, and another KC-135 landed. It had a probe basket connected to its boom. I gathered that the French were using Abidjan as the tanker and logistics base for the war in Mali.

The aircraft for my scheduled flight arrived at 14:30, and I thought we would leave on time, but we did not depart until 15:30. I was seated at the window on the first row of economy seats. I was able to take additional pictures of the French military aircraft and saw there were a lot more than I had been able to see from the terminal. A hot meal was severed in route. It was pieces of very tough beef, noodles, and string beans.

When we approached Bamako, I saw a lot of buildings with no roofs. It was unusual in that I saw no thatched roof huts or villages as I saw in other West African countries. The buildings with roofs I did see appeared from the air to have flat or slightly sloping metal roofs.

When we landed, I saw two C-17s parked near the terminal. As we taxied by them, I was surprised to see that one was from the USAF Dover AFB, and it had three armed guards. The other C-17 had RAF markings. I had read that the RAF was helping the French logistically because the French do not have the airlift capability that a C-17 provides, and the RAF have C-17s. In the same article, it said that the US was studying whether to commit logistic support to the conflict in Mali. I guess the US did not want to publicize their supporting the French in Mali.

Immigration processing was not efficient. We bused from the aircraft parking spot to the arrivals hall and lined up for a visa check, then we were supposed to fill out an arrival card, but no one was handing out the cards. there was one small counter where there apparently were cards, but it was crowded with passengers filling them out. In many countries, the airlines provide the cards in flight, so you have them filled out before you land. In other countries, airline staff stands at the door to the arrivals hall and hands them out, or there is a rack of cards near the entrance. The method here of placing them on a small counter is easily the least efficient. I went straight to passport control and handed him my passport. He asked where my card was, and I told him that there were not any available. He told me to return to the counter, but instead an immigration officer standing close by obtained a card for me.

There was a short line in front of me once I completed the card, and I breezed through passport control even though my visa was not valid until the 27th. My bag was one of the first to arrive on the belt, and Herb was waiting for me outside baggage claim. He had flown earlier in the day on another airline that routed him via Tome. We boarded an SUV, and it was not until we were close to the city and the driver exited the boulevard did Herb find out that the local agent had changed our hotel.

I have stayed in worse rooms, and this room at least had an electrical outlet next to the bed for my CPAP. There was free Wi-Fi, but it was too weak to work in the room. The restaurant dining area was outside with a large screen set up on a stage at one end with a soccer game projected on it. The African Cup matches were being held, and at this point Mali had won one and lost one. The game being displayed was between Togo, one of the smallest countries in Africa, and Algeria, the largest country in Africa.

Herb had a pizza, and I had spaghetti with meat sauce for dinner. Togo was ahead 2-0 when I returned to my room.

My long day in Mali

Sunday, January 27, 2013, my day in Mali started earlier than scheduled. The plan was to have the local tour guide meet Neal, who was flying in from Conakry, Guainía, at the airport. Then he would drive him to our hotel where Herb and I would check out, load our bags in the back of the SUV, tour the city, and have lunch before we were dropped at the airport at 14:00 for our 15:55 flight to Burkina Faso on Air Burkina. We estimated that the tour would start at about 09:30. I had breakfast outdoors with Herb at 08:00. During breakfast, a young lady dressed in a lovely new dress (I could tell because there were fold creases as though it had just been taken out of a package) crossed through the area. When we finished breakfast and I started back to my room across a courtyard in from of the hotel, I came upon a group of young ladies and men all dressed up and posing for pictures. It was a wedding party getting ready to leave for the ceremony. I was later informed that in Mali, weddings could only take place on Thursdays and Sundays. We ended up seeing many wedding parties during our city tour.

Neal arrived slightly ahead of schedule and was able to clear passport control and meet the guide earlier than we had anticipated, so the tour was ready to start at 09:00. They were not driving the new SUV that had transported us the day before, but instead, they were driving a much older, somewhat beat-up SUV. I guess we would blend in more than if we were in the new SUV with the tour agency logo on the doors. We drove down the heavily guarded road past embassies to the main street from the airport and on it drove across a bridge into the city of Bamako, past the beautiful grounds of the hotel we were supposed to stay in if the war hadn't started. The tour company thought it was safer to stay in a hotel off the main drag in the heavily guarded embassy area outside of the city.

Across the bridge, we were greeted by a large arch with a world globe on top, Honoring the Martyrs. We rode through the city, which has clean, smooth roads and a design of straight streets crossing at ninety-degree angles. (Based on the roads, I could tell it had been a French colony). The traffic flowed very well, and I saw no signs of any military. At the north end of the city, we started to drive up to the mountains that overlook the city. The president's palace could be seen on the top of a mountain looking down on the city.

Riding up, enjoying great views of the city below, we passed the Botanical Gardens, the Zoo, and the American Embassy, which had been relocated from the heart of the city to a point next to the Army camp. We looked down on the football (soccer) stadium that the Russians built. At the top of the mountain, we rode past the hospital and medical school and then a wall with 25 panels painted with scenes of historical events ranging from the first discovery of the country by Europeans to the present administration. We stopped at the end of the wall to tour the Explorer Park, constructed in 2000. The park had a lovely garden and was ringed with pedestals that had at one time displayed the busts of the explorers who established the country. Unfortunately, most of the French and other Caucasian busts had been vandalized, and only the native and Arab busts remained. At one end of the park were 192 flag poles which used to fly the flag of each of the UN countries, but no flags were flying.

We rode back into the city past the markets and government buildings. At the National Assembly building, we were stopped by a policeman. Our driver had a difficult time finding the paperwork for the vehicle. He was used to driving the newer SUV and had to call his office to find out where the paperwork was stored in the old clunker. Eventually it was resolved, and we rode on to the National Museum, also built by the Russians, where we were scheduled to have lunch after touring the museum. Unfortunately, the café was closed, but the tour was interesting. Not the best museum, but it did show some artifacts of the country and an impressive collection of textiles. It was full of school children making drawings of the exhibits (no photos allowed) and answering questions on a test sheet.

On the grounds outside the museum were replicas of the major architectural landmarks that we were to see if we had been able to travel upcountry. From the museum, we rode by the Catholic cathedral on our way to lunch at bistro restaurant Le Bafing. I had carp fish and chips. The fish was fried whole, and I had to be careful to separate the bones.

On our way to the airport, we passed the massive new monument to culture. The road to the airport is smooth, straight, and tree-lined once you leave the suburbs. As we approached the airport entrance, we saw our first hint of the war. A long backup of vehicles was at the entrance because each passenger's papers were being checked, and then the vehicles undercarriages were checked with mirrors. Further compounding the situation, a convoy of new military APCs was exiting the airport and the officials halted entries until they had passed by and left the area.

When we tried to enter the departure hall, Herb and I were turned back because we did not have tickets, just a paper copy of the reservation. We had thought we would be able to pay for the ticket at the check-in counter. After a go-around with the security policeman and our guide, we were told to purchase the ticket at the Air Burkina office in a building off the main waiting area. When we found the office, it was closed. Next to it was a general travel agency and he told us he could issue the ticket, but he did not accept credit cards. I had to go to an ATM in another part of the waiting area to get the money. Neal had gone in, and when he received his boarding pass, he asked the agent if we could purchase the tickets from him, but the agent had to check with his manager. Neal and I could see each other through a glass wall but could not talk. I finally told the travel agent to issue the ticket. He took my money and disappeared. It was getting close to the scheduled departure time when he finally returned with printed paid e-tickets. Herb and I gathered our luggage and passed through security and proceeded to the check-in counter. At the counter, the agent looked at our tickets and told us to stand aside. We had been issued "waitlist" tickets. At one hour to departure, he accepted our bags and handed back our passports, reservation, and a form to complete for immigration. It was now ten minutes to scheduled boarding time, and I rushed to immigration only to be turned back because I did not have a boarding pass. I rushed back to the counter, and the agent sheepishly handed me my boarding pass. It did not take long to pass through immigration and on to security.

There I had to remove my shoes which we had not had to do on most of the trip. I was surprised when my artificial knee did not set off an alarm and thought I had it made, but as I passed by a row of desks, I was motioned to have a secondary bag check. The agent checking my bag claimed that flashlight batteries were not allowed. I had been getting a warning that the batteries in my laptop mouse had only 1% left, and I had two fresh batteries in my power cord pouch to use once my mouse stop working. He took those batteries first, then started through my bag and found several flashlights that he emptied and a package of batteries. I was furious, and while he was digging into my bag, I quickly switched out my mouse batteries. Fortunately, he did not realize it used batteries. At one point, he told me he would hand the batteries to the pilot so I could get them when we landed in Burkina Faso but then reneged on that statement. Herb was standing there and informed the agent it was our boarding time. The agent gathered up all the batteries, handed back my flashlights, and let me go. I was steaming at the total arrogance of the agent who undoubtedly knew that batteries were not listed on the prohibited items list.

Upstairs in the gate area, I looked out the window and did not see an Air Burkina aircraft. An agent with an Air Burkina vest told us the plane was delayed. Herb went back to security and talked to the head agent who returned some of my batteries, but not enough to refill my flashlights. Herb asked me to return with him, and we found that the agent who had taken them was not around, and the head agent let me retrieve all the rest. What a fiasco!

After I filled my flashlights and repacked my carry-on, I looked out the window to see a USAF C-17 from McCord AFB. Soon the C-17 from Dover than I had seen the day before in Abidjan, Ivory Coast, landed and taxied in, then a British C-17 landed followed by a British C-130. Airmen in French and British uniforms were coming and going to the snack bar in the airport lounge area. The USAF C-17s departed, and a Russian aircraft of similar size landed, and two of its crew came into the terminal to have a drink at the snack bar. At one point, a row of French airmen was sitting in a row with identical Apple laptops using the Wi-Fi in the area. One had a headset and boom mike on talking to someone through his computer. Half the airmen that flowed in and out of the terminal were females.

I sat there waiting for my flight watching this bit of the Mali war. I also was on Wi-Fi and read that the USAF had committed KC-135s to assist the French. I did not know what base they would be operating from, but I had seen two French KC-135s in Abidjan the day before.

The wait for our Air Burkina flight dragged on, and twice they gave us free drinks and once a tasty tuna sandwich. They would give us an ETA, and it would pass and then another ETA. At 21:15, eight hours after we had entered the airport, a Canadian Regional Jet landed and taxied to the terminal. It was dark, but I jumped for joy and ran to the window only to discover that it was an Air Mali CRJ. I turned to the gate agent and asked her if there was a new ETA for the Air Burkina flight, and she responded that we would be flying on the Air Mali aircraft. I grabbed my bag and stood in line. We had been told that it would be open seating on the flight, but when I handed the agent my boarding pass, she wrote a seat number on it. Strange, but it worked. On the bus across the ramp to the aircraft, I noticed that all the military planes had departed.

We took off at 22:05 and landed in Ouagadougou, Burkina Faso, at 23:05. We checked in to a Libya-owned hotel called the Laico Hotel, one of the fanciest hotels I have ever stayed in. Gadhafi's brother built it.

I did a little research on Air Burkina and Air Mali. Both airlines have only one CRJ-200. Air Mali stopped operations on December 27, 2012, due to the war, parked their CRJ-200 and furloughed its flight crews. Since Air Burkina had only one CRJ-200, when it was grounded for maintenance they must have spent the eight hours we were waiting to arrange to borrow Air Mali's aircraft, get it ready to fly, and ferry it to Bamako to pick us up.

I had survived the conflict in Mali without hearing any shots, but saw a lot of military activity, and was disappointed that I was not able to get to visit the famous Timbuktu.

CHAPTER 10

YEMEN

Friday, April 19, 2013, I started a visit to Yemen and Socotra Island some 350 miles off the coast of Yemen by flying from Baku, Azerbaijan, early on the morning of Friday, April 19. I changed planes in Dubai and arrived in Sana'a, the capital of Yemen, at 09:00. The local tour agent met me and assisted in my obtaining a Yemen visa. Munir, my assigned local guide, met me at the baggage claim and took me to the Sheba Hotel.

Walking tour of Bab al Yemen

After check-in, Munir and I visited Bab al Yemen (the old city of Sana'a), considered to be the oldest living capital in the world. We spent hours walking the narrow streets, stopping for lunch at a kabob stand for minced lamb kabob and a salad of ground tomatoes, onions, cucumber, and lettuce (they use an old-fashioned meat grinder). It was delicious. At 12:30, I sat in the shade of a bookstore while Munir took part in Friday prayers at the Grand Mosque. He was praying in the street with a group of men since the

189

mosque was full. It was a good thing we had lunch before prayers because, after the service, the streets were packed and all the eating stalls crowded.

Daggers

Munir stopped at a "friend's" stall to introduce me to Yemen daggers. Every man I saw in the old city was wearing a dagger in a "j" shape inside a broad jeweled belt. I was told that a dagger that was not in a "j" shape was reserved for a judge or government official. Later, we stopped for hot tea and sat with a couple of Saudis. Just to be on the safe side, I told them I was from Calgary, Canada. They talked in English about business opportunities they were investigating in Yemen.

Khat

After our four-hour walking tour of the old city, we met at the car. The assigned driver's son was at the wheel with a big wad of khat in his mouth. Khat is a stimulant drug that comes from a shrub that grows in East Africa and southern Arabia. Like chewing tobacco, leaves of the khat shrub are chewed and held in the cheek to release their chemicals. Cathinone and cathine are the stimulants in khat that make a person feel high. The main effects are like amphetamine (speed), but less potent.

After lunch almost everyone chews khat in this city. Even though it has been several years since fighting rocked the city, there were checkpoints all over the city where soldiers check your car for suspicious cargo. After lunch, all the soldiers at these checkpoints have a big bulge in their cheek full of khat.

Quick View of Al Saheh Mosque

We rode out to see the huge Al Saleh Mosque. The afternoon rains arrived about the same time as we did, so I skipped a walking tour of the exterior and took a few pictures through the fence and hopped back in the car. Traffic was terrible in the city. Nobody stays in their lane. There were few stoplights but a lot of roundabouts. Some intersections have police directing the flow, but it is chaotic with a lot of horn blowing. Driving in the rain with flooded streets compounds the situation, especially when most of the drivers are chewing khat and getting high.

The ride to the mosque and back to the hotel allowed me to see the architectural beauty of the city, considered by some to be one of the most beautiful cities in the world. I would not quite say that, but it's what the brochures say.

The Sheba Hotel where I was staying was very European looking and had decent but expensive Wi-Fi in the rooms. I was a little irritated that, just to get a couple of hours of Wi-Fi both before I went to bed and when I got up in the morning, I had to buy two days' worth since the period of usages ends at midnight.

Saturday, April 20, 2013, I had to get up at 4 am to get to the airport for a 7 am flight to Socotra Island. I exited my shower with the TV on CNN just as the Boston Bomber was captured. It had been a terrible week for Boston. I had been following the events on my phone and the TV and was glad one of the bombers was caught alive. Robert MacLaughlin, my son-in-law, had run in the Boston Marathon. He had finished and was around the block when the bomb exploded, so it was news I had been avidly tracking.

My flight to Socotra Island had a stop in Al Mukalla on the coast of the Gulf of Aden. The flight was on Felix Airways (ever heard of it?) in a CRJ-700. It was open seating, and half the passengers were young men carrying bags of khat—I guess to sell in the Al Mukalla area because they did not fly on to Socotra.

Sitting next to me on the first leg was a Yemeni project manager with a US passport. He studied at the University of Michigan and has his family living in the Detroit area. He gave me a lot of insight on his challenges to complete a project in Yemen, between the workers getting high every afternoon and the government not paying the bills. He also gave me some background on Al Mukalla. It is the fifth-largest city in Yemen with a population of approximately

192 | ED REYNOLDS

300,000 and is a main seaport. Al Mukalla is the capital city of the Hadramaut coastal region in Yemen in the southern part of Arabia on the Gulf of Aden, close to the Arabian Sea. It is located 300 miles east of Aden and is the most important port in the Governorate of Hadramaut, the largest governorate in South Arabia.

On the second leg of the flight, my seatmate was a young man in the tour guide business. Socotra Island is a popular tourist destination for Europeans. He looked at my schedule and gave me some pointers on the sites. As we approached the Socotra airport, he pointed out several of the sites from the air, which helped me later to understand where I was and where I was going on my two days on the island.

Dixam Plateau

I was met at the airport at 09:15 by Amir, my local guide, and Abdullah, the driver of a Toyota Land Cruiser with four-wheel drive. We immediately started on a tour of the island by driving up the mountains to the Dixam plateau. There we had a view of the canyon below. The plateau area is known for native Dragon Blood Trees.

They are not in fact trees, but an herb belonging to the lily family. The shape of the plant changes as it grows. It starts as a clump of green grass shoots like the beginning of a palm tree. It then grows a thick stem and looks like a shaving brush with the green pointed leaves on top. Then short limbs branch out with the green pointed leaves on the end of the branches. The branches are close together and form a crown shape like an umbrella. They provide excellent shade, and I saw several instances of men and children sitting under them and goats gathered under them. It is difficult to determine how old a plant is because the trunk is fibrous and has no tree rings.

The Dragon Blood name is the result of the red sap that oozes from the tree. It is made into a medicine that is used to stop bleeding in women during childbirth. It is also used to color pottery and as a dye in cloth.

The viewpoint provided a fabulous vista overlooking Daerhu Canyon, with many unusual rock formations.

Picnic Lunch in Daerhu Canyon

From the viewpoint, we drove down into the canyon to a picnic area near the freshwater swimming hole. There Amir and Abdullah set up a gas stove and fixed lunch. The stove was to heat the traditional tea and bread. The lunch was chopped up tomatoes, onions, carrots, and cucumber (they did not have a grinder like in the old city) with canned tuna and plain yogurt. They gave me a dish, fork, and spoon, but they ate from one dish using pieces of the flatbread to scoop up the salad. Dessert was slices of orange.

After lunch we rested for an hour and then rode back out of the canyon. It was a good thing the vehicle had four-wheel drive. I had not been on as rocky, rough road since my trip to Lesotho.

Stuck in sand at Omaa Beach

From the plateau, we rode down to the coast and stopped at Omaa Beach, which had beautiful sand dunes and a little hut for tourists where we stopped and finished the tea. While Amir and I were having tea, Abdullah got stuck in the sand even with the four-wheel drive. He let some air out of the tires and was able to move forward, only to get stuck again heading back out. Amir and I were able to push this time, and we continued our tour to Hadiboh, the main village on the island.

Summerland Hotel

I checked into the Summerland Hotel, where they had a strong Wi-Fi signal in the rooms. The room was small but functional. There was no English-speaking channel on the TV.

194 | ED REYNOLDS

Adeeb Resort

The young men returned at 18:30 to drive me to dinner at the Adeeb Resort, which was halfway between Hadiboh and the seaport terminal on the east end of the island. The "resort" was on the beach with huts for backpackers. We sat on a large mat with a pillow up against a palm tree trunk with our shoes off. A piece of plastic was laid down in front of us, and large plates of food (fish, rice, beans, and bread) were placed on the plastic. Amir and Abdullah ate by taking a piece of fish and mixing it with the rice and beans on the plastic and scooping it up with a piece of bread. I used a fork and spoon and had a dish to mix the food, butI did use the bread to scoop up the mixture at times.

After this meal, we returned to the hotel. It had been a long, eventful day.

Hotel Breakfast

Sunday, April 21, 2013, a tour of the island was scheduled to start at 07:30. The hotel advertised that breakfast was served at 06:30. When I got down to eat breakfast at 06:40, I found the dining room empty and the kitchen empty. I called out a loud "hello," and someone finally arrived to take my order since there was no buffet food laid out. They served me an omelet and a plate of beans.

Ras Shoab Beach

The reason an early start was required was that we were driving over an hour to the west end of the island to the fishing village of Qalansiyah, where we would board a 20-foot open boat to take an hour ride to Ras Shoab Beach. The sea was a little rough as we rounded a point west of the village, but the trip was worth it. The beach was spectacular, with fine white sand and no rocks or shells. There was only one other boat there, and their passengers were two ladies that were swimming a long way down the beach from where we dropped anchor. I had a good swim while the young men talked with the men from the other boat. I never saw the women up close.

Oalansiyah Village Tour

When we returned to Qalansiyah, we rode around the village. There was an Army post nearby with rusty Russian tanks with their guns pointed out to sea and several rusty howitzers.

Detwah Lagoon

We then drove to Detwah Lagoon, a protected area with several picnic huts. Throughout the area, signs were describing the protected plants, shells, and creatures that exist near the lagoon.

We had the same lunch as the day before, and Amir said the schedule called for us to rest for an hour. Abdullah went to visit a group in another hut, and I was lying down when I heard an American woman's voice. I went to investigate and met two young ladies, graduates of Stanford, both working in Washington DC, one for the government and the other for a consulting firm. They told me Socotra Island is the dark secret exotic travel destination for single women in DC because it is secluded, and the Muslim guides are very respectful of female tourists.

They had spent a week camping on the island and were the two ladies swimming down the beach that morning. They were surprised to meet another American on the island. We talked for a while, and I found that they did not know about the events of the week in Boston, West Texas, and the ricin-laced letters addressed to President Obama and Senator Wicker.

More sites to see and a power failure

After the little visit with fellow Americans, I returned to the tour. Our next stop was a cave in the side of the mountain. It was large (high and wide) but not very deep. A vehicle could drive around in it. A man was taking a nap when we arrived, and we gave him a lift back to the highway when we left.

We stopped at a rock-lined lagoon, and a young boy swam across the 100-yard wide lagoon to see us. He looked to be no older than 10.

We visited another beach, but I declined to swim as it was rocky, and you could not easily get to deep water. Amir and Abdullah started to return me to my hotel, but I asked to visit the seaport. I wondered if the island could support a cruise ship since there were things to see, especially the Dragon Blood Trees and beautiful beaches. The seaport consisted of a rock jetty with a crane at the end to offload cargo from small ships. There was a gas station and large fuel tanks but no houses in the area. It did not look inviting for tourists.

When I returned to my hotel room, I found that it had not been serviced and I had to go down to get a clean towel (I had taken the room towel to the beach). Then when I returned to my room, the power went off. The hotel had a backup generator, but when the power in the city failed, the internet connection from the island failed. I could get a strong Wi-Fi signal but no internet.

Dinner was again at the Adeeb Resort. The menu was similar, except there was a platter of spaghetti in place of the rice. Amir and Abdullah drove me back to the hotel after dinner.

The return flight fiasco

Monday, April 22, 2013, the flights from the island to the mainland did not run every day. Yemeni Airlines flies only one flight a week on Mondays. Felix Airways flies Mondays, Wednesdays, and Fridays. Originally I was scheduled to return on the Yemeni flight at 11:30, but the Yemen tour agent scheduled me on the Felix flight at 09:55. With two flights leaving near the same time from the small terminal, we decided to get to the airport at 08:30. That meant leaving the hotel at 08:00.

I arrived at the hotel dining room at 06:30 to again find it empty and the kitchen empty, and no one responded to my loud "hello." I saw a hallway next to the dining room with a man sleeping on a couch at the end. After calling out and receiving no response, I turned on the hallway lights and the cook got up. This time I ordered one egg over. He brought the one egg but also the omelet and beans.

I finished packing and carried my luggage down to reception before 08:00 and found that Amir and Abdullah were waiting across the street, parked in the shade. Therefore, we arrived at the airport early, and I was one of the first to have my bag checked at the entrance. Once inside, Amir checked with Felix Airways and was informed that the flight was canceled, but everyone was booked on the Yemeni flight at 11:30.

What a fiasco. When check-in time came, the Yemeni scheduled passengers were at one end of the counter in a somewhat orderly line, but the Felix passengers were a mob scene at the other end with no order or line. Amir fought the battle for me and got my boarding pass, which had no seat assignment and no name, just a handwritten number and a stamp with the Sana'a code of SAH.

I then had to go through security again to the waiting room. It was hot in the terminal with no air conditioning, but the departure room was air-conditioned. Once we were sitting in the departure room, we were told the flight was going to be an hour late.

We boarded at 12:20, which meant I had been at the airport for 4 hours. The plane was an A-320-200 and had open seating. I wanted a window seat and ended up in the next to last row. The two American girls were in front of me. My seat companions on both legs were paired off with the person on the aisle, so they never talked to me. I was listening to a book on tape anyway.

When I landed in Sana'a at 15:05, I found that Munir had not been informed of the change in airlines or arrival time. He and the driver (also named Abdullah) had been waiting for hours. The terminal has no arrivals display to give them an understanding that the Felix flight had been canceled and that the Yemeni flight would be late.

Bait Bous

We loaded my bags in the car during the end of the afternoon rain shower and headed out on tour. I was supposed to visit the National Museum, but it closed at 15:00, so we rode out of the city and up the mountain to Bait Bous, an ancient village that overlooks the west side of the city. It is a marvel that the buildings were constructed on the side of the mountain and on the mountain top. From there, we rode down to the valley, then up another plateau that also had a commanding view of the city. The parking lot was full of cars containing men chewing khat and enjoying the view. Munir told me it was like that every afternoon. The itinerary called for me to observe the sunset, but the clouds from the afternoon rain were lingering, which prevented my seeing the sunset, so they deposited me at the hotel. I had the same room as the previous Thursday.

Visit Thula, Yemen

Tuesday, April 23, 2013, the tour scheduled for Tuesday was the area north of the city. Abdullah picked me up at the hotel, and on the way north, he picked up Munir. The traffic was as chaotic in the morning as I had seen in the afternoon. The city needs a traffic engineer to recommend more stoplights and re-engineer the flow. Of course, the numerous checkpoints do not help as they require that multiple lanes of traffic narrow down to one or two lanes to stop at the checkpoint.

Once outside the northern edge of the city, we headed to the UNESCO nominated world heritage site at Thula, located 33 miles northwest of Sana'a. Along the way, we traveled through the Dhahar valley, where we stopped to tour the famous Dar al-Hajar (Rock Palace), which stands atop a protruding rock formation in the middle of Wadi Dhahr, a fertile and pleasant valley of small villages and clay-walled orchards. It is pictured in many books about Yemen and has become a symbol of the country itself.

Imam Yahya (1911-48) built the five-story palace in the 1930s as a summer residence. Building a palace in such an extraordinary place was not his idea; there were already ruins of a prehistoric building on top of the hill. The well penetrating the rocks next to the house is said to date from prehistoric times. The palace served as the summer palace of Imam Yahya. It was a group of palaces famous for its delightful location and its beautiful gypsum ornamentation in the Sana'a style.

From Wadi Dhahr, we rode up a winding road to the gate of Thula. Munir and I were greeted by two locals that Munir has known since they were ten years old. One of the locals, named John, provided me with a running commentary on the city as we walked the narrow stone-paved streets. I was fascinated by the old wooden doors, some of which were over 1,000 years old and still in use.

The houses of the city are high-rise structures built of stones which harmonize with the mountain overlooking the city. The façades of the houses are embellished with decorations and mouldings with arch-shaped windows decorated with pieces of marble stained-glass. In the city center lies the Great Mosque, which had a distinctive small stone minaret. There was a bath, and nearby were several reservoirs next to a small stream that flowed from beneath the fort high on the plateau. Thula was surrounded by a solid stonewall with just two gates.

We walked up a beautiful stone staircase to the fort, which contained water reservoirs and grain stores and could thus sustain itself in times of siege and is therefore considered to be the most unconquerable fort in Yemen.

Back down from the fort, we walked through a row of shuttered stalls, one of which John opened to show me his shop of tourist attractions. I felt obligated to buy a necklace for $10 since he had been so informative during the tour of the city and the castle.

Thula had been a significant tourist attraction in the past. Since the hostilities in 2009, the tourist trade has dried up, and the shop keepers were hurting. I was surrounded by vendors once the word got out that Munir had brought a tourist into the city.

Visit Hababah, Yemen

A few miles from Thula we visited Hababah, another fortress village set on top of a plateau. There we walked through the gate to view a large water cistern fed by water from a spring above. The water was green with algae—not very appealing. I even saw a small frog in the corner of the pool. We walked around the village then drove on to Fort Al Zakatain, another of the many villages and forts that were built in medieval times on the many plateaus in the area.

Lunch in Shibam

We stopped for lunch in Shibam (there are two Shibams in Yemen, and the one we didn't stop at is a UNESCO site.) The building looked like a multi-story family house, and we climbed to the fourth floor into a large room with nicely decorated walls and ceiling, including a chandelier. There were two large, low tables, and the walls were lined with low cushions. We had to remove our shoes to enter the room. The window overlooking the street was full of tour agency stickers from all over the world. I then realized that this was a standard tourist lunch place. They served a wide range of local dishes, including two types of rice, boiled potatoes, goat, and some dishes beyond description. All the dishes except the meat, which had a lot of bones, were eaten by scooping with pieces of the flatbread. Dessert was a pizza size flatbread cooked and soaked in honey.

Kawkaban, Yemen

After lunch, Munir and Abdullah prayed, and then we drove on to Kawkaban, an ancient historical center and fortified citadel about 9,000 feet above sea level. The city is walled from the north and is fortified naturally from the other directions and is known for its beautiful architectural design. It had stunning views of the villages below. After taking some pictures of the buildings and the villages below, we headed back to the city and the hotel.

The tour, at least in the area northwest of Sana'a, left me with the impression that the country is full of rocks. All the buildings in these ancient villages were built of stone on top of rocks. The fields and sides of hills were terraced with stone walls. Another observation was that the paved roads were well constructed (although very winding up to the fortresses). In the villages, they were not paved and littered with trash. We only visited one village that was free of trash, so I know they could clean up if they wanted to but either do not care or are too lazy.

Ride to Al Hajjarah, Yemen

Wednesday, April 24, 2013, my last full day tour of Yemen was to the west of the city. The road we took is the main route for trucks from the Red Sea port of Al Hudaydah, slowing our drive. We stopped in the Souq Alman to buy fruit and water. While I was waiting for Munir to buy the fruit and Abdullah to buy the water, a young boy less than ten years old tried to sell me a bag of khat. When I brushed him off, a man with his mouth bulging with khat approached and insisted that I purchase a bag. He would not take no for an answer. The window was down and electric, so I could not raise it. I moved to the other side of the car, and he finally got the clue that I was not interested in purchasing or chewing khat.

We rode on past the highest mountain in Yemen, Jabal and Nabi Shu'ayb, at 12,028 feet, up to the 6,500-foot high village of Al Hajjarah, whose name means "the stony one." The slopes of the mountains in the area are terraced, and coffee, almonds, khat, and fruit trees grow in addition to vegetables. It was a breathtaking scenic ride. The village is also considered to be one of the most beautiful, with four and five-story decorated houses hanging on the side of the mountain.

Dawoodi Bohra Muslims

From there, we drove to Manakhah, which was another village built on the top of a plateau, and then we rode another winding road to Hutayb, a village of the Dawoodi Bohra Muslims from India. I found that interesting since there is a Dawoodi Bohra Mosque just two blocks from my house in Woodland Hills, California. Going up and back down the winding road from Hutayb, we saw men in the white caps worn by the members of the sect.

An anxious lunch in Sanaahh, Yemen

On our way back to Sana'a, we stopped at a local eating establishment in Sanaahh, a small village. We were seated on a second-floor terrace overlooking the street. A pickup truck pulled in below, and two men got out and retrieved rifles from the back-window rack. They entered the restaurant and sat at a table next to the wall but in line with our table. When they sat down, they placed their rifles in their laps with the muzzles facing our table. This made me a little nervous, so I excused myself to wash my hands in the men's room. I think Munir or Abdullah got the sense of my discomfort, and when I returned, the rifles were now upright against the wall.

Now, more relaxed, I ate a lunch consisting of fahsa, a Yemeni stew made of lamb cutlets with lamb soup, spices, and fenugreek cooked in an iron pot. I scooped the stew up with pieces of flatbread. It was delicious.

After lunch, we stopped at a small mosque alongside the road for Munir and Abdullah to pray and then the long drive back to the hotel.

Summary

My tour was over, and I had safely completed a tour of Yemen, one of the most conflicted countries in the world.

From a safety viewpoint, I never saw any out of ordinary activity except the last lunch. The many checkpoints deter weapons from being transported from village to village. The hotel conducted a detailed bomb search of the vehicles entering the compound, and all bags are x-rayed at the entrance to the hotel lobby. Outside the city, we had to show a police authorization to exit the city and, at times, when we crossed into a new area.

CHAPTER 11

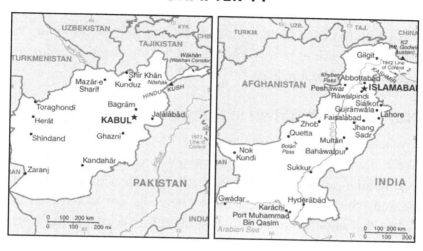

AFGHANISTAN AND PAKISTAN

Thursday, April 25, 2013, my short tour of Kabul, Afghanistan, and Lahore, Pakistan, started in Sana'a, Yemen, when I had to bid farewell to Munir, my tour guide in Yemen for a week, and to Abdullah the driver who—despite his heavy chewing of khat every day after lunch—had somehow driven the rough roads and crowded city traffic without a scratch on the Toyota Land Cruiser.

To fly to Kabul from Sana'a, I had to spend a night in Dubai, where I would rejoin the Universal Travel Systems (UTS) tour group that I had left to visit Yemen. At the check-in counter for Emirates Airlines, I asked to be seated in an aisle seat with no bulkhead in front of me so I could put a bag under the seat in front and stretch out my legs.

Airport security went very smoothly. The local tour agency's airport terminal man (Munir did not have a pass to enter the terminal), shepherded me through check-in, passport control, and security. We were bused to the A-330-200, and when I arrived at my seat, I discovered it was a bulkhead. I was not a happy camper.

The flight attendant reseated me in the last row on the aisle where there was an empty seat next to me. They served a hot lamb and rice meal with red wine on the two-and-one-half hour flight. Emirates was a good airline; now if I could just get the check-in agents to understand my seat request.

Not a smooth arrival in Dubai

We landed in Dubai on schedule at 13:40, and then the fun began. We had a long walk from the arrival gate to the stairway down to immigration, where they had 20 stations, each with a single line packed with a mass of passengers stretching out to the hallway below the stairs. There was no distinction between UAE residents, foreigners requiring visas, and those not requiring a visa. Only wheelchair passengers had an individual line. I lined up in the line next to the wheelchair line, thinking that when there were no wheelchair passengers inline, the agent would take someone from my line. I was wrong, and for whatever reason, my line was the slowest. An hour after landing, I complained to what appeared to be a supervisor. He mumbled something about a shift change, but he then led me and the passengers in front of me to the business class line, and I was finally able to get to the luggage carousel where there were only a few bags left. When I exited the baggage area, I saw a row of hotel stalls. I asked the agent in the Hotel Al Bustan Rotana stall to arrange transportation to the hotel. He put the fee on my room bill, thus avoiding exchanging money for the overnight stay.

In a few minutes, he led me to the parking garage, and I was on my way to the hotel one hour and forty minutes after landing! The hotel was not far from the airport, but we took a strange route of highways and switchbacks and side streets to get there. It was a 5-star hotel with a large atrium and a piano player in the middle. It had many restaurants and bars. I settled in my room, bought 24 hours of Wi-Fi service, then walked around the hotel and the neighborhood. Next door was a high-class food court with a dozen fancy outdoor restaurants and bars.

When supper time arrived, I elected to eat at the pool bar and have a nice cold Amstel Light beer—the first beer in over a week. When I returned to my room, I finished my Yemen journal and emailed it to my travel group and retired early.

At 23:00 the phone rang, and I was informed that the UTS tour group had finally arrived and was awaiting my appearance in the hotel bar. I got dressed and checked several bars in the hotel and could not find the group. I was about to give up but decided to ask the front desk first. He pointed to an out of the way bar I had not known about, and I found the group. They told me that they had as long a time processing out of the airport as I had had. They had an even longer stay at the airport because one member got separated from the group. He eventually traveled to the hotel on his own, leaving his bag at the carousel.

At 00:45, the party broke up and I returned to my room.

Fly to Kabul, Afghanistan

Friday, April 26, 2013, reunited with the UTS group. I ate breakfast with them and traveled with them to the airport for what we thought was a 13:45 flight on Flydubai, only to discover the flight had been re-scheduled for 14:10. Our group was the first to be checked in. When my turn came, instead of asking the agent for an aisle seat with no bulkhead, I asked for an aisle seat with a row of seats in front of me. The agent assigned me to row 13, which no one likes to sit in, so I had the row to myself, allowing me to slide over to the window and take pictures out the window as the flight landed in Kabul.

Flydubai is a low-cost airline with a strict baggage allowance of 32 kg for checked and hand-carried bags. They also charge for food onboard. Not knowing what I would experience for dinner, I purchased a delicious ham and cheese sandwich (since I would not be tasting ham in Afghanistan) and a bag of mixed nuts.

Arrival in Kabul, Afghanistan

We landed in Kabul at 17:45 and walked across the ramp to the immigration hall. I found a line for foreigners with no one in line and was through in seconds. What a contrast from the day before! The rest of the group had been sitting in seats behind me, and they soon were at the baggage carousel with me. It took a little time for our bags to arrive, but Rolf, The UTS tour escort, had arranged for porters to pick our bags off the carousel, and off we went to the hotel bus. It was a long walk past the parking lot and several checkpoints to where the bus was parked. Hotel buses are not allowed in the airport terminal parking lot and must park a long way away. It reminded me of a similar situation I encountered in Baghdad. There the bus parking area was so far from the terminal we had to take a shuttle bus to it. There were guards who told us we could not take pictures of the terminal or the area along our walk.

By the time we loaded up the bus, which was just a Toyota van with three rows of seats, it was getting dark. We arrived at the Hotel Serena in the dark, passing by a brightly lighted building with the sign that it was a wedding hall.

Hotel Serena

Hotel Serena is highly secured with several walls and courtyards between the street and the rooms. When our van stopped to enter the first gate, it was checked for bombs under it. Then we rode along the wall to a second checkpoint where we got out and were sniffed by a dog trained to detect explosives. Next, we entered through a heavy metal door into a courtyard and from there through another heavy metal door to a room with an x-ray machine. I was hand-patted after my metal knee set off the alarm on the metal detector. We then crossed a large courtyard to the entrance of the hotel lobby, also a large room. Check-in was fast, and the Wi-Fi was free. I found my room and discovered a bed turned down and an envelope on the desk with my name. Inside was a welcome note from the hotel manager. Next to the desk was a small table with a bowl of fruit and a dish of almonds, raisins, and pistachio nuts. The bathroom had a large tub, two sinks, and a separate room for the toilet and the shower. I rate the large room with twin queen size beds as elegant as any hotel room as I have ever stayed in.

My luggage had not been delivered to my room, so I went down to the lobby to check and Rolf told me to report to the security office to open my luggage. When I got there, they wanted to see the knife that the x-ray had seen in my luggage. When they saw it was a camping jackknife with a corkscrew, they said OK and let me close it up and wheel it to my room.

This resulted in my being a little late for dinner, which was a marvelous buffet with a large salad bar, local lamb dishes, Indian food, Asian food, Japanese sushi, and a fabulous dessert table. They served non-alcoholic beer and wine. BYO was allowed, but Rolf had not thought of buying any wine at the duty-free shop in Dubai.

Tour Kabul, Afghanistan

Saturday, April 27, 2013, we departed the hotel at 09:00 to tour Kabul. The same van that took us to the hotel was used for the city tour. I sat alone in the third seat. This allowed me to take pictures out of both sides and the rear. We were told by the driver when and where we could take pictures. The city was a little more westernized looking along the main divided street than I had expected, especially having just come from Yemen.

King Darul Aman Palace

From the hotel, we rode down Darulaman Road to the former king's Darul Aman Palace, where we got out of the van and walked around, taking pictures. The palace was built in the 1920s by King Amanullah Khan to modernize Afghanistan. It was first gutted by fire in 1969 and restored to house the defense ministry during the 1970s and 1980s. During the Communist coup of 1978, the building was set on fire. It was damaged again as rival Mujahideen factions fought for control of Kabul during the early 1990s. Heavy shelling by the Mujahideen after the end of the Soviet invasion left the building a gutted ruin. The palace was reportedly part of the targets in the attacks launched on April 15, 2012, for which the Taliban claimed responsibility. On the southwest side of the palace complex across the palace grounds and sports fields, a new building was under construction to hold the parliament. Behind the parliament building is the mansion that housed the king's family. It was also gutted.

Several soldiers guard the grounds and eagerly talked to us and posed for pictures.

National Museum of Afghanistan

On the north side of the palace across a road was the national museum of Afghanistan, also known as the Afghan National Museum or Kabul Museum, and our next stop on the tour. When we arrived, we were given the option to pay $6 to take photographs inside. I had read that it had lost most of its items during the wars, so I elected not to pay the fee and not take pictures.

Inside, I learned that its collection had earlier been one of the most important in Central Asia, with over 100,000 items dating back several millennia. After the collapse of President Najibullah's government, and then during the start of the civil war in the early 1990s, the museum was looted numerous times, resulting in a loss of 70% of the 100,000 objects on display.

In March 1994, the museum, which had been used as a military base, was struck by rocket fire, and was largely destroyed. It was rebuilt by the Greeks and, slowly, artifacts have been found and put back on display. The hall devoted to the Buddhist era was the most interesting to me.

In an area where I could take pictures, I found another interesting collection: cars belonging to the country's leaders. They were in terrible shape, having been shot-up during the wars. There were two 1920s era Rolls Royces, a 1930 Ford convertible, a Russian limo that was a Packard knock-off, and several 1950 to 60 era Cadillacs. It is a shame that there were shot at and gutted.

Gardens of Babur

From the museum, we rode back to the city on Sarak-e-Chilsitun Street, another main boulevard in the city, to the Gardens of Babur, locally called Bagh-e Babur. It is a historical park and the last resting-place of the first Mughal emperor, Babur. The gardens are thought to have been developed around 1528 AD when Babur gave orders for the construction of an 'avenue garden' in Kabul. It is surrounded by a high wall, and we had to pay a fee to enter. Past the entrance gateway was a courtyard with vendors selling local handicrafts, primarily necklaces, rings, and bracelets. I was surprised that I could buy a United States Army Afghan service medal in the military box. Our group lingered in the courtyard, bargaining for items. I was shown a necklace which I admired. The asking price was $50. I told the seller I would pay only $10, and he lowered the price to $20, then $15, and finally accepted the $10. When the others in the group heard that they started bargaining, and I think one of them bought a similar necklace for $5.

We entered another gate into the garden from this courtyard, which has a long stone path leading up a gentle slope. On both sides were picnic areas in trees (cherry blossoms were in bloom) with people having picnics. Our guide told us not to take pictures of the right side without permission since that was the family and women's area. The left side was the men's area and all right to take pictures. Near the end of the long walkway was the garden pavilion, which was under renovation. The pavilion was built at the turn of the 20th century for the entertainment of royal guests. It was the court physician's residence before the garden was opened to the public in the 1930s. Past the pavilion was the Shah Jahan Mosque, one of the most important historic monuments in Kabul. The marble mosque was dedicated by Mughal ruler Shah Jahan during a visit to the garden in 1647. The mosque was restored by an Italian team in 1966 but severely damaged during the fighting in 1993. In 2003 it was repaired, and the west wall replaced. Continuing up the slope was Babur's grave enclosure. Babur was initially buried in

Agra, but his body was moved to the site in 1540. Inside the grave enclosure are the graves of his son, Hindal, one of his grandsons, and the daughter of Alamgir II. It was a beautiful building!

Outside the enclosure we met a young couple. The father, who was carrying a baby, agreed to let us take pictures of the family. Then a group of 13- year-old girls approached us, speaking excellent English. After a while, they agreed to let us take their picture. Inna Baker, a dentist from New York, was such a hit with them that they returned with a camera to have their picture taken with her and invited her to their home.

On the way back to the gate, another couple with a baby allowed us to take their picture. The mother had a stunning green dress and shoes. Next, a group of boys with an older man posed for a picture. One of the boys begged for money, but we continued to the van.

After leaving the Gardens of Babur, we rode along a street of lumberyards and building materials to a goat market and stopped at Bala Hissar, an ancient fortress, to take pictures. The guide did not think it was safe for us to leave the van. We had to jockey positions inside the van to take our photos. The estimated date of the fort's construction is around the 5th century AD. Kabul's walls, which are 20 feet high and 12 feet thick, start at the fortress and follow the mountain ridge in a sweeping curve down to the river.

Wazir Akbar Khan

From the fort, we rode up a mountain to Wazir Akbar Khan, a vista point above the city. Several men were riding and galloping horses around in a large dirt area. We stopped for photos of the city below and then were surrounded by a group of young boys begging. Inna had a packet of chewing gum and was handing it out but stopped when she realized that the aggressive ones were taking more than one piece. I got a good picture of the military intelligence balloon that flies over the city.

Our tour's last stop was a small bookstore that sold postcards and stamps and would mail the cards for us. I bought one to send to the third-grade class that had requested cards from all over the world. My daughter, Robin, had sent me the request.

It was a short ride back to the hotel. My brief tour of Kabul was over. I spent the afternoon writing my journal, then had another excellent buffet dinner, then said farewell to the tour group. I prepared for my flight to Pakistan in the morning, while they would fly to Kashmir in the afternoon.

Fly to Pakistan

Sunday, April 28, 2013, I checked in and received my boarding pass and proceeded to passport control but had to send my carry-on through an x-ray machine, and I was patted down. After my passport was stamped, I was able to go upstairs to a waiting area. There I sat listening to a book on tape for several hours. The plane for my flight on Pakistani International Airlines (PIA) arrived over an hour late. I was scheduled to change planes in Islamabad with just one hour between flights and was concerned that there would be no later flight to Lahore if I missed my connection. There was no one from PIA around to discuss the options.

They finally called our flight, and we were bused out to our aircraft, a Canadian Regional Jet. While I was standing in line waiting to board, I took a picture of the aircraft registration markings as I do on every flight. A policeman ran up and said no pictures and had me delete the picture. When I boarded the plane, a man patted me down and searched my carry on. The female passengers had to go into the aft baggage compartment to be patted down as they boarded the aircraft.

The flight took an hour to Peshawar, Pakistan, during which we were served a sandwich. Very few departed the plane in Peshawar, and only a couple of passengers got on. The next leg took forty minutes to Islamabad, where everyone got off. We landed ten minutes after the scheduled departure time for my flight to Lahore. I did not see any other PIA aircraft on the ramp and figured I missed my flight.

Missed Connection

I was sitting in the last rows of the aircraft, so I was one of the first off and immediately approached an official on the ramp to explain my problem. He took my reservation paper, looked at a printout in his hand, and told me not to worry: the aircraft I had just arrived in would be the aircraft for the flight to Lahore. He then had me board the VIP bus with him. When we reached the immigration hall, he took me to the head of the line. He had my passport stamped for Pakistan and then took my baggage tag. A porter retrieved my bag and led me through an x-ray and pat-down into the arrival hall, and from there, into the check-in hall, where my bag was x-rayed again and I was patted down again. I finally made it to the check-in counter and was given a boarding pass, and my bag was tagged to Lahore.

I then had to go through security again, but finally reached the waiting hall. There I was able to take a picture of the aircraft registration markings (a habit of mine for my flight log) without someone objecting. When I boarded the plane, they did not check my carry on or pat me down like in Kabul. I was assigned a seat in the first-class area.

Argentine Ambassador to Afghanistan

My seatmate was a distinguished-looking man in a business suit. He struck up a conversation in a French accent. He was fascinated that I was a tourist visiting Pakistan. I showed him a Traveler's Century Club brochure and told him about my travels and the group I travel with. He was surprised that we visited North Korea last summer. He once worked in South Korea and has wanted to visit the North. After a lengthy discussion about world travel, I finally asked what he was doing in Pakistan, and he informed me that he was Rodolfo J. Martin-Saravia, the Argentine ambassador to Afghanistan and Pakistan, based in Islamabad. He was flying to Lahore to attend a dinner at the same hotel where I was staying, hosted by the president of a Chinese company doing business in Pakistan. He also told me he was a good friend of Pope Francis; he had coffee with him in Rome just before he was elected and will be traveling to Rome next month and will see him. At one time, he was the Argentine ambassador to the Vatican and used to meet then-Cardinal Bergoglio at the airport whenever he flew to Rome.

Missing luggage?

When I landed at Lahore, I was impressed with the airport compared to Kabul, Peshawar, and Islamabad. A representative from the Pearl-Continental Hotel was there to greet me. I had a little trouble when I thought my bag had not arrived. I reported it to an agent, but in fact it had just fallen off the carousel belt out of sight. The agent was calling Islamabad when the hotel representative found it off the belt in the back of the room.

Pearl-Continental Hotel

I had a short ride to the hotel, and the representative and driver pointed out sights along the way. The hotel is very impressive, with a large lobby and many restaurants and a large shopping mall attached, with jewelry, handicrafts, and custom men's tailor shops. It reminded me very much of a Hong Kong hotel. The room was spacious, and there was an outlet on the wall by the bed! The bathroom was like the hotel in Kabul with both a tub and a separate shower stall.

The hotel also had security, first for the vehicle to enter the parking lot and then for my bags and me entering the building. All told, I think I was patted down 15 times between the hotel in Kabul and the hotel in Lahore.

I walked around the hotel and the mall shops and then had the buffet dinner for $15. When I finished eating, I ran into the ambassador in the lobby. He immediately shook my hand and introduced me to the men with him as the man he had been telling them about. The president of the Chinese company asked me how many countries I had visited. Then the commander-in-chief of the Sri Lanka Air Force shook my hand and talked about his days attending the USAF Command and Staff Course in Montgomery, Alabama. I was a little embarrassed talking to all these distinguished men in their business suits, and I was in my touring outfit and New Balance running shoes.

The hotel had a strong free Wi-Fi signal, and I was able to talk with Judy and catch up on my email before retiring.

Tour Lahore Fort

Monday, April 29, 2013, Lahore has a couple of great sites to tour. I left the hotel at 08:30 to visit the Lahore Fort, a marvel of Moghal architecture begun in the 11th century and completed finally by the end of the 16th century. Among the Emperors who contributed to its splendor are Emperors Akbar, Jahangir, and Shah Jahan. It is a World Heritage Site and has excellent English signage.

At the fort, I picked up a local guide to give me a tour and explain the sights, such as the beautiful Palace of Mirrors, Shah Jahan's Quadrangle, and the Pearl Mosque. The elephant steps, gate, and bridge were interesting to see. The steps start so high off the ground that only a large animal like an elephant could use them. The gate is large to allow an elephant with a sedan and passenger on top to enter, and the bridge has added beams to hold an elephant's weight.

Overlooking the fort is Badshasi Mosque—the world's largest. It was constructed during the reign of Emperor Aurangzeb. Pakistan's famous poet-philosopher, Dr. Mohammad Iqbal, lies buried outside the mosque. My guide took showed me a room in the mosque where, if you stood in one corner facing the wall, you could hear a person speaking in the opposite corner facing that wall. In another location, the guide sat on the floor, and I sat opposite him in the hall, and when he hummed, the sound was amplified in stereo into both my ears as though I was sitting between a set of speakers. Incredibly, architects were able to design these rooms so many years ago.

Ride to the Border

After the visit to the fort and mosque, I rode on to the Shalimar Gardens and had a brief view. It was then time to ride straight to the border. The traffic was unbelievable. Not so much for the congestion, which I have experienced in all the cities on my trips, but rather for the variety. Mind you, we were on the major divided highway to the border and had to weave around buses large and small, trucks large and small, horse-, mule-, and donkey-drawn carts, bicycles, motorcycles, motorized rickshaws (also called tut-tuts), herds of sheep, and a pair of ducks crossing the highway without a care in the world. My service driver handled this with ease and a lot of horn blowing.

I was dropped off at the Pakistan side of the border about 10:30. My car service could not take me any further. A porter took my bags and directed me to the immigration office where the bags and I went through a security check. Then things started to become complicated. My Pakistan visa was in my ten-year passport and my India visa in my two-year passport. I handed the Pakistani official my ten year, but he wanted to see my visa to enter India, so I handed him my two-year passport, and he affixed the exit stamp in that one.

Changing of the Guards

I then had to wait for a shuttle bus to take me to a fancy gate with soldiers in fancy uniforms and headdresses. Just past the gate was bleacher seating on both sides of the road. I had been told by Ambassador Martin-Saravia that every afternoon the Pakistani and Indian guards put on quite a show at the changing of their guards. Since the area was set up for tourists, I asked the guard in the fancy uniform who was checking my passport if I could take his picture, and he posed for me. I witnessed a small changing of guards without the fancy performance. Afterwards, I was cleared to walk on across a large parking lot to a big brick building on the India side. There I had to go through a security checkpoint and then to a custom and immigration desk. There were only two of us crossing the border currently (I had been the only one on the shuttle bus), and a middle-aged man with a younger supervisor was processing us. First, I filled out a form and handed him my two-year passport with the India visa, but he also asked to see my Pakistani visa, so I handed him my ten-year passport. He seemed to be having a lot of trouble entering the data on his computer. The supervisor finally took my two-year passport to another desk, had to log in, wait for the proper screen to appear, and enter some info, before he handed me the passport and waved me through.

Mix-up at the Indian Border

By now, I realized that there was a time change, and in India it was thirty minutes later and was now noon. It had taken me one hour to be processed, just as they had told me in Lahore. Outside the building I found several cabs and a dispatcher. I told him I need to get to the airport ASAP. He assigned a cab, loaded my bags, and off we rode to a gate at the end of the parking lot. The driver asked for my passport, and I gave him the two-year passport. He walked up to an official at the gate, and the official leafed through it page by page several times. The driver returned and asked me to see the official. I carried my ten-year passport, and he went through it—page by page—and then told me he could not find the India entry stamp. I told him I had just processed through customs and immigration, so he called them and sent my driver back to the building. He returned with the middle-aged agent who had a stamp and stamped my other passport, and the gate official could then manually enter my information in a logbook. My driver then had to drive him back, and by the time I was on the road to the airport it was 12:10, so it had taken me an hour and ten minutes to cross the border.

The Road to Amritsar

The road to Amritsar is a straight divided toll road. The traffic was not as congested as it was in Pakistan, but more bicycles and carts with bicycle front ends. We arrived at the airport at 12:40, which was two hours before departure. I had to pass through a security check to enter the terminal and then another after I got my boarding pass. The second check had me dump the contents of my carry-on. They almost took my laptop security cable. I had to appeal to a supervisor to be allowed to keep it.

I then waited on the first floor of the terminal and ate lunch of nuts, fruits, and a Pepsi that I had kept from earlier flights. When they called our flight, we had to take an escalator to the second floor, and before we stepped on the escalator, we had another security check. Once I got to the second floor, I was in a line that processed my boarding pass, and I walked onboard the aircraft.

The flight departed early, and I had visited Yemen, Afghanistan, and Pakistan safely and without incident.

CHAPTER 12

LIBYA

Prologue

The purpose of this trip was to finish visiting all the UN countries in Africa. In the past I had visas issued for Libya, Algeria, Chad, Central African Republic, Equatorial Guinea, Sao Tome and Principe, and Eritrea but had not been able to visit those countries for various reasons. In the spring of 2013, I arranged with Klaus Billep, *Universal Travel Systems (UTS)* to plan a trip to visit those countries plus some additional areas in the African area. He scheduled an itinerary that visited all those countries, and we set about obtaining visas and flights.

As the planned departure date of October 13 approached, we started to have difficulty in following the planned itinerary. First, the Algerians held my passport for three weeks without affixing a visa, so with less than a week before my departure, *Passport Visas Express* in Washington, DC, had to retrieve the passport from the

220 | ED REYNOLDS

Algerian embassy and FedEx it back to California, canceling the Algeria visit.

Second, the seizure of Abu Anas Al-Libi, a wanted terrorist in Libya, changed the Libyan agreement with UTS's Tripoli travel agency, *Treasures Tours,* to issue me a tourist visa upon arrival in Tripoli. *Treasures Tours* could get me the approval for a "work visa," but it had to be issued in the worker's country. I agreed to that idea, which meant I had to FedEx my ten-year passport to Washington, to have *Passport Visas Express* obtain the visa issued by the embassy of Libya in Washington.

Those two events required significant last-minute changes in my itinerary. The first change was to schedule something in place of the visit to Algeria. I decided to visit Ceuta, Spanish Morocco, and then travel on to Madrid, where I had never spent time and which was a safe place to have my ten-year passport sent with the work visa.

I had some decisions to make: if I got the Libyan visa, I could fly to Tripoli to tour the Roman ruins and continue the original schedule, visiting Chad, Somalia, the Sinai, and the Canary and Madeira Islands before flying back to LA. If I did not get the Libyan visa, then my first desire was to visit my daughter, Robin, who was just starting a new job in Berlin. I stayed up late Thursday night to work out the flights, only to learn the next morning that Robin was going to be back in the US to attend a high-level trade meeting in Washington, DC. My next plan was to visit Northern Spain and, on Friday, UTS arranged a train trip to San Sebastian for a tour and then a flight from Bilbao, Spain, to Somaliland with a change of planes in Tripoli.

The details of the two alternative schedules required UTS to work through Friday and Saturday morning. UTS owner, Klaus Billep, had to drive out to my house Saturday afternoon with the revised airline tickets and my two-year passport.

We reviewed the itinerary, and I was informed that due to Tripoli's situation, I would have to pay the local agent in cash and would need to make cash payments in several other countries as well. I had not planned on carrying that much cash, so after Klaus left I made a mad dash to a Wells Fargo bank in a local supermarket to withdraw several thousand dollars in $100 bills dated 2006 or later and not marked up. It was not a quick withdrawal. So many bills are marked that it was difficult on a Saturday night to find bills that would be accepted in Africa.

Cash in hand, I then spent most of the night entering the revised itinerary and flights in my Outlook and Gmail calendars, so my family would have them, and I would be alerted on my smartphone with flight details.

Arrival in Madrid

Wednesday, October 30, 2013, I flew into Madrid from Morocco to await my Libyan visa. When the plane landed, I saw that Madrid's airport is one of the largest airports in the world in size of land. We taxied a long way to a parking spot, and there we were bused to a large arrival hall where we processed through passport control. Then we had to walk a fair distance and take an escalator to a train station to take a train to the baggage area. Even with the time all that took our bags and not arrived.

I stopped at an information booth to ask how best to get to the hotel I had written on a piece of paper. That was a big mistake. The information clerk recommended that I take a Metro. It was easy to get to, and the hotel was a short walk from the station.

I purchased a ticket and waited on the platform for the train to arrive. I waited and waited, and when the train finally arrived, I boarded, and again waited and waited. An hour after I had retrieved my luggage, the train departed. My stop was four stops from the airport, and when I exited the train, I found only steps, no escalators to reach the street level. It was a lot of lugging with my 50 lb. bag and my carry-on. Once I was on the street, it was not too bad and I could enjoy the walk was past the National Museum with its beautiful statues adorning the front of the building.

The place the information clerk had marked on my map for the hotel turned out to be the Hard Rock Café. I had to walk around the block for the entrance to the hotel. When I checked-in at registration, they had no reservation in my name. I checked my voucher and discovered that I was at the wrong hotel. I then remembered that I had asked Klaus to book me into a Marriot hotel, where I figured that my Silver status would provide some amenities. The reservation agent printed out a Google map of the Marriot hotel, the AC Bristol, to show to the taxi.

The taxi ride took me through the city's center past many monuments and beautiful buildings and park areas. On the city's tourist map, the AC Bristol was at the very south edge next to the Puerta de Atocha train station.

The hotel did not provide free Wi-Fi in the rooms for Silver status customers. Breakfast was not included in my fare, and the dining room didn't open until 20:30. The World Series' sixth game started at one am, and I planned to sleep for a few hours before listening to the game, so I wanted an early dinner.

I walked the neighborhood around the hotel and found that many of the restaurants didn't serve until 21:00, and the café menus were not appealing, so I settled on a Burger King as the quickest and safest place to grab a quick dinner, and it had free Wi-Fi.

As I was eating, I received a message from UTS that my Libyan visa had been approved and would be ready for pickup at 14:30 DC time. I quickly finished my burger and returned to the hotel. There was a strong free Wi-Fi signal in the lobby, and between Vonage calls and emails, Klaus and I worked out the schedule for the remainder of my trip.

The revised schedule had three nights in Tripoli, visiting the UNESCO sites at Sabratha and Leptis Magna. With a plane change in Mogadishu, a night in N'Djamena, Chad (which was the last UN country for me to visit in Africa), a day in Sharm El Sheik, and several days in the Canary and Madeira Islands, I was set!

Klaus then informed me that FedEx could not guarantee delivery of my passport in Madrid until Tuesday, November 5, so he switched to DHL for guaranteed delivery by Monday. My flight out of Madrid was scheduled for Monday at midnight to fly to Tripoli via Istanbul.

With the schedule agreed to, I returned to my room, set my alarm for 01:00, and went to sleep.

Tour Madrid

Thursday, October 31, 2013, I awoke at 01:00, purchased 24 hours of in-room Wi-Fi, and tuned in the World Series on my laptop. It was exciting to watch. The Cardinals' pitcher had been excellent in previous games, but today the Red Sox got to him, and he gave up walks and hit a batter for the first time since becoming a professional ballplayer. He left the game early, and the Red Sox won 6 to 1.

As I listened to the game, I revised my pocket schedule and flight log with the new itinerary.

The game and post-game activities finished before 05:00, and I returned to bed and slept until after 09:30. After a shower and shave, I dressed and went to the hotel business center to print out my e-tickets and my pocket schedule. It turned out to be more difficult than I expected. The business center desktops required that 1€ coins be put in a slot for ten minutes of operation. By the time I logged in to my email and opened the attachment on the emails with the revised itinerary and e-tickets and sent it to the printer, the time had expired, but the 16-page document was in the printer queue and took a long time to print.

When I had opened the pocket schedule, it came up in an Oracle Excel clone, and I initially could not find the tools to format the document to print. With the print job finally completed, I returned to my room and copied my pocket schedule to a thumb drive.

This time when I obtained coins for the computer, I asked the desk agent if the business center computers had Microsoft Office installed. She said yes, I put in a coin, plugged my thumb drive in and looked for Microsoft Excel. I could not find it, and I had to revert to the Oracle clone. It took some time to discover where to change the print orientation, and I could not figure out how to format the day/date in English. The time was expiring just as I changed the orientation to landscape and sent the job to the printer. I was upset and told the front desk agent that I wanted my money back because the computer did not have Microsoft Office installed as advertised. She called the vendor, they admitted that Microsoft Office is not installed, and she refunded my money. Then she recommended one of the internet cafés down the street who might have Microsoft Office.

I left the hotel, and as I looked for the internet café, I also checked places to eat. I stopped in a place where I had a nice salad and ham and cheese on a roll. The roll was jaw-breaking, but the salad with lettuce, tomatoes, olives, and tuna was particularly good. I gave up on going to an internet café and walked the area.

There was a new desk agent at the hotel, and I asked him about trains to San Sebastian. He had recently visited there and highly recommended that I go, printed out a schedule, and recommended that I go to the Puerta de Atocha train station a few blocks away and purchase the roundtrip ticket.

At the train station, I had to draw a numbered slip and wait for my number to appear on a board with the number of the agent that would sell me the ticket. I drew 563 on my slip and the agents were working on 518. It was a long wait. Eventually, I was able to purchase a round trip ticket, leaving at 08:48 on Friday and departing San Sebastian at 13:33 on Sunday. I noticed they had reserved seats.

I then explored the train station. It had a beautiful botanical garden in the center of the station with a turtle farm at one end. I found a place to eat a light supper and returned to the hotel. I was tired from having listened to the four-hour game in the middle of the night, so I went to bed early.

Travel by train to San Sebastian, Spain

Friday, November 1, 2013, I got up at six, and when I packed, moved some of my things into a smaller bag to be left at the hotel. When I arrived in the lobby to check out, I read my emails and discovered my DHL package was already in Madrid, so I made sure the hotel staff would sign for it and hold it for my return Sunday evening. I stored the extra bag with them and took a taxi to the train station, which was in the very north of the city center.

The station was not as impressive as the one in the south of the city. The track number for my train was not posted, so I bought a ham and cheese sandwich and an iced tea for breakfast. Then I sat in front of a display board and waited for my train's track number. It was 08:00, and my train was scheduled for 08:48. It was not until 08:30 that the track number was displayed.

In each car, half the seats face forward and half face backward and have dropdown trays. In the center where the front-facing and rear-facing seats meet, there is a table. I was assigned a right aisle facing forward with the table.

Between each seat were two power outlets. Initially, I had no one sitting at the window seat next to me. Across from me and in all the rear-facing seats was a group of slightly handicapped teenagers. The train was a local, stopping every thirty minutes or so. Between two stops, I had a seat companion, but most of the trip, the seat was open. Two hours into the trip, the teenagers left, and then our coach got a lot quieter.

I set up my laptop and caught up on my journal. I should have purchased an extra sandwich to have for lunch. There was a vending machine that ate my coins without delivering any snacks.

The train traveled northeast toward San Sebastian with stops in: Villaba, Avila, Arevalo, Medina del Campo, Valladolid Campo Grande, Venta de Banos, Palencia, Burgos Rosa de Lima, Brivsca, Miranda de Ebro, Vitoria Gasteiz, Alegria-Dulantzi, Agurain/Salvatierra de Alava, Araia, Altasu, Legazpi, Zumarraga, Beasain, Ordizia, and Tolosa before arriving in San Sebastian/Donostia at15:58.

I saw a lot of variety in the Spanish countryside—small villages, large towns and cities, open farmland, hills, woods, and wind turbines. One thing that surprised me was the vast amount of graffiti that I saw along the way. It was not just scribbling of words and sayings but elaborate scenes with multiple colors, which indicated that it took some time to complete. Some were beautiful works of art, but for the most part I thought it cheapened the beautiful scenery along the way. The weather was bright and sunny most of the way, but as we got close to the coast, it started to cloud up.

I took a taxi to my hotel, Barcelo Costa Vasca, high on a hill above the Miramar Palace. When I checked in, I asked about taking an English-speaking tour the next day. The desk clerk gave me a map, circled the tourist office, and told me they provided the information on daily tours in many languages. My room was on the top floor at the end, facing the sea. It had a small balcony, and I was able to see the surf waves breaking beyond the Palace.

After depositing my luggage in my room, I left the hotel to walk to the tourist office. The walk started with a set of stairs from the hotel parking lot down to the street and then down the hill to the Miramar Palace Park, where I climbed steps up to the Palace and toured the Palace grounds. It afforded great views of the city. Below was a highway that ran along a promenade. Below the promenade was a wide yellow sandy beach. Although there was an island guarding the bay, the waves were high enough for surfing, and there were dozens of surfers below the Palace Park end of the beach. I walked down the road from the Palace and crossed the highway to the promenade. It was crowded with people strolling in both directions, along with joggers. There was a bicycle path between the promenade and the highway, and it had a steady flow of bicyclists. Many of the bicyclists were carrying surfboards, as were people on the promenade. The surfers were in wet suits, and I was surprised at how many were young girls. The surfing diminished as I left the Palace end of the beach but picked up again as I approached the center of the city.

By then, the sun had set, and I left the promenade when the streets intersecting it started to look interesting with various shops. As I wandered the streets window shopping, I came upon the Urumea River, and I turned back to the park in front of the Town Hall.

The tourist information office was a half block from the Town Hall, and they gave me brochures for both walking tours and bus ride tours. I continued to explore the center of the city, taking pictures of the fine-looking buildings and the cathedral. Starting back to the hotel, I deviated from the promenade, and it started to rain. Eventually, the streets intersected with the highway alongside the promenade. The surfers were leaving the water and carrying their surfboards back to their rooms. The young ladies would double up carrying a surfboard under each arm.

When I approached the road leading to the Miramar Palace Park, I walked by and through a tunnel under the Palace Park and climbed steps at the west end of the tunnel. When I reached the hotel, I was thirsty and hungry, having not eaten since I left Madrid. The dining room did not open until 20:30, so I had a sandwich and a couple of beers.

The Wi-Fi signal in my room was strong, and I was able to call Judy on Vonage. There were no English language TV stations. It was kind of comical to see Two and a Half Men in Spanish. They matched the tone of the actors very well. I unpacked, washed clothes, and started to update my calendar with the revised schedule so Wendy and Judy could follow my travels.

Tour San Sebastian

Saturday, November 2, 2013, I did not set the alarm and slept until after 09:00. My room rate did not include breakfast, so I worked on my computer, continuing to update my calendar and my pocket schedule. When I finished, I went down to the front desk to see if I could print the pocket schedule. They had a free workstation and printer but only a couple of sheets of paper. They also were using the open source Oracle Microsoft Office clone. I had the same problem with my Excel spreadsheet that I had in Madrid. I could not determine where to change the printer orientation and to set the dates to English (in Madrid they displayed in Spanish, here they displayed in Turkish).

I returned to my room and converted the dates to text on my laptop, then returned to the printer. It took a while, but I finally found a screen where I could set the orientation and printed the pocket schedule. It was then after 13:00, so I decided to each lunch in the hotel. They offered a three-course set special meal. I had a delicious octopus salad and a half a small baked chicken. The dessert was four macaroons and a golf ball size scoop of ice cream.

Fortified, I headed to the city. It was too late to take the English language walking tour, so I followed the route on my own and then followed the Tourist Tram tour route on foot. I saw the city!

It was dark when I returned to my room, and my shirts were damp from the long walk. I opened the door to the patio and hung my damp shirts up in a strong breeze. After calling Steve, Marc, and Judy I decided to watch the last episode of the *Canadian Amazing Race* which I had on my laptop. All of sudden it started to rain, and I barely was able to get my shirts in before they got wet. Fortunately, the breeze had dried them.

Return to Madrid

Sunday, November 3, 2013, it rained heavily during the night, waking me up several times. In the morning, it had stopped, but the patio was wet and there were still a lot of clouds in the sky. I showered, shaved, packed, checked out, and took a taxi to the train station. At the station, I had a meal at the café and waited for the train to Madrid.

On the train, I set up my laptop and caught up on my journal. The weather improved as we rode south, and I was able to see the same magnificent scenery that I had seen on the way north. I was in the front coach in one of the seats facing forward. Only a few passengers were in my coach until Miranda de Ebro, when the four seats across the aisle from my seat filled, and someone sat in front of me. She set up her laptop and watched a video.

At Burgos-Rosa de Lima (the halfway point), I finally got a seatmate. The coach filled all seats at Palencia and then at Valladolid Campo Grande it emptied and the sun set. At Avila, my seatmate left, the coach filled, and I gained another seatmate who left at Villaba de Guadarrama. During the trip, I watched five episodes of *60 Minutes* that Wendy had taped for me earlier in the year.

We arrived in Madrid on time at 21:08, and I took a taxi to the hotel. By the time I checked in and dumped my luggage in my room, I was starved, and I left the hotel in search of food. I returned to the always open Burger King. I had spent all my remaining Euros on the taxi, so I needed a place I knew would accept a credit card.

Back in my room, I washed my underwear and two shirts. I had not realized how dirty one of the dark shirts had gotten until I saw the water. After rolling them in towels to ring out the water, I hung the four items in the closet and went to bed.

The Good and the Bad leaving Madrid

Monday, November 4, 2013, when I awoke at 08:30, I checked the washed clothes and they were still damp. In the past, they had always dried in eight hours, but my mistake was closing the closet door. The towels I had used to wring out the water were dry because I hung them over the shower door. Usually, they are damp in the morning, and the clothes dry. Lesson learned—**DON'T CLOSE THE CLOSET DOOR** with wet items inside!

I used the hairdryer to dry the underwear and rolled the shirts up tight in the dry towel, opened the window wide, and laid the shirts on the bed. I then showered and shaved and rushed down to the lobby to check email. I had a message from DHL that my passport was "Out for Delivery" at 08:54. I checked the front desk, and it hadn't been delivered, so I walked over to the Atocha railway station to eat breakfast and exchange money. When I returned, the

230 | ED REYNOLDS

DHL letter had arrived. I tore it open, and inside was my ten-year passport with a Libyan visa. I confirmed that checkout was noon, and even though my flight did not leave until midnight, I elected to save the money and checkout. I planned to go to the airport, check-in early, and hang out in the Star Alliance lounge, which would have free Wi-Fi, food, and drink.

Right at noon, I checked out and dragged my bags to the Puerta de Atocha train station and up to the top to the bus station and, for 5€, took the Yellow Airport Express bus to the airport. I sat upfront in a handicap seat where I could take some pictures. The bus was about half full, and I had my big and little luggage on the rack. I kept hitting my small backpack on the back of the seat as I looked around at the sites, so I took it off and stashed it on a ledge in front of me.

The Puerta de Atocha railway station is on the southeast edge of the city, and the airport is out of the city to the northeast. The bus went north to the city center, then turned northeast at Arc of Independence, soon stopping for another passenger. The bus filled to maximum capacity when a woman came on with a baby in a stroller. The young couple in the other handicap seat was not moving, so I gave up my seat and moved to the back of the bus.

Panic

At the airport, only about half the passengers got off at the first stop. I had a little struggle getting people to move so I could retrieve my two bags and exited the bus. I found a cart, loaded my two bags, and realized I had not retrieved my backpack. It was still on the bus. I panicked and rushed to the information booth where a woman who spoke English told me she would call the bus company. She suggested I ask the driver in the next bus to arrive if he could call my bus.

I had to wait fifteen minutes for a Yellow bus to arrive. The driver did not understand English, but one of the passengers translated on my behalf, and the driver called dispatch and told me to wait there for my bus number to return. I had the receipt with the bus number on it.

I sat on my large bag on the cart and waited an hour and a half for my numbered bus to return, and there on the driver's dashboard ledge by the door was my backpack. I showed the driver my receipt and he had me retrieve the bag. I thanked him profusely. It was a good thing I had a long wait for my flight.

Long Wait

The Turkish Air counter was not open, so I bought some lunch and looked for a place to sit. The check-in hall at the Madrid Airport does not have a single seat! I found that there were a few seats downstairs in the arrivals hall. I did not want to give up my cart, so I went looking for an elevator. When I found one and entered with others and pushed the button for the first floor, the elevator did not move. I pushed the door open button and exited. I wandered around, pushing my cart, looking for a place to sit, when the second elevator opened its doors, and two men exited wearing the elevator name on their back. I tried it and that it worked, so I wandered around the first floor and saw that they had a cafeteria with many tables.

I took one of the slope-type escalators that allows you to use a cart up to the first floor and found that Turkish Airlines was checking passengers in for their 17:00 flight. When there was no one in line at the Star Alliance Gold counter, I asked the agent if I could get on the 17:00 flight. She told me it was oversold, and they were looking for people to volunteer to take the midnight flight. Next, I asked her if I could check-in for the midnight flight. She replied, not if I was going to check a bag. She then told me they would open the counter at 21:00 for my flight. Bummer, I had five hours to kill!

I returned to the arrivals level and set up my laptop and updated my journal. For a fee, I could purchase Wi-Fi, but since California was still asleep, I decided to wait until I could call Judy and Klaus to inform them that my passport with the Libyan visa had arrived. I spent the afternoon listening to a book on tape and reading the international *New York Times* cover to cover. The *Times* had a lengthy article on the NSA and another on Secretary of State John Kerry's visit to Cairo. At 20:00, I went to the Turkish Airlines check-in counter and stood first in line reading the paper. Eventually, the agents came and set up their stations and started to check us in a little after 20:30. Security was a breeze because they had many stations and no one in line.

Passport control was something else. I used my ten-year passport with the Libyan visa to obtain my boarding pass, but I needed to leave the country with the two-year passport I used to enter the country.

The Star Alliance Lounge Wi-Fi was a little cumbersome. I had to get a 30-minute card with a scratch-off username and password. Every thirty minutes I had to log in again with a different name and password. It was a bureaucratic pain when you have two devices and two hours in the lounge.

I called Judy and Klaus to inform them that I had the passport and Libyan visa and was checked in. The food was not substantial for a lounge of the size, with nothing more than premade sandwiches of the type you would find in a US gas station food mart. It did have a variety of booze, with large bowls of peanuts, olives, and potato chips.

When it came time to board the plane, I walked to the gate and found long lines at every gate snaking around the departure hall, which made it tricky to navigate to the correct departure gate. It appeared to be not well organized. It was not obvious where to line up as a Star Alliance Gold member at my gate, so I asked an agent, and she just told me to board with the first group.

There was a delay in boarding, and they called the passengers by group number printed on their boarding pass. The first group to be called was business class and Star Alliance Gold, so I lined up with them and was the first person to board the plane in the economy section. Every seat on the plane was taken, but I was surprised that there was not the problem with bags being loaded in the overheads, as is often the case with the last to board on full flights.

Fly to Tripoli via Istanbul

Tuesday, November 5, 2013, the flight departed almost an hour late. I was assigned an aisle seat in the row just forward of the exit row, so my seat did not recline. I inflated my neck pillow and was able to get some sleep on the three-hour flight. At Istanbul, I passed through passport control quickly and then through security. I have yet to understand the rationale of having passengers who are just getting off a plane that required them to pass a security check to get on that plane, go through security after they land. Where and how could a passenger acquire some prohibited item during a flight? Oh well, most airports require the second check, so it is one of those things that make flying less fun than it was before 9-11.

I entered the vast departure hall at the Istanbul Airport. I was amazed at the crowds at 05:30. When I entered the large Turkish Airways Lounge, I found every table occupied. It was mind-blowing to see the number of people in the lounge. I know that Turkish Airlines flies to more countries in the world than any other airline, but I was surprised at the number of people so early in the day. I doubled up at a table with an open power outlet and plugged in my laptop and smartphone. Having eaten a small meal on the flight from Madrid and knowing I would be served another on the flight to Tripoli, I did not chow down on the food in the lounge with its many food stations and variety.

The lounge is at the end of the departure hall, and I left a little before my boarding time, anticipating a long walk to my gate. I was right; my gate was at the other end of the departure hall, downstairs where passengers are bused to their aircraft.

When I boarded the bus, a man insisted that I sit next to the door. Did I look that old and tired? I guess so. Anyway, when we arrived at the aircraft, I was one of the first off the bus and up the stairs. This time my seat was the row behind the exit row so I could recline if I wanted to, though I generally do not.

I fell asleep after take-off and my leg relaxed, so my knee was protruding into the aisle. When the flight attendant pushed the meal cart down the aisle , the cart hit my knee, and I awoke in a scream of short-duration pain. It was not that it hurt so much, more that it startled me awake. The attendant was so apologetic she gave me extra drinks, water, juice, and tea, which I had no room to put on my tray table.

Libya at last!

We arrived in Tripoli fifteen minutes ahead of schedule. Since I had a work visa, I was a little concerned with what kind of questions I would be asked at passport control. The agent did take a little time scrutinizing my visa but did not ask any questions and stamped the passport, and I was cleared to pick up my luggage.

As I exited the baggage hall, a young man at the railing called out Edward? His name was Adnan Eshibany from *Treasures Tours*. He led me to his new BMW compact and drove me to the Jakarta Hotel. He explained to me it was less expensive than the Corinthia, Intercontinental, Radisson Blu, Four Seasons, or the Sheraton, but assured me I would be happy with the room. He was right. The hotel was not large, but I had a two-room suite with a Jacuzzi bath and shower. The Wi-Fi in the room was free and had "good" signal strength.

After dropping my luggage in the room, we departed for a tour of the city. Adnan showed me the Bab al-Azizia barracks, Gaddafi's former residence, which had been partially destroyed, and other buildings damaged during the revolution. We then went on a walking tour of the center of the city crossing the Martyrs' Square where the revolution started, showing me where Gaddafi gave one of his speeches claiming everybody loved him, but also where many people were killed; the Marcus Aurelius Arch; the market similar to the ones in Casablanca and Istanbul; the fish market which was one of the cleanest I have seen in Africa with a set of peaked roofs like the Denver Airport. It was tiled and washed down continuously.

For lunch, we rode out on the highway east of the city past a burned-out car, the result of a gun battle between the leaders of a drug-smuggling gang and the local police, past an office building with several windows shot out during the gun battle, past the restaurant where Gaddafi gave another of his "everybody loves me" speeches, past the former Wheelus AFB which still has a military aircraft operation; and finally to a row of fish restaurants. There we walked past displays of fish: the customer selects the fish there and tells the vendor how they want it prepared and it's then served inside the Tripoli Seafood Restaurant. We selected two fish to be barbecued and some calamari, to be fried with a tangy coating. We helped ourselves to a salad bar and were given a basket of fresh-baked bread. The calamari were outstanding, the fish OK. To drink, we had a large bottle of water and fruit-flavored soda. Adnan had a red grape-flavored soda, and I had peach.

After lunch, Adnan pointed out some more landmarks on the way back to the hotel. The highway ran alongside the very wide beach, which had many makeshift small structures and a few children's parks. The government owns the beach and allows the parks, but the other structures are just shelters to change clothes or to hang out in the shade.

I was able to take a two-hour nap before Adnan picked me up for diner. On the way to the restaurant, we stopped to walk to the American Soldiers gravesite. It has high walls around it, and the door was locked, so I could not find out if they were graves from WWII or Wheelus AFB.

The Libyans dine late, so when we entered the Ghazala Restaurant at 20:30, we were the only customers. We ordered Libyan soup and shish kabob. The soup was very spicy, but Adnan showed me that in his house, they eat the soup by soaking bread in it, and that seemed to diminish the spiciness. The kabob was tasty.

Adnan told me he had spent time in Taiwan and Hong Kong with a young lady from a Taiwanese tour group that he had taken to this restaurant. He also told me that he had just returned from the American Embassy in Casablanca, where he had been turned down to get a tourist visa to the US to visit a Muslim woman from Texas he had met on Facebook.

When we returned to the hotel, Adnan introduced me to the owners and manager of the hotel. They were in the manager's office discussing real estate deals and showed me a brochure of small, attractive houses they were building. I was exhausted from having flown all night and retired to my room, where I was able to call Judy. The Vonage connection was fair. I washed my underwear and took a shower. I was not able to use the Jacuzzi tub because there was no stopper. From previous experience I carry a sink stopper in my toilet kit but it was too small for the tub. I did use it in the sink to wash my underwear. When I went to brush my teeth, the top of my water bottle fell down the drain. It stopped just at the point the drain narrowed. As I tried to figure out a way to retrieve it, I remembered that I had a small roll of duct tape in my bag. I wrapped the tape, sticky side out, on a toothbrush, and was able to retrieve it.

Enough fooling around, so I went to bed.

The Lone Tourist at Leptis Magna

Wednesday, November 6, 2013, my alarm was set for 06:00, but the call to prayer from a mosque close by awoke me before the alarm did.

I was the only one at breakfast when I arrived at 07:00. The breakfast buffet was not large, so I would not say I had a hearty breakfast, but it was enough. When I checked outside, the streets were wet and there were dark clouds in the sky, so I packed my raincoat in my backpack. At 09:00, Adnan arrived with his brother, Yousef, in Yousef's Jeep Wagon. Adnan felt that his little BMW 1 series 5-door would not be as comfortable on the rougher roads on the way to Al-Khums, where Leptis Magna is located.

It was an hour and a half drive, and we encountered a variety of weather from overcast to light rain to heavy rain to sunshine and back again. The road was flooded in some parts. We rode east past Wheelus along the beach and then turned southeast away from the coast inland past Castelverde until we intersected the coast again in Al-Khums. Along the way, we passed an overturned milk tanker truck with milk flowing down the street mixed with the muddy rainwater. It was an interesting sight.

One thing that I found fascinating is that people had spray-painted over the pre-revolution license plates, covering the old country name in Arabic of the "Great Socialist People's Libyan Arab Jamahiriya" that Gaddafi had used. Some of them pasted decals of the current official name of "State of Libya," or plain Libya, in Arabic over the old name.

Adnan had told me to carry my passport, and we passed through several checkpoints but were never interrogated. At the Leptis Magna parking lot, we rendezvoused with Abraham, the site caretaker and guide. He was a retired history professor and had been taking care of the Leptis Magna site for 22 years. Just as we were about to start, the rain started again. Abraham put on clear plastic rain gear. I was happy to have a hurricane jacket. The rain stopped, the sun came out, and we started the tour.

The first site was the Septimius Severus Arch, but the route Abraham wanted to take down a set of stairs was flooded, so we skirted the Arch, staying on high ground past the work area where copies of the figures were being made. We then descended to walk through the sports arena; the swimming pool; the warm room with its once heated basement; the Apodyteria; and the latrines. The male seats were larger than the female seats. It was too bad that the elaborate water flow and sewage system that had existed to flow black water to the sea no longer operated. It could have reduced the flooding we encountered throughout the tour, causing us to deviate from Abraham's route and, in many spots, wade through water up to our ankles.

We walked up the colonnaded street through the Byzantine

Gate to a temple. There on the floor by a stone bench was a carved game board. The University of Pennsylvania performed some of the archeological reconstruction in the 1960s, and the remnants of railroad tracks to cart the excess dirt away still existed.

The tracks ended at the seacoast, where we encountered strong winds that made it difficult to walk on the uneven ground. The surf was high from the stormy sea. When we ventured back inland, we visited the Temple of Serapis, the Hunting Baths, and the Market. At the market, Abraham showed me a copy of the Units Lengths of Measure based on the length of a person's arm.

From the market, we walked to the Arch of Tiberius, the Arch of Trajan, through the Chalcidicum Market Place, and past the Schola to the Theater.

To me, Leptis Magna had many of the same characteristics as Ephesus in Turkey without the crowd of tourists. Having the whole site and a guide just for me was uniquely mind-blowing, even with the flooded areas and occasional rain. The walk along the seashore was unforgettable because of the high surf and strong winds, which made the balancing act of navigating the flooded areas a challenge. I was especially impressed by the market and then the theater. We could not stand where one tests the acoustics of the theater because of high water. Abraham encouraged me to climb to the top of the theater, and as I started up, he bid me farewell and said he hoped to see me again. I thought it was a strange thing to say, and he disappeared, stage left, as I climbed to the top and took pictures of the theater and the rest of the site and raging sea. When I finished and descended back to the stage, Abraham was nowhere around, so I walked out of the site on my own. He was not at the office, and when I told Adnan what had happened, he called Abraham on his cell phone and made a plan to meet. When Abraham saw me, he asked me where I went. He claimed he was calling my name and was concerned that I might have fallen. He continued by saying that in 20 years, he had never lost a person he was guiding. I apologized for making him uncomfortable.

We all piled into the Jeep Wagon and drove to the amphitheater, a short distance away. It was another amazing site, about 80% restored. Again, Abraham encouraged me to walk around the stands and, as before, bid me farewell and said he hoped to see me again. I do not think he understood the meaning of his statement. This time I kept him in sight. He and Adnan smoked a cigarette, and it dawned on me that since he had gone hours leading me around the site without smoking, he most likely had sneaked off to get a smoke when he disappeared back at the theater. Our tour of Leptis Magna complete, we dropped Abraham off at the site office and went in search of a place to eat lunch. Adnan said that the places he used to eat in before the revolution had closed due to a lack of tourists .

We stopped at a Libyan restaurant with a life-size statue of a camel and its baby in front. I had the typical Libyan lunch of a small salad, bowl of spicy soup, a lamb bone with some meat on it, and boiled potatoes and cabbage on a bed of couscous.

A Tour of Confiscated Seashore Land

On the way home, we visited Yousef's summer home, recently built on the seashore near the Tripoli suburb of Tajoura. The land had been the encampment of one of Gaddafi's son's armies. The army had confiscated the land from its rightful owner, and after the revolution, the government signed the land back to the original owner, who sold it to Yousef. The road to his house was not paved and often needed a four-wheel drive to make it through the sand. The house was yellow with a cinder block wall bordering the lot in a wide-open area with no close neighbors. Yousef is an active surfer, ski boater, and motorcyclist. His driving was nail-biting as he drove the speed limit of 60mph right up to the rear of slower cars and often squeezed between cars.

He delivered me safely back to the hotel by 16:30, where I had four hours before Adnan picked me up for dinner.

Adnan chose a nicely decorated restaurant that he had n᷄ in since the revolution and was surprised to find that i᷄ into an Indian restaurant. We had spinach soup and a half chicken tandoori.

Back at my room, I wrote in my journal and retired about midnight.

The Lone Tourist at Sabratha

Thursday, November 7, 2013, the weather was bright and sunny when we headed west of the city in Adnan's BMW to Sabratha and the World Heritage archaeology site of Sabratha. On the way, Adnan drove me through Gaddafi's compound, which was severely destroyed. Along the way, I saw other buildings that had been destroyed during the revolution. One was hit by a NATO bomb. At Sabratha, we met up with Fathi, a local guide. He was a young man with a beard who had been a guide for ten years.

We started out walking past the Roman and Punic museums, both closed since the revolution, through the Ancient Residential Quarter to the Southern Temple and the Statue of Flavius Tullus. There we had close views of the Mausoleum of Bes, in my opinion, the most stunning structure in the area west of the theater. Sabratha is known for its elaborate mosaic tile floors, many of which are intact. Sections of the tile floors have been removed intact and are on display in museums throughout the world. Common people's homes had black and white mosaic floors, while the upper class had colors in their designs.

One of the interesting designs was the picture of left and right "flip flops" on the floor of the entryway to baths. Another typical design was the reverse swastika, like the American Indian design.

From the Mausoleum of Bes, we walked by another mausoleum under discovery. We walked past and through the Southern Temple; the Baptistery; the Basilica of Apuleius of Madora; Antonine ᵔle; and the Temple of Liber Pater to the Forum. Across the pres ᶠ the Forum, we visited the Capitolium; the Temple of ᵔ House; the Basilica of Justinian; the olive oil ᵈ for a rest and picture taking at the latrine.

We then walked past the Flavius Toulouse Fountain, a pair of Christian Basilicas, the Baths of Oceanus, then on to the Lighthouse, and finally the Temple of Isis at the extreme east end of the complex. Then we walked up to the major attraction of Sabratha, the three-story-high theater. It was reconstructed by the Italians in the 1930s and had hosted a visit by Mussolini in 1936. Fathi told me that his grandfather attended the show to hear Mussolini address the people of Sabratha.

The theater is an impressive structure with a large stage, a huge area for the performers' dressing rooms, seating for VIPs, and about 17,000 spectator seats. It is currently used for historical productions. The wall below the stage had many beautiful relief figures of gods and performers.

After I climbed to the top of the seats and took pictures of the area, I rejoined Adnan and Fathi. The tour was over. We walked back to Adnan's car and drove to the city to eat lunch. We stopped in front of a chocolate store where Adnan bought some chocolates, and then ate in a Turkish restaurant next door. Out of curiosity, I ordered a Turkish pizza, and a small mixed salad. The mixed salad was a mix of humus, tabouli, olives, and some other things I couldn't identify. The bread was good and went well with the salad. The pizza was no different than the US. It had ripe olives, sliced tomatoes, sliced green pepper, and lots of cheese. It was a small plate size and was enough for one person.

A Discussion of Gaddafi's Reign

During lunch, we discussed politics, Gaddafi's reign, the good he initially did, and the bad that followed. He was in office too long, in their opinion. Fathi was one of the guides waiting for the cruise ship that Gaddafi banned, refusing to let the Americans on board depart for shore tours. Both Adnan and Fathi had recent experiences of having the US deny them US visas to attend schools in the US. Fathi had been accepted by American University to enroll in the MBA program. He had all the paperwork for the departure and yet was not granted a visa, with no explanation. Adnan had been sponsored by a travel agency in California to attend a tour manager's course in Los Angeles and was, in his opinion, rudely rejected with no explanation at the US Embassy in Casablanca the week before my arrival. They told me that before the killing of the US ambassador, it used to take just two days to get a US visa if you had the proper paperwork. Now they told me they must apply in person in Casablanca and they told of other rejections that made little sense. I guess my problems obtaining a visa pale in comparison.

After lunch, we dropped Fathi back at the site and returned to Tripoli. Along the way, I saw a lot of anti-Gaddafi graffiti on the walls of buildings and walls.

The Last Night in Tripoli

Back in my room, I wrote in my journal until Adnan called at 20:00. He was picking me up early because he had to stop at his family's apartment to pay his respects because his sister was getting engaged that night. It was a traditional Muslim marriage, arranged by the mothers. It would be just the third meeting between Adnan's sister and her soon to be fiancé. The stop took longer than expected. Only Adnan knew the fiancé. He got drawn into escorting him to the meeting and staying with him as he was questioned by a room full of women. Adnan came down at one point and apologized and invited me to have dinner with his family.

Adnan's brother, Anis, who had recently returned from six years in Vancouver, sat with me and some male neighbors on a patio. Anis was not a supporter of Gaddafi and could not return to Libya while he was in power. We had a long talk about the safety and dangers in Libya and he said that it is a safe country around Tripoli. He said everyone he knew did not hold any animosity against the Americans over the snatching of the terrorist out of his car and whisking him away to the US to stand trial. Anis said the attitude among his friends was that the guy had it coming because he killed a lot of innocent people in the bombings of the American Embassy in Tanzania.

We also talked about the Libyan people's frustration that the new government is not moving fast enough to establish control of the country. There are many factions (clans, tribes, unions, and militia) that are upset that they are not adequately represented in the new government, and they are causing a lot of continued unrest.

As we talked, I heard gunshots, but Anis said they were probably fired in the air at a party. He said one of Libya's problems is that too many people have guns they obtained during the revolution. As the time got later, I felt uncomfortable about dominating Anis' conversation at the important family gathering. When Adnan and the fiancé reappeared, I asked Adnan to take me back to the hotel so I could pack for the next day's flight. This gave Anis a chance to get to know the fiancé better.

He agreed and dropped me off at the hotel. I called Judy and wrote in my journal and continued to hear fireworks in the distance. An hour later, Adnan called from the lobby and asked to meet me in my room. When he arrived, he told me that two gun battles were raging in the city between the rogue militia and the police. A leader of the rogue militia had died that afternoon, and the rogue militias were out for revenge. Both locations were several miles from the hotel, but he invited me to stay at his apartment with his brothers. I thanked him and showed him that a stray bullet could not hit me in my bed since it was lower than the window and, since I was four stories above the street, any bullets would penetrate the window at an upward angle, hitting the ceiling. He checked the windows and agreed they were not in the line of possible street fighting and left.

I wrote in my journal and went to bed at midnight. I learned later that the gunfire continued until 02:00 and that two of the rogue militia were killed and 21 wounded. Reportedly no government forces were wounded.

Friday, November 8, 2013, though the gunfire continued

during the night, I still fell asleep and woke to the "Call to Prayer" at 06:00. The streets were deserted and, after the prayer calls, noticeably quiet since it was the end of their week. I was the only one at breakfast, and then I returned to my room and packed.

Adnan picked me up and drove me to the airport. He and his family stayed up until 02:30. His sister's fiancé and his family were afraid to leave until the fighting stopped since they lived in the area of the battle. He told me the people are sick and tired of the militia thinking that, because they defeated Gaddafi, they should continue to fight and not join the new government. It is a shame.

At the airport, Adnan accompanied me to the right check-in counter and then bid farewell. I wish he had stayed a little longer because the agent did not understand English, and my ticket was complicated. I was flying from Tripoli to Cairo with a seven-hour layover, and then to Addis Ababa on Egypt Air. At Addis Ababa, I had a 13-hour layover (where I had a hotel reservation) and then a flight to Djibouti on Ethiopian Airlines. At Djibouti, I would fly to Mogadishu and back on Turkish Airlines, change airlines and fly to. Addis Ababa to spend the night, before flying to Chad on Ethiopian Airlines. My e-tickets did not show the places where I would check into a hotel and need my bag, so the agent first tagged my bag to Mogadishu. That was the last place I wanted my bag to end up. I tried to tell him I wanted just to check my bag to Addis Ababa. He was confused because I was laying over in Addis Ababa twice. In desperation, he switched counters with an agent that understood English and, with a little help with one of the men in line behind me, we finally got it straight.

During the switch in agents, I did not have my Star Alliance number recorded and they did not give me the pass to the lounge. The passport control was quick, but the agent was surprised at the US passport. He told me he had not seen many of them recently.

The lounge would not let me in just on my Gold Star Alliance Card. I needed an invitation from check-in. It was not a long wait anyway, and the boarding announcement was made. It surprised me because the plane had just arrived, and the passengers were still exiting when I got to the gate. It was a rapid turnaround, and they soon started to load the plane. It surprised me, and I was the last to leave the gate area. The plane was not full. The only middle seats occupied were with families or groups of men traveling together. They served a beef dinner and handed out newspapers. I read the Cairo newspaper, and it was disturbing. The headline read: "Putin due here soon to restore military ties." The article described that the Egyptian government was unhappy with the US cutting military aid. Despite John Kerry's visit earlier in the week, they were turning to Russia to reestablish ties that existed in the 1970s. Other articles discussed the confusion and apprehension of the countries in the region over Obama's changes in attitude about Syria and Iran. There were articles about Mubarak remaining under house arrest; the status of the Muslim Brotherhood; Libya; US-Saudi relations; US-Iran relations; and the Syrian situation. None of the articles described the US in a favorable light.

At the Cairo airport, they have several Star Alliance Lounges. The first one I visited was closed, the second one was for smokers, and the third was open. I set up my laptop, charged my smartphone, processed emails, and watched videos of TV shows I had missed since leaving on the trip. Wendy copies them and uploads them to our shared Dropbox folder.

When the time came to go to the gate, I found it was at the far end of the G wing of the terminal. I had to pass through security at the gate. The plane was full, and I was assigned a seat amid a group of ladies. Despite the late hour, several of the ladies talked throughout the flight, making it difficult to get a sound sleep. They served a meal, and I think I did sleep a little, but at times I wanted to tell the ladies just to shut up.

Layover in Addis Ababa

Saturday, November 9, 2013, when we landed at Addis Ababa and were exiting the plane, the talkative ladies from my flight continued to talk and walk very slowly up the exit ramp, holding up the passengers behind them. In the immigration hall, there was a line for "Visa on Arrival," which I first got in. I then flipped through my passport and found that I already had an Ethiopian visa, so I exited the line and got in the immigration line. I was again among the young ladies who were still gabbing away and not moving forward. I then noticed that there was an exclusive line for Star Alliance Gold, so I got in it and was quickly at the immigration counter. I was rejected because the visa I had from two weeks ago was for a single entry, so I had to go back to the end of the "Visa on Arrival" line. They would not sell me a multiple entry visa, so I will have to pay the $20 again in two days when I return.

Back at the immigration agent's desk, I was quickly processed. I picked up my luggage, only to have to stand in a line for customs check. Again, I was caught up among the gabbing ladies. When my bag flowed through the x-ray machine, the operator had me open it and show her my CPAP machine. In the meantime, another customs inspector was going through the ladies' bags and throwing out boxes of perfume and other cosmetics which I was surprised were not allowed to be brought into the country.

Finally, I exited into the arrivals hall and went to the Harmony Hotel desk to see when the next shuttle was due. No one was at the desk, so I decided to take a taxi. The taxi situation is not very well controlled. I found a taxi, and the coordinator told me it would cost $20 to take me to the hotel. I told him that it had cost me just $15 two weeks ago, but he said the late hour cost $5 extra. I got in the cab, and the driver wanted 20€, but when I got to the hotel and the bellman had my bags, I gave him a $20 bill, and he left.

The hotel could not find my reservation, but the clerk remembered me from the 28th and looked up that record and gave me a room key. It was 4 in the morning. I set my alarm for noon and went to bed. At 08:00 someone called my room twice, so I took the receiver off the hook. There was a new hotel being constructed next door, and I awoke several times to hammering and other construction noises. I did not get a restful sleep.

Fly to Djibouti

At 10:00, I awoke for a bio break and called Judy. She had been out when I called before bed. I slept another hour, and at 11:45, called the Manager to get a two-hour extension on the noon checkout. I took a shower and updated my journal.

My flight to Djibouti was not until 16:00, so I checked out and took the hotel bus to the airport at 14:00. Even though Djibouti is another country, Ethiopian Airlines considers it a domestic flight, so I checked in at the old domestic terminal. I already had a boarding pass from the day before, but it did not have my United Star Alliance Gold number in the record. I put my bag on the check-in belt, handed the agent my passport, e-ticket, Star Alliance Gold card, and my boarding pass. I asked her to enter the numbers in my record and, in doing that, she forgot to affix the baggage tag on my bag, which started moving towards the luggage room without a tag. I called out, and she jumped from her counter and went running down the belt and got to the bag just before it turned the corner into the luggage room. She completed adding my numbers to my record and affixed the luggage tag receipt to the back of my ticket. She also gave me an invitation to the Star Alliance Lounge. It was a familiar lounge because it was where I watched Romney give his concession speech on TV the prior November.

When the time came to go to the gate, it also stirred memories from last year. On one of the flights last year out of Addis Ababa, the door to the stairs that the passengers have to take to get to their aircraft was locked, and the gate agent couldn't find the right key on a ring that had a dozen or more keys on it. This time the door was not locked, it was just closed.

We walked to the aircraft, and it left on time. My seatmate was a young US Navy seaman on his way to join his first sea deployment. He was from Grand Prairie, Texas, a suburb of Dallas, where I had worked at Chance Vought Aircraft before I joined the Air Force.

We had a good conversation during the short flight.

Arrival processing at Djibouti was a mess. They had lines for VIP's, Nationals, Foreigners with Visa, and one for Foreigners without Visa. Many of the men on the plane did not understand either English or Arabic and got in the wrong line or had the wrong paperwork. It took me over thirty minutes to get processed. My bag was just coming on the belt, and I loaded it on a trolley and headed for the taxis. One of the locals on my plane told me the rate was $12 to my hotel. I quoted that rate to the taxi that loaded my bag, and he wanted more. As we were leaving the airport, I told him to turn back if he was not willing to take $12. He shut up and delivered me to my hotel. The hotel was in the center of the city, facing one of the two town squares in Djibouti. I would rate it one star. The furniture in the room was cheap and dated. It had a Wi-Fi signal, but even standing in the hall below the modem, I could not make a Vonage call. I went down to the restaurant for dinner. The menu was limited, and the salad I wanted was not available, so I played it safe and ordered spaghetti with meat sauce. It was a big pile on a medium-size plate. It tasted OK.

I retired without writing in my journal and set the alarm for 04:00.

CHAPTER 13

MOGADISHU, SOMALIA

Sunday, **November 10,** 2013, the town square in Djibouti was noisy and I was wakened many times. At 03:00 I gave up and got up and checked my email. The shower had no enclosure. A curtain stopped the spray from wetting down the whole bathroom, but the floor was wet. I packed and checked out, leaving my bags at the hotel. They called a cab, and the bellman told the cab driver not to charge more than $12. The cabs are a mix of cars with taxi signs and rundown wrecks from Japan with right-hand drive. From the airport I had the wreck, but to the airport a taxi with a sign on top.

Entering the terminal, I had to pass through security. They did not like the fact that I keep setting off the alarm. I showed them the scar for my artificial knee and told them even if I removed all my clothes, I would still set off the alarm. Finally, they went into a closet and returned with a wand and confirmed that the only thing on my person that set it off was my artificial knee.

The check-in agent was not going to issue me a boarding pass without a Somalia visa until I told her I was going to be leaving and returning on the same plane. She was confused and took me to the Turkish Airlines station manager to explain what I was doing. He OK'd my plan, giving me a boarding pass, and I processed through immigration and upstairs to pass through another security check. Again, I was given a hard time about my knee. The security agent wanted to see a letter documenting the implant. I told him I did not carry one, and he was the first ever to ask it in ten years. His response was times have changed, and I needed a letter. As he was lecturing me, I put my shoes and belt back on and stood in line to board the plane, ignoring his lecture. The line started moving, and I just continued and boarded the aircraft.

The aircraft was an A-321-200 and was full of passengers who had originated in Istanbul. I was disappointed that all the window seats were occupied. The plane had seatback video, and I watched a movie on the flight, but we landed in Mogadishu before I could see the end.

I was able to see out a window as we landed, and it was a beautiful view. The airport is on the coast and parallels a beach. The ramp had several planes and helicopters with UN markings. We walked across the ramp to the arrivals hall on a route guarded by armed private security men with jackets marked Turkish Airlines Security on their backs.

Mohammad Ali

At the door to the hall, they handed us a form to fill out, and inside the hall was chaos. One pair of immigration agents was processing passengers without visas, one pair handling Somalia nationals, and the third pair for passengers with a visa. I asked several officials which window I should go to for Transit, and a young man named Mohammad Ali took me to the agent for passengers without visas. The agent asked me how long I was going to be in the country. I told him a couple of hours, and he handed back my passport and form without stamping the passport. He was not going to allow me to enter the country without an overnight stay. A lesson learned. I should have had a hotel reservation to show the agent. He would have granted the visa and I could have visited the city, cancelled the reservation and still taken the afternoon flight. Instead he instructed Mohammad to lead me to the departure hall and tell them I needed a boarding pass.

Mohammad led me out the door of the arrivals building past the security check points. Everyone appeared to know Mohammad and did not question me since I was with him. I told him I wanted to see as much of the area as I could, so he led me out of the airport to walk around the area outside the parking lot before heading back to the departure building. Ali was reluctant to cross Wadada Garoonka Diyaaradaha, the highway to the city center.

I did not see much of the locals. The area had commercial buildings, a bank, rental car lot and, under the trees, several beverage stands serving taxi and truck drivers waiting to enter the airport parking lot. The people I observed were primarily the male drivers of the cars and trucks and the women that sold the beverages under the trees. The stands had a variety of coverings (blue tarpaulins and sheets) to shield the sellers from the sun or rain. I could see a hotel along the perimeter road, but it was too far to walk safely with no entry visa.

We did not stay outside the airport area for long and returned to the departure building, entering via a side door to bypass the regular departure entrance security. We walked down halls where everyone appeared to know Ali, and finally to the check-in area. It was a larger mob scene than passport control with two flights checking in and no signs for lines. Everyone was crowding the counters. Mohammad found the Turkish Airlines check-in agent and pushed to the head of the line (oops! head of the mob, because there was no line) using my Star Alliance Gold card and the fact I did not have a bag. He "duked it out" with another handler that was performing the same function for a diplomat. Mohammad won because I had no luggage to check, and he obtained my boarding pass.

Boarding Pass

After he handed me the boarding pass, Mohammad led me to a counter where it was to be stamped by immigration. The immigration agent would not stamp the boarding pass and told Mohammad I needed an entry visa and told him to take me back to arrivals to get the visa. Mohammad knew that they were not going to grant me an entry visa, but he led me past the security and gate agents and exited the departure hall. Once we were outside, he stopped and said, "Let's wait here." We sat under a tree and talked. He told me he worked at the airport every day as a "greeter" and assisted passengers to process in and out like he was doing for me.

When the time came for the passengers to walk to the aircraft, he pushed me into the line, I bid him farewell and handed him $10 discreetly in my handshake. Near the plane, they were collecting the boarding passes and checking passports. They asked me why I did not have an entry or exit stamp. I told them I was transit and had arrived on the same aircraft, and they said OK and let me board.

I would have liked to have had my passport stamped and taken a taxi into the city, but with the mob scene I experienced, I let it ride. Mohammad had at least provided me the opportunity to walk around the village outside the airport and see a little of the life in Somalia.

I was able to sit in a window seat and had great views of the city and surrounding area on the departure climb. Mogadishu did not appear to be as bad as was depicted in "Blackhawk Down" or in the special I saw about the recovery of the Blackhawk helicopter parts. The central city had paved streets and nice-looking buildings. I guess the firefight was in a suburb.

Another country on the "Do Not Travel" list had been visited. Not as extensively as I had planned, but at least I had left the airport grounds and had a safe visit with an exciting story to tell about my experience with "Mohammad Ali" from Mogadishu, Somalia, and the immigration officers.

CHAPTER 14

SHARM EL SHEIKH, SINAI

Wednesday, **November 13, 2013**, the last area to visit on the "Do Not Travel" list was the Sinai. In November of 1996, while working for the Canadian company SHL Systemhouse on a project in Israel, I had visited the Gaza Strip from the north. I wanted to visit from the south, but due to hostilities in the Northern Coastal area of the Sinai. the best that *Universal Travel Systems* could arrange was a visit to Sharm El Sheikh, Sinai, Egypt.

I flew into Cairo from Chad, the last country for me to visit in Africa. It was my second visit to Egypt on the trip and, because I had neglected to request a multi-entry visa on my first flight, I had to purchase another visa for $15. After exiting the baggage area, I was reminded of why I hate the Cairo airport: you are immediately hounded by men. Salesmen are trying to sell you a tour, taxi agents are trying to get you a taxi, and rental car agents are trying to get you to rent their cars. I planned to take the Novotel bus to the hotel, store my luggage, and return to the airport on the Novotel bus. I had to laugh at the rental car agent that tried to convince me that

I should rent a car to drive to the Novotel, since you can literally see the sign from the terminal; it's that close. In most airports the information booth is staffed by women who are eager to assist you. At the Cairo airport, the booth is staffed by men who appear to be continually conducting personal business. They appeared annoyed when I asked them to call the hotel since I was not sure if they were operating on their thirty-minute schedule at 02:00. The bus arrived and took me to the hotel where I told the receptionist that I was going to check-in that evening and asked to store my luggage until then. The bellman took the bags, and I got on the bus back to the airport.

This time I processed through the domestic end of the terminal and was on a level above the international level. The Star Alliance Lounge was not open on the domestic level. Right next to my gate area was a children's play area with the only power outlet I could find. I sat in a little kid chair and read a newspaper until my smartphone was fully charged and then proceeded to the gate, which was downstairs on the same level as the international gates but separated by a glass wall.

Multinational Force Organization

We were bused to our aircraft, an Embraer-170. My seat companion was Mike Phillips, an American from Miami, working as a technical manager for the Multinational Force Organization (MFO) tasked to keep the peace in the Sinai. He had served in the US Army in Iraq and then had become a contractor in Kuwait. His job was to program the e-proms on the equipment used by the MFO for the Sinai environment. For example, the fuel used in vehicles in the region does not contain the same mixture of additives as in the states, and Mike's job would be to tune it for the local mixture.

We discussed the political situation in the region. Mike believed that the Egyptian Muslim Brotherhood was a terrorist organization and that the Palestinians were their own worst enemy by their refusal to recognize the state of Israel. He told me of the challenges the MFO had covering such a large area, and how Hamas and other pro-Palestine terrorist groups had become isolated in the Sinai when the Egyptians shut down the tunnels they had used to move in and out of the Gaza strip.

Mike also told me what to expect in Sharm El Sheikh. He said the only place open to buy breakfast was a McDonald's in a shopping strip not far from the airport. He also told me that the taxi drivers would try to overcharge for a ride to the city and, in the city, beware of the aggressive shop keepers becoming nasty when you turn them down.

Taxi to Town

When we arrived in Sharm El Sheikh, we bid farewell, and I crossed the street to the taxi stand. There was a sign posted with the rates to various destinations. When the first taxi quoted four times the posted rate, I moved to the next taxi. I continued to bargain with different cabbies, and despite the posted rate, all the cabbies were united in wanting more. Their rationale was they had waited all night and slept in their cars waiting for a plane to arrive. Not my problem. Finally, the second taxi agreed to take me to McDonald's for $1 over the posted rate, and I agreed. When were arrived, he asked for a tip. Since he was not a metered cab and I had no luggage for him to handle, I told him a tip was not included in the rate we agreed to.

The area along the road to the city looked like a mixture of Las Vegas and Palm Springs with an ocean beach. Every major brand of hotel had a resort there, several with golf courses, and many of the Las Vegas casino names had casinos there. The McDonald's was open 24 hours but was just switching over to breakfast, and I had to wait a bit.

When I finished breakfast, I started to walk to the center of the city. Down the four-lane divided boulevard, I saw a camel just slowly walking across the boulevard back and forth, stopping in the grassy median to munch on the short palm trees that lined the center of the median.

I stopped at the Novotel and told them I was from the Cairo airport Novotel and was just in town for the day and asked what tours they would recommend. They gave me a map and referred me to their tour office on the beach. I walked through their beautiful property to the beach and found that the tour office was not open, and from the signs it appeared that they were offering just various boat and water sport tours.

The Marriott Resort was next door, and their tour desk was also closed. I crossed the boulevard and purchased some drinks at the A2Z store. The next hotel resort was the Hilton, and it had an amusement park situated in the back of it. I noticed a sign across the boulevard that said "Sun'NFun," so I figured they had tours. They had the signs for them all discounted, but again they were not open for business. It was only 08:00, and it appeared that the establishments did not open until 09:00 or later. I walked back to the boulevard and was heading again toward the city center when I came upon a sign that said Public Beach.

I walked back to the beach on the "Public Beach" road and found a paved lane along the beach with no walls between resort properties. The lane was lined with open-air restaurant/bars and tourist vendor stalls and shops. I stopped to use a WC at a "Dive Shop," which was very actively outfitting their first group of the day. A few restaurants away on the lane, I saw a "Free Wi-Fi" sign. A man was setting up the cushions in the open-air bar and I asked him if I could use the Wi-Fi. and He said OK and typed in the password on my phone.

I checked my email and caught up on the news of the world. I then updated my Google map of the city, thanked the man, and walked on toward the center of the city.

Food Chains in Sharm El Sheikh

I came upon an open area with a large parking lot lined with various vendors and restaurants. There was a big Hard Rock Café, next to a TGI Fridays, next to a Pizza Hut, and then a KFC. I crossed the road after checking out a 1950s era pink Ford sedan in front of the Hard Rock Café, and came upon a Chili's, which had both indoor and outdoor seating. I stopped to check out a stand with a row of power outlets when a man on a balcony over the restaurant called out a hello. I asked if I could plug in my smartphone. He replied, "Wait," and came down and unplugged a drink box and told me to use that outlet. He then sat with me and had a long talk. He was from Cairo and could not find work there, so he commutes to Sharm El Sheikh to work in the Chili's. He had just one wife and three children. He wanted to know why Americans were not visiting Egypt anymore. I told him that the travel agencies were not scheduling trips because they are afraid of the demonstrations. We talked for about thirty minutes, and then I unplugged my charger, thanked him, and walked on.

Concerns over lack of Americans

When I reached the main boulevard, there was a large taxi parking area and a tourist police station. I was hounded by taxi drivers, and after waving them off was asked by a bystander where I was from, and then he too asked why Americans are not visiting Sharm El Sheikh as they did before. I repeated that the tour agencies do not think the country is safe. He argued that they get tourists from Russia and European countries, but he likes Americans and wishes they would return. We briefly discussed the negative impression the US has of the Muslim Brotherhood and how we do not think that Morsi should have tried to impose strict Muslim beliefs into the country's Constitution. He agreed and hoped the political situation would get better so American tourists would return. We then parted, and I continued my walk.

I returned to the hotel area and checked with the Marriott tour desk and discovered the one tour that I wanted to take, to Ras Mohamed National Park, had already left. Bad timing—first they were not open, then the tours for the day had left. He told me most people reserve the day before.

Discussions on Religion and New Governments

I continued to the Novotel, where I ate their buffet lunch. It was nice to have a salad bar with ripe tomatoes, iceberg lettuce, and other goodies of my own choice. Before lunch, they let me start charging my smartphone in their business center. After lunch, I retrieved the phone and continued my walk around the area. At one point, I returned to the "Sun'NFun," where I engaged in an hour-long conversation with Ahmed, one of the tour salesmen. He also wanted to know why the Americans were not returning. I repeated what I had told the others. We discussed the Muslim religion and other religions that try to impose their beliefs on others while some of the most populist religions in the world, such as Buddhists, do not. We discussed the treatment of females in the Muslim religion and of homosexuals and how many of the American Christian Right have similar beliefs but do not go around blowing up people who do not agree with them. Extreme beliefs in any religion and any country should be between the individual and his religious leaders and not imposed on others.

We discussed the political situation in Egypt, and I pointed out that it took the United States 13 years after starting the Revolution before it elected its first president, and several more years to add the Bill of Rights to the Constitution. The countries that ousted their dictatorial leaders during the "Arab Spring" should not be in such a big hurry to get it right that they start fighting each other again. It takes time and compromise, something the United States can also be impatient about.

Sharm El Sheikh is an interesting resort with lots to do, great beaches, and diving, but I will remember it best for meeting and having lengthy discussions with its people. It was a memorable visit.

Return to Cairo

I returned to the Novotel and recharged my smartphone, reading newspapers as I waited. The sun had set, and I had a 20:45 flight, so at 18:00, I took the Novotel airport car to the airport for $12. When I was dropped off at the front of the terminal, a bus had just discharged a large group. I thought, "What bad timing!" I had to queue up behind them and then I noticed they were going to the international departure door and I needed to go to the domestic departure door where there was no line. I quickly obtained my boarding pass and processed through security. They had no Star Alliance Lounge, but I was given a chit for a free drink at the café downstairs in the waiting area.

Change in Flights

I obtained my drink and was looking to see if a small plane was on the ramp when I noticed that there was another flight to Cairo posted on the board at an earlier time than mine. Looking around for someone from Egypt Air, I saw two men in business suits with Egypt Air/Star Alliance pins on their lapels. I asked them if I could change my flight, and one said sure and had me take an elevator upstairs, where he vouched for me through security to the check-in counter, let me to the head of the line, and talked to the agent. I had not shown him my boarding pass and my Star Alliance card. He issued a new boarding pass with my Star Alliance number printed on it which the other one did not have. I then breezed through security again and returned to the gate. When the time to board was announced, I happened to be standing right at the gate, trying to see the tail numbers of the plane, so I was the first one processed. I was about to board the bus when the ticket agent ran down to me and told me my ticket was for a different flight. I was escorted back to the gate counter, where I explained to another agent that "Yes, I was booked on the 20:45 flight but then rebooked on the 19:15 flight." The agent called someone on the phone and told me to wait. It took what seemed a long time for the agent to appear and tell me the plane's business class was full. I told him I was in economy class. This led to a big discussion between agents at the gate counter, and finally, they hand wrote a boarding pass and allowed me on the bus.

The plane took off twenty minutes late because of me but landed only five minutes late. Since it was a domestic flight, I did not have to go through any processing to get out to the main lobby and up the stairs to wait for the Novotel shuttle bus.

Rides to the hotel

A man standing at the shuttle bus area asked me which hotel I was going to, and when I told him it was the Novotel, he told me he was the Novotel driver for single passengers and led me to his car. I said, "Wait a minute, you're a taxi driver, and I am not paying to go to the hotel when the bus is free." He said, "No, the car is free for single passengers; they want ten people for the bus." I asked to confirm again that the car was free, and he said yes, so I got in and started to the hotel. As we approached the toll booths where you exit the airport, the driver told me that I had to pay the toll. I told him: "No way, you told me it was free, and if it is not, take me back to the terminal." He kept arguing that the car was free, but I needed to pay the toll. When he realized I was not going to pay, he reversed direction in the toll booth plaza and started driving back to the terminal in oncoming traffic. Fortunately, there were very few cars, and we made it back to the terminal. I kept telling him to be honest and tell passengers the truth. He dropped me off, and I went in and downstairs to the information booth, where the men were still conducting their private business, but I finally got one to call the hotel to determine when the next bus was due. The 21:30 bus was departing soon, and they would tell the driver to look for me. When the bus arrived, the driver recognized me and asked me, "How was Sharm El Sheikh?" I responded that I had an "interesting day" and left it at that.

Eat what is native to the country

I checked into the hotel, asking for a non-smoking room. They assigned me a room at the end of a long hallway 40 rooms from the elevator next to a construction area for the installation of additional elevators. I dropped my backpack in the room and went down to eat a light meal. I saw the chef making small pizzas, and a man at a table was having a salad with tomato and iceberg lettuce, so I told the waitress I wanted a salad like his, plus oil and balsamic vinegar, and a small pizza.

It seemed like it took a long time, but I finally got the salad, which was delicious, but they didn't serve the pizza until I finished the salad (I would have liked to have both at the same time). The cheese on the pizza was not melting hot, and the pepperoni was not round but red strips without a spicy taste. I had violated my own rule: order what is native to the country. Pizza is not one of this Egyptian chef's expertise.

When I returned to my room, I found the internet cable missing, so I used my own. I discovered that even though I was connected, I could not get any internet apps to work. I turned on the TV, and it did not work either, so I figured there was a wiring problem in my room, most likely due to the construction next door.

It had been 36 hours since I had slept in a bed, so I called it a night without updating my journal.

POSTSCRIPT

Following the last long trip to Africa, I continued to travel, but to safer countries. Most of the trips were to islands such as Madeira, islands south of New Zealand, islands off of Australia (Mawson, Davis, Macquarie, Heard, Christmas Island, and Cocos Islands), Vanuatu, Sri Lanka, Maldives, Lakshadweep, Andaman-Nicobar, Christmas, Kiribati, Tarawa, Samoa, American Samoa, Niue, Wallis, Fernando do Noronha, Tristan de Cunha, St. Helena, Ascension, Rarotonga, Aitutaki, Penrhyn, Tahiti, Tuamotu, Austral, Gambier, Pitcairn, and Easter Island.

In addition to those islands, I returned to India and traveled on to Bangladesh, Myanmar, and Laos. To finish a "bucket list" adventure, I traveled to Sochi, Abkhazia, and crossed from Vladivostok to Moscow on the Trans-Siberian Railroad.

The adventures and experiences on those trips and the trips surrounding the visits to countries on the "Do Not Travel" list are too numerous to be included in this book.

INDEX

Made in the USA
Monee, IL
23 March 2021